KHOMEINI ON PALESTINE

Compiled by

The Institute for Compilation and Publication of Imam Khomeini's Works

INTRODUCTION

In the Name of Allah, the All-beneficent, the All-merciful

From various aspects, the victory of the Islamic revolution in Iran resulted in the intensification of the Muslims' campaign against the Zionists and changed the method of the Palestinians' struggle. The Shah's regime was considered a powerful ally for Israel and the West in the sensitive Middle East region. During his reign, Iran was a market for the import of large amounts of Israeli goods causing the economy of the occupying regime to flourish, and in the area of oil, the Shah rushed to its aid by exporting enough to meet its needs. As a result, in the Israeli economic and industrial sectors, Iran's oil was transformed into arms and bullets used to pierce the chests of the Palestinians.

Under the Shah, Iran had become a base for Israeli espionage activities and one from which the Zionist regime could keep watch over the Arabs of the region. To disclose the nature of the Shah's open and secret relations with Israel and to protest at the unsparing aid the Shah's regime was giving this common enemy of the Muslims constituted just two of the reasons behind the uprising of Imam Khomeini. As he himself said, "One of the reasons why we oppose the Shah is the assistance he gives Israel. I have constantly repeated in my discourses that the Shah has co-operated with Israel from the day it came into being, and when the war between Israel and the Muslims reached its climax, the Shah illegally took the oil of the Muslims and gave it to Israel. This in itself has been one of the factors behind my opposition to the Shah."[1] The fall of the Shah and the rise of the Islamic system in Iran was the first devastating blow to the expansionist aims of the Zionists, putting them seriously at risk.

The effect of the message of the Islamic revolution and of its leader on public opinion was so widespread that when Anwar Sadat signed the peace treaty at Camp David, the Egyptian government was rejected by Arab circles, even by the reactionary Arab regimes, and was totally isolated.

Following the bitter experience they had in their confrontation with Imam Khomeini's movement, America and the European governments - the main supporters of the regime occupying Quds[2] - set to trying to bridle the Islamic revolution and change the situation. To this end, they even went so far as to pursue the same policies as their Eastern adversary (the now defunct Soviet Union). The crystallisation of this co-operation was seen when Saddam occupied the land of the Islamic Republic at the instigation of the two superpowers and in their all-encompassing support for him in all stages of the Baathist regime's long war with the newly-established Islamic system in Iran.

The imposed war was started with the aim of occupying and dividing Iran and annihilating the Islamic revolution. The Islamic republic system, which was determined to play its spearheading role in the struggle against the enemies of the Muslims and to materialise its cries of "Today Iran, Tomorrow Palestine," was forced to unwillingly enter the field of battle to defend its revolution. It was a war which the heads of both Eastern and Western governments admitted took place to totally destroy the Islamic revolution and to dash any hopes of uprising or revolution the Muslim nations may have had. In this way, Saddam, at the instigation of the enemies of the Muslims and with their support, became the director of a long-running and bitter saga which Imam Khomeini speaks of thus: "That which causes great sorrow is that the superpowers, America in particular, by deceiving Saddam into attacking our country has forced the powerful government of Iran to busy itself with defending its country so as to give the criminal, usurper Israel the opportunity to pursue its evil plan which is the creation of a greater Israel stretching from the Nile to the Euphrates."[3]

The bitter realities, the conspiracies and the obstacles which the enemies of Islam put in the path of the progress of the Islamic revolution, along with the changes which were becoming manifest in the Eastern bloc, enabled America to once again present compromise and surrender to Israel as the only solution to the crisis in the Middle East, and not only return Egypt to the Arab fold, but place it at the head of the queue of willing compromisers, a queue which now comprised a vast spectrum of Arab governments. However, with all of this, that which took place in Lebanon and that which we are witnessing today in the lands of occupied Palestine show that the Palestinian nation has received the message of the Islamic revolution despite all the obstacles, and Imam Khomeini's enlightening and rousing words are bearing fruit as the *intifadah* takes shape. Despite the treachery of the compromisers in the Arab world, today even the leaders of the occupying regime and America admit that the essence of the ideology of the Islamic revolution and the ideas of Imam Khomeini have found an undeniable presence in events taking place in Palestine.

The present book contains the guidances and positions adopted by a great man who transformed his divine movement into a great revolution in the Islamic world by reliance on God and faith in the great power of the people. That which has been compiled in this work are selected excerpts from Imam Khomeini's speeches, messages and interviews, given at different periods during the history of the Islamic revolution, reflecting his opinions on Palestine.

A study of the present anthology clearly reveals that at the height of the power of the oppressive imperial system in Iran, Imam was the divulger of the secret relations which existed between the Shah's regime and Israel, that he considered confronting the danger posed by Israel to the Islamic world to be a very serious issue and that he continually pursued this issue.

Imam Khomeini was the first *marja-i taqlid* (source of religious guidance) and great religious leader to authorise the use of monies received for charitable disbursement to support the Palestinian combatants. When the Quds-occupying regime perpetrated yet another crime in its long list of crimes and set fire to the al-Aqsa mosque[4], Imam Khomeini, with complete foresight and in stark contrast to the policy adopted by others on the matter, which was to endeavour to have the mosque rebuilt, stressed the need to preserve the vestiges of Israel's crimes as a symbolic factor to incite and encourage the Muslims to rise up against the existence of the main reason for the crime, that is the occupying regime. He said, "They set fire to the Masjid al-Aqsa. We cry out: 'Leave the Masjid al-Aqsa half-burned to the ground; do not erase all traces of the crime!' But the Shah's regime opens an account, sets up a fund, and starts collecting money from the people supposedly to rebuild the Masjid al-Aqsa, but really to fill the pockets of our rulers while also covering up the crime committed by Israel."[5]

From the very beginning, he introduced the Islamic aspect and the ideological dimension of the struggle with Israel as the most effective factor in the movement for mobilising the oppressed Palestinian nation and attracting support for them from the Islamic *ummah*[6]. He considered other methods of struggle, such as reliance on Arab nationalism and nationalist views along with other imported and non-Islamic ideologies, as a departure from the path of struggle for the freedom of Quds. He had a clear insight into the internal problems besetting the Islamic world, amongst them the weakness, inability or subordinate nature of some of the heads of Islamic states. Consequently, he emphasised the importance of public knowledge and awareness in the Islamic world stemming from the principles of belief and the *ummah*'s common faith and culture, and of avoiding sectarian differences. He called on the heads of the Muslim governments to accept this approach too, and believed that as long as the governments were of the same mind as their people and went along with Muslim public opinion and demand, they were to be entrusted with the authority of leadership and with the responsibility for guiding the struggle, otherwise the Muslim nations should do to them what the Muslim nation of Iran did to the Shah.

Now briefly some of the aspects of Imam Khomeini's views relating to the Palestinian problem and confrontation with the Zionist enemy will be discussed. With a quick look through the present anthology, one can briefly summarise the different aspects of Imam Khomeini's views on Palestine and other concomitant issues under the following headings:

The need to use the oil weapon against America and Israel:

At a time when the experience of the many Arab-Israeli wars, in particular the defeat in the Ramadan war, had, for some of the Arab leaders, strengthened the argument for compromise, Imam Khomeini stressed the need to continue the struggle using an oil embargo as a weapon against Israel and its supporters. In a message to the Muslim governments and nations on 7 November 1973 (16 Aban 1352 AHS), following the Ramadan war, he wrote: "It is the duty of the governments of Islamic oil-producing countries to use their oil and the other means they have at their disposal as weapons against Israel and the imperialists, and to refuse to sell oil to governments supporting Israel."

This stance of Imam Khomeini's was pursued vigorously at different periods and even after the victory of the Islamic revolution. Unfortunately, however, for various reasons, amongst them the weakness and subjection of many of the heads of the Islamic countries, his words were not heeded and not translated into action. If we consider the special conditions which prevailed at that time and the importance and vital role oil played in industrial development, more so at a time when the Western industrialised world had not come up with any viable means of defence against the oil-embargo weapon, we can understand more fully the importance of this stance of Imam's.

The freedom of Palestine is to be found in the rediscovery of Islamic identity:

The necessary requirements for being able to adopt a basic stance on Israel and pursue a serious struggle against it are that the people, while being aware of the facts, should at the same time not be stricken with consumption fever and should trust their leaders to the extent that they go along and co-operate with them. However, the suppression and despotism prevalent in most Islamic countries at the time was such that the people did not support their governments. Imam knew this and realised that the main buttress of the struggle would be the people's Islamic faith, he said: "Until the time that we return to Islam, the Islam of the Prophet of God, our problems will remain. Until that happens, we can solve neither the Palestinian problem nor the problems besetting Afghanistan and other places. The nations must turn to the earliest age of Islam, if their governments do so with them there is no problem, otherwise the nations should detach themselves from their governments and do to them what the nation of Iran did to its government so that the problems can be solved."[7]

Repeatedly disclosing the plan for a Greater Israel:

The main slogan of the Israeli parliament was: "Israel, your borders reach from the Nile to the Euphrates," and was put forward at a time when Israel was weak and newly-established, when the occupiers were fewer and had little power compared to the Islamic world. It was obvious then, that at a time when they had power, they would strive to realise this dream. Imam Khomeini repeatedly pointed out the danger of Israeli expansionism and the fact that Israel would not be satisfied with its present borders, and he informed the people that any kind of denial or cover-up by Israel of this aim was merely done to deceive public opinion in the Islamic world and allow it to pursue its step-by-step policy to achieve its ultimate aim. If this warning of Imam's alone had been understood properly, the way for the various conciliatory plans - which naively sought to make Israel the captive of international agreements and resolutions and, at the cost of giving it most of the occupied lands, obtain a kind of limited self rule in a corner of Palestine - would have been blocked.

The distinction between Judaism and Zionism:

It is known that Zionism is a political phenomenon with expansionist, racist and colonialist aims that under the cover of the Jewish religion takes on a religious appearance and tries to pursue its goals as the saviour of the Jewish people. But it is not hidden from the perspicacious thinkers that the fanciful claim of the racial unity of the Jews of the world is made by Zionists who want to justify their usurpation of Palestinian land and their crimes in the occupied territories. It is obvious that the director of this drama was, in the beginning, British colonialism, but later that position was entrusted to the officials at the White House and today they are the ones who call the shots. And it goes without saying that the neo-colonialism of the West cares little for the religion of God and the pious people, the only thing that matters to the colonialists of today being their own imperialist interests. Aware of these realities, Imam Khomeini, by always making a distinction between Judaism and Zionism, confronted this trick and removed the mask of hypocrisy from the faces of those claiming to defend Judaism. He introduced Zionism as fundamentally a political movement antithetical to the principles of religion and the aims of the divine messengers.

The way to save Palestine is through the unity of Islamic nations:

Imam Khomeini always considered returning to Islam and uniting as a prerequisite to saving Palestine and blocking Zionism's expansionist plans. Consequently, while stressing that the main goal of Israel is the destruction of Islam, he repeatedly called on the Muslims to put aside all their differences, including the religious ones. Even though the majority of the Arabs and Muslims living in Palestine belonged to the Sunni sect, Imam Khomeini, in his role as Shi'ite jurisprudent and *marja*[8], did not refuse them any kind of help. He considered the issue of Palestine as one that was related to the very existence of Islam, and stressed it was a problem which concerned the Islamic world as a whole. He encouraged all Muslims, especially the Shiites of Lebanon, to extend their help to the Palestinians. Imam Khomeini saw the rule of a small number of Zionists over more than one billion Muslims of the world as something shameful and said: "How can Israel, with such a small number of people, come and prevail over these countries which possess everything and have all kinds of powers, the way it has? Why should it be this way? Is it not because the nations are divided and stand apart from their governments, and the governments are disunited, that a population of one billion Muslims with all the means they have at their disposal are sitting by while Israel perpetrates these crimes in Lebanon and Palestine?"[9]

In the words Imam Khomeini, the great leader of the Islamic revolution, made famous, if all the Muslims came together and each one of them threw a bucket of water over Israel, it would be washed away. He said: "There is something which puzzles me and it is that all the Muslim governments and nations know what the problem is, they know that the hands of foreigners are involved in disuniting them, they see that this disunity will weaken and destroy them, they see how the frail government of Israel has stood against the Muslims, and they know that if united and each one of them threw a bucket of water over Israel it would be washed away, yet still they are helpless before it."[10]

Taking advantage of opportunities and the potentials of the Islamic world:

In defending the rights of the oppressed people of Palestine and in order to mobilise support for the Palestinian uprising from the Islamic nations, Imam Khomeini believed that instead of turning to grounds, topics and issues which had no roots in the culture of the Palestinian nation, one should take advantage of the ideology of Islam and the potentials it offered. Declaring the last Friday of the holy month of Ramadan "World Quds Day" is an example of this enlightened attitude of Imam Khomeini's. The month of Ramadan provides the Muslims with an ideal opportunity; spiritually inspired by a month of fasting and attending religious and educational ceremonies, the believers gain a readiness to turn their attention to the great responsibility borne by the *ummah* to free the first *qiblah*[11] of the Muslims. Were the political and propaganda obstacles of the imperialist powers and their agents in the Islamic countries to be weakened through the efforts of the Muslims, then World Quds Day could play a very determining role in uniting the Muslim nations as well as mobilising and inspiring the Muslim forces for the freedom of holy Quds.

In Imam Khomeini's view, another example of the potentials of the Islamic world was to be found through reviving the Abrahamic *hajj*, observing the true philosophy of *hajj* - which in the holy Quran is called "the uprising for the people" - and ensuring that the disavowal of pagans ceremonies became an integral part of the spirit of true *hajj* and its rituals. Based on this view, whenever the global congress of *hajj*, which is the focus of attention of millions of Muslim people from all over the world and from all denominations, discovers its true philosophy and is transformed into a centre for recognising the problems of the

Islamic world and revealing the treacherous plots of the enemies of Islam and their agents, then the question of Palestine and the occupation of Muslim lands by a handful of Zionists will, as a matter of course, be placed at the top of the agenda as one of the most important problems facing the Muslim world. And through the *hajj* congress, the support of the Muslims of the world can be found, unanimity created and the resources of the Islamic world put to use for finding a fundamental solution to this old problem. Indeed it is the existence of these very potentials and the enlightening messages of Imam Khomeini that have led America, Europe and Israel in past years to employ all their might against Imam's policies and the Islamic republic system. Taking advantage of the dependency and shaky position of some of the anti-people governments in the Islamic countries, they strive to prevent the message reviving the pure Islam of Muhammad (upon whom be peace) from spreading. And through their use of different methods of disseminating malicious propaganda against the goals of the Islamic revolution on the one hand and calumny, assassination, international pressures and the killing of pilgrims to the House of God for the crime of shouting "Death to America and Israel" on the other, they try to stem the rising tide of the Islamic revolution and consolidate the usurping government of Israel in the heart of the Islamic world. However, the Islamic uprising of the Palestinian people is a sign of this reality that the message of Imam and his movement for God has reached its main audience. ?

The Institute for Compilation and Publication of Imam Khomeini's Works

SECTION ONE
THE NATURE OF ISRAEL

Israel the Enemy of Islam and the Muslims

The plot to destroy the ideals of the Muslims

Today Israel and its close friend Egypt are thinking up ways of creating a united front to destroy the Muslims and their lofty ideals. Recently Iraq, along with some of the heads of the other regional countries, approved of this plan. For nearly twenty years now, I have been informing people of the danger of international Zionism. Today, I feel the danger for all the freedom-bestowing revolutions of the world, including the recent Islamic revolution in Iran, is no less than it was in the past, for at the present time these world-devouring bloodsuckers using various techniques to defeat the oppressed and weak of the earth have risen up and are active. Our nation and the free nations of the world should bravely and vigilantly resist these dangerous plots.

Imam's message, 11 February 1981 (22 Bahman 1359 AHS). *Sahifeh-ye Imam*, vol. 14, p. 66[12]

Evil propaganda against Islam

The agents of imperialism are busy in every corner of the Islamic world drawing our youth away from us with their evil propaganda. They are not converting them into Jews and Christians; rather they are corrupting them, making them irreligious and indifferent, which is sufficient for their purposes. In our own city of Tehran now there are centres of evil propaganda run by the churches, the Zionists and the Bahais in order to lead our people astray and make them abandon the ordinances and teachings of Islam.

Islamic Government, p. 176.

The destruction of the first qiblah of the Muslims is the vile wish of Israel

Today, with the widespread arrests of the Muslim brothers in Egypt, Sadat has completed his service to Israel. His alliance with America and Israel has shamed the Arab people. (He has formed) an alliance with an Israel which at this time, in addition to the crimes it carries out in the region, has committed another great crime, that is excavation work at the site of the al-Aqsa mosque, the first *qiblah* of the Muslims; and with the weakening of the foundations of this mosque, the first *qiblah* of the Muslims will, God forbid, be destroyed and Israel will achieve its vile wish.

Oh Muslims of the world! Oh oppressed people under the sway of oppressors! Beware! Rise up and offer the hand of unity to one another, defend Islam and your destiny and fear not the hue and cry of the superpowers, for this century, by the will of God the all powerful, will be the century of victory of the oppressed over the imperious and haughty and of truth over falsehood.

Imam Khomeini's message to the pilgrims to the House of God in Mecca, 6 September 1981 (15 Shahrivar 1360 AHS). *Sahifeh-ye Imam*, vol. 15, p. 146.

Israel's effacement of Islam

The Muslims should realise that in the wake of the Islamic revolution, and the attention it brought to the miraculous power of Islam, all America's plots and machinations from the creation of dissension among the Sunni and Shiite brothers and the attack on Iran - which is the hub of the Islamic movement - to the comprehensive and extensive plan for the attack on Lebanon and those great crimes, are all hatched with the sole intent of effacing Islam and weakening this divine power. They should realise that America's plan, which is being implemented by the malicious Israel, will not end in Beirut and Lebanon, rather Islam everywhere, in the Islamic countries and in particular in the Persian Gulf region and the Hijaz, the centre of divine revelation, is targeted. Its primary aim is to make the rulers of the region submit themselves completely to the command of America and, more distressing than that, of Israel, and accept the shame of any form of degradation and servitude. In such a climate and faced with such a great tragedy, the Islamic nations should not remain indifferent and should not spare any effort in protecting Islam and the Islamic countries. How painful and distressing it is that in the proximity of the Muslims and the so-called Islamic governments, the usurper Israel can so outrageously and presumptuously attack the innocent people of Lebanon, the dear brothers and sisters of Beirut, and rather than rising up in their defence, which is a divine ordinance and a human duty, the governments of the Islamic countries display meekness and instead rise up to act for the vile aims of America and Israel by training their sights on Islamic Iran and Islam in Iran rather than the oppressor Israel.

If today they can create excuses for their silence (in the face of these crimes) and their help for the vile aims of this criminal (regime) and its overlord, can they also distort their history? Can they deceive the free nations of the world? Can they convince God the Avenger with these implausible excuses of theirs? And the way that they have played with the great religion of Islam as if it were some kind of toy, is this mortal sin of theirs forgivable? How will they answer for the blood of the innocent men, women and children of Beirut?

Imam Khomeini's message on the auspicious occasion of Id al-Qurban **[13]**, 20 September 1982 (29 Shahrivar 1361 AHS). *Sahifeh-ye Imam*, vol. 16, pp. 437-8

America and Israel bear malice towards the very basis of Islam

The Muslims present at the noble stations, from whichever nation and religious denomination they may be, must be well aware that the main enemy of Islam, the Noble Quran and the exalted Messenger, may the peace of God be upon him and his descendants, is the superpowers, in particular America and its corrupt offspring Israel. They have set their avaricious sights on the Islamic countries and will not balk at committing any crime or hatching any plot in order to plunder the huge amounts of resources these countries have both underneath and above the ground. And the secret of their success in this satanic design lies in the creation of disunity amongst the Muslims which they bring about in whatever way they can. It is possible that during the hajj ceremonies, they will persuade some people, such as the clergymen who are in their employ, to sow dissension among the Shiites and Sunnis and to fan this satanic phenomenon such that some naive people will believe it and they themselves will become the instigators of disunion and decay. Brothers and sisters, both sects must be vigilant and realise that these sightless, stipend-receivers, in the name of Islam, the sacred Quran and the customary practice (sunnah) of the Prophet, want to pluck Islam, the Quran and the sunnah out of the midst of the Muslims, or at the very least to lead the Muslims astray. The brothers and sisters should realise that America and Israel bear malice towards the very basis of Islam, because Islam, its book and the sunnah are a thorn in their side and an obstacle to their plundering and because it was by following this book and this sunnah that Iran rose up to confront them, embarked on a revolution and was victorious. ?

Imam's message on the occasion of the *hajj* pilgrimage and the auspicious Id al-Qurban, 29 August 1983 (7 Shahrivar 1363 AHS). *Sahifeh-ye Imam*, vol. 19, p. 24.

Israel's Expansionism (the Plan for a Greater Israel)

The occupation of Israel is not an end to the affair

Everyone must know that the goal of the great powers in creating Israel does not end with the occupation of Palestine. They are planning to make all the Arab countries share in Palestine's fate, God forbid. Today, we are spectators of the Palestinian combatants' struggle in their holy war (*jihad*) to place the destiny of Palestine into the hands of the Palestinians; we are onlookers as these freedom fighters take their lives in their hands and bravely rise up in holy war against occupation and aggression and to free Palestine and the occupied lands; we are spectators of that which the hands of the imperialist appointees did to these freedom fighters yesterday in Jordan and what they are doing to them today in Lebanon; we are spectators of the propaganda that is instigated by the imperialist appointees and the machinations that are carried out by them, in various ways, all with the aim of distancing the Muslim groups from the Palestinian combatants and of throwing the battle out of the strategic areas - for it would have given them a prime opportunity to deal a serious blow to the forces of Israel and Zionism, this usurping enemy.

Under such circumstances, do the Muslims and the heads of the Islamic states not have a duty and a responsibility before God? Morally and rationally are they not obliged to help? Is it right that the Palestinian freedom fighters be massacred by imperialist appointees in areas under imperialist sway while others remain silent in the face of this crime and even collaborate and conspire together to throw this freedom-bestowing *jihad* out of its most suitable and strategic zone? Do not the Arab governments and the Muslim residents of this region know that with the annihilation of this *jihad*, the other Arab countries will not be safe and secure from the malevolence of this perverse enemy?

Imam's message in support of Palestine, 10 November 1972 (19 Aban 1351 AHS). *Sahifeh-ye Imam*, vol. 2, pp. 479-80.

The danger of Israel is one facing all Middle Eastern and Islamic countries

The heads of the Islamic countries should be aware that this germ of corruption which has been planted in the heart of the Islamic countries has not been put there merely to suppress the Arab nation; rather it is dangerous and harmful to the Middle East region as a whole. The plan is for the domination and supremacy of Zionism over the Islamic world and the further colonisation of the rich lands and abundant resources of the Islamic countries. Only through self-sacrifice, perseverance and the unity of the Muslim governments can freedom from the evil of this black incubus of colonialism be found. If one government fails to act as it should in this vital matter which now faces Islam, then it is incumbent upon the other Muslim governments to persuade it to co-operate through reproaches, threats and the severing of relations. It is the duty of the governments of Islamic oil-producing countries to use their oil and the other means they have at their disposal as weapons against Israel and the imperialists and to refuse to sell their oil to governments supporting Israel.

Imam's message to the Muslim governments, 7 November 1973 (16 Aban 1352 AHS). *Sahifeh-ye Imam*, vol. 3, p. 2.

The fate of Lebanon awaits other Islamic lands

It is obvious that the heads of the Muslim governments, and in particular the Arab governments, should unite and try to get rid of Israel, this corrupt entity, for if they procrastinate, then it is feared that, God forbid, this affair will be repeated in other similar countries. I ask God the Exalted to sever the hands of the foreigners and their supporters (from the Islamic lands) and I pray for the independence of the Muslim governments. May God's blessings and peace be upon those who follow the guidance.

Imam's message in support of the Palestinians and the people of southern Lebanon, 22 March 1979 (12 Rabi II 1398 AH / 2 Farvardin 1357 AHS), vol. 3, p. 372.

Israel is not content merely with the Golan Heights

With your union you should pluck this germ of corruption out from amongst you. If you do not, then this cancerous growth will spread to other places. For it will not be content merely with the Golan Heights, for they (the Zionists) are of the opinion that the Jews are superior to all other races and the land from the Euphrates to the Nile belongs to Israel and should be returned to it. Yet you are sat arguing over an unimportant, a very insignificant matter, and you are focusing all your energy on Iran, lest Iran should at some time say something. All the organs in Iran are shouting out: we have no designs on other governments or other nations save to unite with them and drive the corruption out of the region. Yet still you bear animosity towards Iran. Why should this be so? The nation's leaders, the nation's intellectuals, the region's *ulama*[14] and the *ulama* of countries everywhere should think seriously about just who the enemy is and who the friend. They must throw the enemy out and offer the hand of unity to the friend. This problem must be solved with the help of all the Muslims, and as long as unity fails to exist amongst all Muslims, this problem will remain.

Imam's speech dated 24 January 1982 (4 Bahman 1360 AHS). *Sahifeh-ye Imam*, vol. 15, p. 433.

Israel will not be content with its present boundaries

Time and again attention has been called to this point that Israel will not be content with its present position, it will go forward a step at a time and with each step it takes it will say: 'we don't have any further designs, this is an end to it now.' Tomorrow it will go one stage further. Today it is Lebanon, tomorrow, God forbid, it will be Syria, the day after Iraq and so on.

Unfortunately these governments, instead of rising up against these people, these inhuman people, instead of opposing them, instead of uniting to stop them, don't even repudiate them. At present, they (the governments of the Islamic world) are rushing to strengthen Israel's position, and this has brought shame on everyone in the Islamic countries, on the leaders directly, and, indirectly, even on the people of those countries, for they have chosen leaders to represent them who do just whatever they like and pave the way for whatever humiliation they want for Islam and the Muslims, while they do nothing to stop them. To whom should we turn with these problems?

The Muslims, especially the oppressed of the region, should know that by replacing one pawn for another - which is perhaps meant to deceive the Palestinian and Lebanese fighters - Israel will never be dissuaded from its malicious aim which is sovereignty over the countries of the Muslims from the Nile to the Euphrates, and that America, which is baring its talons and showing its teeth in the region, will completely support a pawn such as Israel, the executer of all its crimes in the region. One should not lose sight of their political games. Those who back Israel should know that by doing so they are strengthening a biting, venomous serpent which if given half the chance will, God forbid, destroy the progeny of the region. They should not give this dangerous creature such an opportunity.

Imam's message for the pilgrims to the sacred House of God, dated 3 September 1983 (12 Shahrivar 1362 AHS). *Sahifeh-ye Imam*, vol. 18, p. 83.

Greater Israel

This is the second pawn now to have been brought into play. Yitzak Shamir, who is now set to be the prime minister, has announced his plan from the start saying that Greater Israel should become a reality, Palestine should be completely destroyed and all the places in Israel's hands are an integral part of Israel. Greater Israel means an Israel stretching from the Nile to the Euphrates or in other words encompassing all the regions inhabited by Arabs, which besides Egypt surely includes the Hijaz too. Yet they (the Arab governments) sit by looking on, while a large number of them even co-operate and want to officially recognise Israel and so on. These are disasters which have come to pass in our century, but unfortunately the Muslims, or rather the Muslim governments, are indifferent and do not allow their own countries, the ordinary people (in these countries), to speak about this matter. Truly this world exists in a suppressive environment, a suppression created by these two superpowers.

Imam's message dated 6 September 1983 (15 Shahrivar 1362 AHS). *Sahifeh-ye Imam*, vol. 18, p. 93.

Israel will not be content with these agreements

On 5 June 1983 (15 Khordad 1362 AHS), when, praise and thanks be to God the Exalted, the power of Islam and the government of the Islamic republic is the talk of the region, I warn the governments of the Islamic countries to desist from making past mistakes and call on them to offer one another the hand of brotherhood, and by humbling themselves before God and relying on the power of Islam, to sever the oppressive hands of the world-devouring tyrants and plunderers, in particular America, from the region, to condemn this American/Zionist/Lebanese accord which strengthens American dominance in the region and will allow Israel to conquer the Islamic country of Lebanon and subsequently the other Arab and Islamic countries, and to nullify it through action. They should know that Israel, as I have said again and again and as you have heard time and again, will not be satisfied with these agreements. It sees the Arab governments from the Nile to the Euphrates as usurpers, and sooner or later with the help of America it will put its malicious plan into action if, God forbid, it should find the opportunity and if the Arab governments do not awaken from their deep slumber. Is it not a source of shame for the Muslims and the governments of the Islamic countries that America, from the other side of the world, can govern their destinies and through the usurping infidel, Israel, can ensnare and ruin them all.

Imam's message on the anniversary of the 15 Khordad uprising dated 5 June 1983 (15 Khordad 1362 AHS). *Sahifeh-ye Imam*, vol. 17, p. 445.

From the Nile to the Euphrates

What could be better than for all the governments of the region to muster all the power at their disposal to wipe Israel off the map? This maleficent Israel which has put the innocent Palestinians in the state they are now in, which has committed all these outrages against brave Lebanon, has encroached upon the countries of the region and has transgressed their borders. What could be better than for regional governments to take hold of one another's hands and free the region from the iniquity of Israel and its supporter America? As I have reminded you time and again, Israel considers the area from the Nile to the Euphrates to be its own and it sees you as usurpers of its lands - although at present it does not have the nerve to explicitly state this - in the same way as Saddam, the brother of Israel, also strives to dominate the region; and if supposing he achieves this - which will never happen - he will deprive everyone of peace. ?

Imam's message on the occasion of the great religio-politico gathering of *hajj* and the auspicious feast of Id al-Qurban, dated 29 August 1984 (4 Shahrivar 1363 AHS). *Sahifeh-ye Imam*, vol. 19, pp. 26-7.

The Distinction between Jews and Zionists

Jews in Iran

On occasion, the Shah and his regime say they will bring in experts from Israel; we know what to do with these experts if they do bring them in. If even one Israeli... I'm not talking about the Jews here, no one has the right to lay a finger on the Jews in Iran, they are under the aegis of Islam and the Muslims; no one has the right to attack the Jews or the Christians who adhere to a religion revealed by one of God's prophets. Recently the government attacked the Bahais, this was spurred by devilish motives and the Muslims should pay no heed to this devilry of theirs. Their aim is to make other groups rise up against the Muslims. Pay no attention to these things; oppose anything with which the governmental organisations become in any way involved, because they harbour ill intent towards you. If the Israelis come to Iran in order to extract the oil, it will be the duty of all Muslims to throw them out or kill them all. They are at war with Islam, they are at war with the Muslims, they are in a state of war and if we are able, we will cut them all down. If they set foot in Iran, if even one Israeli sets foot in Iran, it will be the duty of the people to destroy them. The Israelis will come! The hell they will!

Imam's message dated 16 December 1978 (25 Azar 1357 AHS). *Sahifeh-ye Imam*, vol. 5, pp. 246-7.

Jews are distinct from Zionists

Any kind of relationship with Israel will be severed, however, the Jews will be free to remain in Iran and live in an environment which will be freer than at the time of the Shah's rule, for Islam respects all religions.

Imam's interview with foreign journalists, 14 January 1979 (24 Dey 1357 AHS). *Sahifeh-ye Imam*, vol. 5, p. 434.

Question: Amongst your demands is the annihilation of the state of Israel; if this leads to Israel's destruction and victory for the Palestinians, what will be the fate of the Jews?

Answer: The issue of the Jews is quite separate from that of the Zionists. If the Muslims are victorious over the Zionists, the latter will meet the same fate as the deposed Shah, however, the Muslims will do nothing to the Jews, for they are a nation like other nations, they will carry on with their lives and they will not suffer dispossession.

Imam's interview with the West German Radio-Television network, 8 November 1979 (17 Aban 1358 AHS). *Sahifeh-ye Imam*, vol. 11, p. 4.

The Zionists are not people of religion

The religious minorities who lived amongst the Muslims from the beginning of Islam, from after the victory of Islam - not those polytheists who were conspirators or those people who hatched plots and wanted to create turmoil, but those who were of the religious minorities - were all treated with the upmost respect by Islam. According to a story, one of the stories that is probably about Muawiyah's army, an anklet was stolen from the foot of a Jewish woman; when he heard, Hadrat Amir[15] said: I have heard that they came and stole an anklet from a *dhimmi*[16] woman, if a person were to die in circumstances such as mine, no one would reproach him. This is how concerned he was that the welfare of all segments of the population should be protected.

We consider the Jewish community to be completely separate from the issue of Zionism and the Zionists; the latter are in no way among the people of religion. The teachings of Hadrat Moses, upon whom be peace, were divine teachings, and Hadrat Moses has been mentioned in the Quran more times than any other prophet. The life of Hadrat Moses has been related in the Quran and it provides valuable lessons and shows us how he acted towards Pharaoh. He was a shepherd with a world of power and resolve who rose up against the great might of Pharaoh, destroying him.

Belief in divine power and turning his attention to the affairs of the weak and oppressed as opposed to the arrogant and powerful, the first of whom was Pharaoh, and rising up against the latter was the way of Hadrat Moses, upon whom be peace, something which is in complete contrast to the plan of this group and these Zionists. They have joined with the arrogant and powerful and act as their spies, their servants; they act against the weak and oppressed and contrary to the teachings of Hadrat Moses, who himself was from the ordinary people, just as all the other prophets were, who took as his supporters individuals from amongst the ordinary people of the bazaars and alleyways etc., and rose up against Pharaoh and the power of Pharaoh.

The weak attacked the arrogant to strip them of their pride and bring them down a peg or two; this is contrary to the way of these Zionists who strike up relations with the arrogant ones and act against the weak. Perhaps those few misled Jews who have come together there from different parts of the world now regret what they have done. Perhaps those Jews who do not want anything other than the lofty teachings of Moses now regret going there, for once they see at first hand what the plan is of this group who call themselves Jews yet who act against the teachings of Hadrat Moses, who kill people for no reason and align themselves with America and others, they will not be able to put up with this. We know that the Jewish community is quite different from the Zionist community; we oppose the latter, our opposition arising from the fact that they oppose all the religions, they are not Jews, they are political people who, calling themselves Jews, perpetrate certain acts. The Jews despise them, as all people should.

Imam Khomeini's speech at a gathering of the Jewish Society of Iran, 14 May 1979 (24 Ordibehesht 1358 AHS). *Sahifeh-ye Imam*, vol. 7, pp. 270-1.

The Jews do not accept the Zionists

Today, you can see what the Zionists, who claim to be Jews - although the Jews themselves do not accept them - and who, unfortunately, claim to be followers of Hadrat Moses, are doing to the people in the world.

Imam's speech at a gathering of representatives of the religious minorities in the Islamic Consultative Assembly, 18 November 1982 (27 Aban 1361 AHS). *Sahifeh-ye Imam*, vol. 17, p. 95.

The false claims of being followers of Hadrat Moses

There is one point I should make and that is out of these well-known religions which are today universally recognised by mankind, those being the religions of Hadrat Moses, Jesus and Islam, when we examine the life of the prophet Hadrat Moses, upon whom be peace, how he lived, the nature of his message and the struggle he embarked upon with the *taghut*[17], and compare this with how his people, how those who say we are the people of Hadrat Moses, we are the followers of Hadrat Moses[18], act, we see there is no comparison. Moses opposed the *taghut*, and these people who say they are the followers of Hadrat Moses are themselves *taghut*s, yet they claim to be his followers. Israeli radio broadcasts many of Hadrat Moses' teachings, but what is Israel like? What is the situation there? How do those who claim descent from Hadrat Moses live? Hadrat Moses was a shepherd with a staff. History has related what his life as a shepherd was like, how he then rose up and went after the greatest power which existed at that time and opposed it, not considering this world for a moment. Compare this with how these people, who consider themselves to be the descendants of Hadrat Moses, cling to this world. Great amounts of America's wealth lie in their hands, they have the financial power in America yet still they say they believe in the religion of Moses. ?

Israel's Supporters

America is Israel's main supporter

It is America who supports Israel and its sympathisers. It is America who gives Israel its strength to make the Muslim Arabs homeless.

Imam's speech on the occasion of the ratification of the Capitulation Bill, 26 October 1964 (4 Aban 1343 AHS). *Sahifeh-ye Imam*, vol. 1, p. 415.

Israel is supported by all the imperialists

Israel was born out of the collusion and agreement of the imperialist states of East and West. It was created in order to suppress and exploit the Muslim people, and it is being supported today by all the imperialists. Britain and the US, by strengthening Israel militarily and politically and supplying it with lethal weapons, are encouraging Israel to undertake repeated aggression against the Arabs and the Muslims and to continue the occupation of Palestine and other Islamic lands. The Soviet Union, by preventing the Muslims from arming themselves adequately, by its deceit, treachery and conciliatory policy, is guaranteeing the existence of Israel.

Imam's reply to a letter from Muslim students in America and Canada, 13 July 1972 (22 Tir 1351 AHS). *Sahifeh-ye Imam*, vol. 2, p. 456.

America's support for the Shah and Israel

By supporting these elements (the Pahlavis) the American government is, in the eyes of the Muslims, the head of all the oppressors and criminals in history. In order to make free use of the Muslims' vast resources, the American government has placed millions of honourable people in the clutches of their crude agents who lack the qualities of human beings... Turning a blind eye to the rights of hundreds of millions of Muslims; establishing a handful of rogues as rulers of their destinies; allowing the illegal regime in Iran and Israel's unworthy government to rob the Muslims of their rights and deprive them of their freedom; and behaviour reminiscent of the Middle Ages, are just some of the crimes which will go down in the records of the heads of the republic of America. The present leader, who has given so many pledges, must avoid committing the criminal deeds of the previous governments.

Imam's letter to the Islamic Students Union in America and Canada, October 1977 (Mehr 1356 AHS). *Sahifeh-ye Imam*, vol. 3, pp. 210-11.

America's plot against Iran because of the termination of oil supplies to Israel

It was reported in the newspaper that the American Senate has, by a unanimous vote, condemned the executions which have taken place in Iran. The person who presented the motion is one of Israel's friends and is himself a Zionist.

It is wrong of us to expect them not to condemn these executions we have carried out. We don't have such expectations of America, particularly since the Iranian government has terminated supplies of oil to Israel and will no longer provide it with oil. We expect nothing other than this for Israel is one of America's close friends.

Imam's speech dated 22 April 1979 (2 Ordibehesht 1358 AHS). *Sahifeh-ye Imam*, vol. 7, p. 341.

America strengthens Zionism

At present, all our problems stem from America, all the problems of the Muslims stem from America. It is America who has strengthened Zionism to such a degree and continues to do so and who kills our brothers group by group.

Imam's speech 29 October 1979 (7 Aban 1358 AHS). *Sahifeh-ye Imam*, vol. 10, p. 273.

The collusion between America and Israel

I have repeatedly warned of Israel's designs, for it will not be satisfied with the lands it has already seized, and now as you see it has taken Quds as its capital. Everything one hears from America, from these human rights supporters and these circles and committees abroad is like unrhythmical poetry; thus, you see that they reject Israel, but Israel pays no attention, they warn Israel, but Israel turns around and condemns them. This is because the matter is not being taken seriously. America is not seriously opposed to Quds being established as the Israeli capital; consequently Israel can do such a thing. This is simply one of their tactics. The human rights committees and the other committees in these countries which are concerned with the same affairs are all hand in glove with one another in plundering us Muslims and the people in Asia and Africa. And unfortunately the Muslims will not be warned.

Imam's speech dated 6 August 1980 (15 Mordad 1359 AHS). *Sahifeh-ye Imam*, vol. 13, p. 64.

Israel will not perpetrate crimes without America's permission

Do not think that this is just about the Golan Heights, there is more to it than this. No one should suppose that these organs which have been established, such as the international organisations, the human rights organisations and the such like, will do something that is to the advantage of the people. And never presume that the opposition of these organisations will go anywhere towards stopping the crimes of Israel and others like her. America has stated its opposition to this annexation, but who in their right mind could believe that Israel would carry out such actions without the prior permission of America and without first coming to an understanding with her over this?

Imam's speech dated 16 December 1981 (25 Azar 1360 AHS). *Sahifeh-ye Imam*, vol. 15, p. 370.

This is a blow which the Muslims were dealt by America

It is regrettable that Islam and those who profess to be followers of Islam are in the state they are in. Islam is very strict when it comes to violators and aggressors, yet these people who say they are the followers of Islam are encouraging such people. America is the leader of all the criminals, and these recent crimes perpetrated in Beirut were done openly by these criminal Zionists, but with the hidden hands of America. America was the main perpetrator. They (the Zionists) themselves have admitted that it was an American plan. If America had not been involved, if it had strongly deterred Israel from doing this, it would have listened. This is a blow which the Muslims were dealt by America, and still these gentlemen claim to adhere to Islam, claim to be on the side of the Muslims as they hand everything they have over to America and apologise to them. Is this not regrettable for our nation, for Islam, for everyone?! Do these nations not see what they are doing? Such things they (the Zionists) did to Beirut, to women, children and the poor, helpless people. They perpetrated every conceivable act, totally disrupted the situation there while everyone just sat and watched. A few did express support, but if anyone said a word it was just that, a word and nothing more, then they left and all the crimes took place.

The presence of the American military is for supporting Israel

Just look at what is happening in Lebanon today. What a bloodbath is taking place in Lebanon as you and I sit here. What a situation this usurping and unjust government in Lebanon, this traitor Amin, has brought about for the Lebanese people. Such things Israel did there, now, instead, he and his government are doing them. Yet we have not heard a word from America, on the contrary it sent its troops there to help in these crimes. They say they are there for a purpose, but perhaps they set the stage themselves, perhaps they throw a couple of fire crackers some place injuring one or two people, and even if they don't do it themselves still they storm every house, carry out a house to house search, and arrest, imprison and kill the youths. Such tragedies are taking place in the world and America is sitting by and actually encouraging these. What is more regrettable is that the Muslims too are just sitting by and watching.

Imam's speech dated 6 September 1983 (15 Shahrivar 1362 AHS). *Sahifeh-ye Imam*, vol. 18, pp. 93-4.

The collaboration of the superpowers in the confrontation with Palestine

Today, all of the powers and superpowers have joined hands to stop the Palestinian Muslims from reaching their goal. Even many of those who claim to be devoted to the Palestinians, their devotion does not extend to seeing the Palestinian Muslims gain victory over Israel and unfortunately, by keeping silent, compromising and looking on, they have joined hands to stop the Palestinian Muslims from gaining victory. For their victory would be Islam's victory, and these powers are afraid that just as Islam was victorious in Iran and upset their apple cart there destroying their interests, so too if Islam were to be victorious in Lebanon and Palestine all their plans would be foiled there as well. Therefore, all the satans have come together to stop the growth of Islam. ?

Imam's speech at a meeting with members of the Central Council of the Lebanese Hizbollah, 28 February 1988 (9 Isfand 1366 AHS). *Sahifeh-ye Imam*, vol. 20, pp. 461-2.

SECTION TWO

THE RELATIONSHIP BETWEEN IRAN AND ISRAEL UNDER THE SHAH'S REGIME

The Links between the Shah's Regime and Israel

The economy during the Shah's rule in the clutches of the Zionists

A great danger exists for Islam, the independence and very existence of the country because of this bill which was perhaps devised by the Jewish spies and Zionists with the aim of destroying the country's independence and disrupting its economy. In the opinion of Mr. Alam's government, this bill is still in force and the government sees itself entitled to act upon it, even though it goes against both *shariah*[19] and constitutional laws and against the sensibilities of a nation of twenty million people in Iran, indeed of all Muslims...

In accordance with the religious duty I have to the Iranian nation and the Muslims of the world, I announce that a danger exists. The noble Quran and Islam are in danger, the independence of the country and its economy are in the clutches of the Zionists who in Iran are manifest in the form of the Bahai party, and in no time at all, if the Muslims maintain their lethal silence, they will, with the help of their agents, seize all the economic institutions of this country and the presence of the Muslim nation in all the country's affairs will be eliminated. The Iranian television has become a base for Jewish spies, and the government is aware of this and supports it. The Muslim nation will not be silent until this danger is removed, and if anyone is silent, then he will be responsible before God the Almighty and will be condemned to ruin in this world.

Imam's reply to questions put to him by merchants and guilds of Qum, dated March 1963 (Isfand 1341 AHS). *Sahifeh-ye Imam*, vol. 1, p. 104.

Iran under the heel of the Zionists

I know that no officer with a conscience approves of these crimes and acts of brutality, and I am aware of and deplore the pressures to which they are subject. I extend a fraternal hand to them in the hope of obtaining the salvation of Islam and Iran. I know that their hearts are troubled by this subordination to Israel, and that they do not wish Iran to be trampled by the boots of the Jews. I declare to the heads of the Muslim states, whether Arab or non-Arab: the *ulama* of Islam, the religious leaders and pious people of Iran, together with its noble army, are the brothers of the Muslim states and share their losses and their gains. They abhor and are disgusted with the treaty with Israel, the enemy of Islam and Iran. I say this quite clearly; if they wish, let the agents of Israel come put an end to my life.

Imam's message dated 2 May 1963 (12 Ordibehesht 1342 AHS). *Sahifeh-ye Imam*, vol. 1, pp. 194.

The penetration of Israel's agents into all the country's affairs

The gentlemen must realise that the danger to Islam today is no less than that once presented by the Bani Umayyad. This tyrannical regime is co-operating fully with Israel and its agents (the misguided and misguiding Bah`ai sect). The propaganda organs have been placed into their hands and they enjoy extensive influence in the court. In the army, the Ministry of Education and other ministries, positions have been opened for them and they have been given sensitive jobs. Point out the danger of Israel and its agents to the people. In the mourning ceremonies, remind them of the calamities which have befallen Islam, the religious centres and the supporters of the divine law. Express your aversion to the treacherous government's act of sending a few thousand enemies of Islam, the nation and the motherland to London to participate in an anti-Islamic and anti-people meeting and for giving them the financial assistance needed for their trip.

Imam's message dated 18 May 1963 (28 Ordibehesht 1342 AHS). *Sahifeh-ye Imam*, vol. 1, p. 233.

The ban on criticism of Israel

I was informed today that a number of preachers were taken to the offices of the security organisation (SAVAK) and were told that they could speak about anything they liked other than three subjects: they were not to say anything bad about the Shah; not to attack Israel; and not to say that Islam is endangered. The problem is that if we don't concern ourselves with these three subjects then what else is there to talk about? All of our difficulties without exception stem from these three issues.

Imam's remarks dated 3 June 1963 (13 Khordad 1342 AHS). *Sahifeh-ye Imam*, vol. 1, p. 249.

Is the Shah an Israeli?

What exactly is the relationship between the Shah and Israel which causes the secret service to tell us neither to speak of Israel nor of the Shah? What is the connection between the two? Can it be that the Shah is an Israeli? Does the secret service believe him to be Jewish? Surely this cannot be so; he professes to be a Muslim. He who claims to be a Muslim, according to the laws of Islam, is thereby a Muslim. The connection between ourselves and Israel... perhaps this concerns some kind of confidential matter. Maybe there is truth in what they say about certain organisations wanting to destroy the Shah. Don't you consider it a probability? If so then resolve the matter in some way. Somehow inform this man of these issues; it may cause him to wake up and become somewhat aware of the situation.

Imam's remarks dated 3 June 1963 (13 Khordad 1342 AHS). *Sahifeh-ye Imam*, vol. 1, p. 250.

The close friendship which exists between the Shah's regime and Israel

And even more regrettable is the control Israel and its agents exercise in many of this country's sensitive matters and the grip they have on the country's economic institutions with the help of the government and the agents of the tyrannical regime. Israel is in a state of war with the Muslim governments, yet the Iranian government treats it as a close friend and provides it with all kinds of propaganda apparatus and facilitates the import of its goods in every way.

I have repeatedly warned of the danger, danger for the holy religion, danger for the independence of the country, danger for the economy of the country. I deplore the term "the infidels are one nation" which has been put on the people's lips by these organisations. It is contradictory to the text of the word of God and is used to support Israel and its agents. It is a premise leading to the recognition of Israel and is used in support of Israel's agents and the misguided, deviating (*Bahai*) sect.

Imam's warning to the Iranian nation on the country's independence, dated 7 April 1964 (18 Farvardin 1343 AHS). *Sahifeh-ye Imam*, vol. 1, pp. 262-3.

Other examples of the relationship between Israel and the Shah's regime

The objective is Islam, it is the country's independence, it is the driving away of Israel's agents, it is the unification of Islamic countries. The entire country's economy now lies in Israel's hands; that is to say it has been seized by Israeli agents. Hence, most of the major factories and enterprises are run by them: the television, the Arj factory, Pepsi Cola etc.

Two of the aeroplanes that were to take the pilgrims to Mecca belonged to Israeli airlines. The Saudi government protested and the regime was forced to back down. Today, even eggs are imported from Israel. Make firm your ranks. These are the agents of imperialism; the roots of imperialism must be deracinated.

Imam's remarks dated 10 April 1964 (21 Farvardin 1343 AHS). *Sahifeh-ye Imam*, vol. 1, p. 270.

The plans of the Shah's regime devised by the Israelis

With this ominous plan of theirs (distancing the people from the clergy) they wish to make the public detest us so that gradually they (the people) obey their overlords. If only it were just a matter of obeying the overlords, they mean to make us subject to Israel too...

What we object to is all forms of corruption. We believe that your reform programmes are in fact devised by Israel and it is to Israel that you turn for help and advice whenever you want to draw up a plan. You bring military advisers from Israel into this country. You send students from our country to Israel. If only they were sent elsewhere, to America or even to England for example. But no, you send them to Israel! These are the kinds of issues we dispute.

We argue that all the Muslim countries have formed a united front on one side, in opposition to infidelity and Israel, whilst you and the Turkish government are stationed on the other side in support of Israel. We hold that this is ill-advised. Don't go against the sensibilities of the Muslim peoples so, for I swear by God this is to your detriment. All of the Muslims on one side and Iran on the other! If this is to be the case, then the nation of Iran will become reproachable and our Sunni brothers will think that Shiites are Jew worshippers... If so then come and explain to us in what way this can be said to constitute reaction. You who boast a history of two-and-a-half millennia of sovereign rule and endlessly crow about those rotten bones which have decomposed and are no more and which you now want to dig up from beneath the soil to use in your confrontation with Islam, have you now at this late hour joined forces with Israel against the precepts of Islam and against the Muslims?! We are the ones who advocate your non-involvement with Israel, yet you now try to accuse us of collaboration with others and of being involved with so-and-so. The Devil take this reasoning!... How can you call a country which is totally dependent upon foreign trade for its every need, developed? You bring specialists to Iran from Israel and send people to Israel to "learn something." Only this year you sent people there from Qum in order to "learn something." What do they have to learn from the Jews, the art of cheating, deceiving and betraying? We believe that sending them there will result in nothing but ruin, and in ten, twenty or thirty years' time you will see that we were right. Send them and see if you gain anything other than ruin.

Imam's speech dated 15 May 1964 (26 Farvardin 1343 AHS). *Sahifeh-ye Imam*, vol. 1, p. 298.

The quintessential Iran-Israel farm

Now, as I am sitting here speaking to you, many of the good farmlands of Iran are in the hands of Israel! People have written to me from Ilam and told me that the good farmlands of this place have been given to Israel for farming sugar beets, and at the side of the road, these people who say we have nothing to do with Israel have placed a sign which reads: the quintessential Iran-Israel farm. In an Israeli newspaper which was given to me recently, there was something written about the Israeli ambassador in Tehran! (And the gentlemen say that we have nothing to do with Israel!) A couple of days ago on 7 September (16 Shahrivar AHS) in the Darvaz-i Dowlat district of Tehran, the Jews created such a hullabaloo. Four or five hundred thieving Jews gathered together, and all that their speeches boiled down to was a eulogy to one and a tirade against another, and then they proclaimed that greatness belongs to the Jews, the Jews are chosen by God, we are a people who should govern, we are against dictatorship, we are against Hitlerism, and so on and so forth. This was the content of their speeches. These people come with the full knowledge of our government and openly say these things… It's wrong for a country to rely on the Jews. Is this that we say now very bad? Of course it's a bitter pill to swallow, it's bitter for you. Nevertheless, it is disastrous for an Islamic country, for Muslims, to rely on, to have relations or make agreements with a government which is now the enemy of Islam, which opposes Islam and has usurped Palestine.

Imam's remarks dated 9 September 1964 (18 Shahrivar 1343 AHS). *Sahifeh-ye Imam*, vol. 1, pp. 390-1.

The reforms of the Shah's regime have created a market for Israel

Today, Iran's economy is in the hands of America and Israel. Its market is now out of the control of the Iranians and Muslims. The dust of bankruptcy and poverty has settled on the faces of the merchants and farmers. The reforms of the gentlemen have created a black market for America and Israel and there is no one who can help this poor nation.

Imam's message on the occasion of the ratification of the Capitulation Bill, dated 26 October 1964 (4 Aban 1343 AHS). *Sahifeh-ye Imam*, vol. 1, pp. 417-8.

Imam's warning to the Shah

Do not conclude a treaty of brotherhood with Israel, the enemy of Islam and the Muslims, which had turned more than a million defenceless Muslims into refugees. Do not offend the sensibilities of the Muslims. Do not permit Israel and its treacherous agents to penetrate further the bazaar of the Muslims; do not endanger the economy of the country for the sake of Israel and its agents... Submission to the demands of the pseudo-state of Israel and endangering the economy of this country are a sign of weakness, servility and treachery to Islam and the Muslims.

Open letter to Prime Minister Hoveyda dated 16 April 1967 (26 Farvardin 1342 AHS). *Sahifeh-ye Imam*, vol. 2, pp. 130-2.

The Shah's Phantoms at the disposal of the Israeli military

Our wretched people subsist in conditions of poverty and hunger, while the taxes that the ruling class extorts from them are squandered. They buy Phantom jets so that pilots from Israel and its agents can come and train in them in our country. So extensive is the influence of Israel in our country - Israel, which is in a state of war with the Muslims, so that those who support it are likewise in a state of war with the Muslims - and so great is the support the regime gives it, that Israeli soldiers come to our country for training! Our country has become a base for them! The markets of our country are also in their hands. If matters go on this way, and the Muslims continue to be apathetic, their markets will be lost to them.

The Islamic Government, p. 167.

Traces of Israel's crime must not be erased

They set fire to the al-Aqsa mosque. We cry out: "Leave the al-Aqsa mosque half-burned to the ground; do not erase all traces of the crime!" But the Shah's regime opens an account, sets up a fund, and starts collecting money from the people supposedly to rebuild the mosque, but really to fill the pockets of our rulers while also covering up the crime committed by Israel.

The Islamic Government, p. 38.

Iran: a military base for Israel

Israel, the universally recognised enemy of Islam and the Muslims, at war with the Muslim peoples for years, has, with the assistance of the despicable government of Iran, penetrated all the economic, military and political affairs of the country. It must be said that Iran has become a military base for Israel, which means, by extension, for America.

Imam's message dated 8 February 1971 (19 Bahman 1349 AHS). *Sahifeh-ye Imam*, vol. 2, p. 334.

The invitation to Israeli experts for help with the monarchical celebrations

While these tragic circumstances and conditions prevail around the country, millions of tumans are to be spent celebrating in honour of the monarchy. According to reports, 80 million tumans are to be spent on Tehran alone, preparing the city for the festivities. Experts have been invited from Israel to take care of the arrangements for the celebrations; from Israel, that country which is the enemy of Islam, which is at present at war with Islam, which destroyed the al-Aqsa mosque - a crime which some people sought to cover up. In addition, according to the world's major radio stations, Iranian oil tankers are on their way to Israel filled with Iranian oil for a country which is at war with the Muslims! These are the actions of the kings that we have to hold festivals for!

Imam's remarks dated 27 May 1971 (6 Khordad 1350 AHS). *Sahifeh-ye Imam*, vol. 2, pp. 374-5.

Measures taken by the Shah to open the way for Israel

Illegal imprisonment, contrary to both the law of the land and *shariah* law, is the revenge which this imperialist-placed regime is taking on Islam and its adherents...

You must go to the barracks, the theological schools must be dishonoured, and as soon as one is accused, imprisonment, exile or execution must follow so that the way is made ever more open for the masters of the left and right and their henchmen, among them Israel!... The Shah's regime has been given the mission to hand over that which is held sacrosanct in the country to Israel and its mentors...

Imam's message to the Iranian nation, dated 11 September 1972 (20 Shahrivar 1351 AHS). *Sahifeh-ye Imam*, vol. 2, pp. 468-9.

The Shah's regime: the agent for crushing opposition to the occupiers of Palestine

At this present time, we are confronted with the heavy blows which are inflicted ever more increasingly day by day on Islam and with the problems and disorganisation which beset the Islamic nations more than ever before. On one side there is the story of Palestine and the al-Aqsa mosque, the displacement of the innocent people of that land and the support given the occupying Jews by the great imperialist governments - and with the perpetuation of this germ of corruption, God forbid, a great danger lies ahead for all the Islamic countries, in particular the Arab governments...

Today there are broader and more extensive plans in the making which reveal the true face of the agents of imperialism and the nature of their mission, plans through which they mean to destroy the strongholds of anti-imperialism and turn them instead into fortresses in the service of Zionism and its servants. Plans through which they mean to push aside the learned *ulama*, the respected preachers and those in the service of Islam and put pseudo-clergymen and agents of the corrupt organisations in their place at the altars and pulpits of Islam and the exalted Messenger, may the peace of God be upon him and his descendants...

Granting immunity to American military personnel and their dependants, shattering the country's prestige, destroying its judicial independence and putting the American and Zionist pillagers in control of all military, commercial, industrial and agricultural affairs and of its markets, are some of the other portentous consequences of this "honourable" revolution of the tyrannical regime...

I don't know if all these weapons have been purchased to drive out the overlords and the imperialists or not, for the regime itself has been put in place by them, has turned Iran into a military base for them and has given them a free hand in all the military, political and economic affairs of the country. Or have they in fact been purchased to carry out the raptorial plans of America who may now have changed its policy, because its economy is weak, to one of strengthening its bases in Iran and crushing the defenceless nation of Iran and other freedom-seeking nations in the region that are struggling against the occupiers of Palestine and other plundering foreigners, using their own power and wealth.

Imam Khomeini's message dated March 1973 (Farvardin 1352 AHS). *Sahifeh-ye Imam*, vol. 2, pp. 500-2.

Disclosure of the Shah's collaboration with Israel

At this time, when the flames of war between the Muslims and the Zionist infidels are blazing and the people of Islam have taken their lives in their hands and are making sacrifices on the battlefields to get what is rightfully theirs from the usurper Israel, the Iranian government have, on the orders of the Shah, initiated celebrations throughout the country on the anniversary of the two-and-a-half-millennia of monarchy festival, a festival for bloodthirsty kings, the likes of whom we are seeing today. The Muslims wallow in blood for the glory and greatness of Islam and the freedom of Palestine, while the Shah of Iran sets festivities and merry-making in motion for the vulgar, imperial regime.

At the same time as the great Islamic and Arab nation is defending the honour of Islam and the Muslims, the Islamic girls schools in Iran are attacked on the orders of this nefarious man and the girls are stripped of their veils and shown great disrespect. At a time when the enemies of Islam are threatening the Islamic countries and zealous men with a sense of honour bravely rise up in their defence and to defend their rights, the Shah of Iran, by creating spectacles across Iran, has brought about a big show, and, in the name of the *ulama* of Islam, has had congratulatory telegrams sent to himself signed with the signatures of court-affiliated, pseudo-clergymen created by the Endowment and Security organisations.

Under these circumstances, when the Muslims are making sacrifices for the freedom of Palestine and their lands, the Shah sends large numbers of prominent *ulama*, scholars and teachers of the theological centres, along with many other Iranian intellectuals, into exile or throws them into jail and subjects them to the most barbaric forms of torture. One could say that these scenes they make and these arrests are simply to keep the Iranian nation preoccupied with their own problems and their minds off the Islamic nation's war with Israel. It is out of fear of the broadening of the struggle, the creation of a consensus among all the classes of society and the expression of support by the Muslim nation of Iran for the just war of the Arab people that the Shah has resorted to these illegal and unwarranted imprisonments and expulsions of *ulama* and intellectuals. He fears lest they should protest as to why the regime in Iran remains indifferent towards such a vital issue with which the Muslims are now confronted, and why, when nearly all the Muslim governments and many of the non-Muslim governments are supporting the Arabs at war, the Iranian government and the despicable Shah, out of obedience to America and to display even more subservience, remain apparently mute on the issue but in reality side with Israel.

It is this Shah of Iran who has given the Israelis a free hand throughout Iran, who has endangered the economy of Iran and who, according to reports in some of the foreign newspapers, sends Iranian officers to Israel for training. It is this Shah who has handed over Iranian oil to the enemies of Islam and humanity to be used in the war with the brave Muslims and Arabs and who, through the recent ignominious agreement and the increase in the production of oil, has risen up to fight against the oil-producing countries who wish to use the oil weapon against America. It is this plundering, this purchase of billions of dollars worth of weapons and this continuous, back-breaking expenditure on celebrations by the Shah which cause living expenses to rise, which bring about a dizzying rise in the price of goods and which threaten Iran with famine. I am afraid that the billion dollar weapons he has bought from his world-devouring masters, dragging Iran into bankruptcy in the process, will now be sent to Israel. I fear that with the ammunition that has been procured at the cost of famine, hunger and the blood of the deprived people of Iran, the Iranian army will be forced to train their sights on the zealous hearts of the combatants of Islam.

I sense danger for the Islamic world because of this unquestioning obedience to America. It is now up to the honourable nation of Iran to stop this tyrant from carrying out these crimes and to the army of Iran and the men of position to humiliate themselves no longer and to instead seek a solution for the independence of their motherland.

It is the duty of the brave nation of Iran to block the interests of America and Israel in Iran and to attack them, even though this may result in their destruction. It is the duty of the learned *ulama* and the preachers to bring the crimes of Israel to the notice of the people in the mosques and religious circles. The learned *ulama* and noble nation of Iran should not keep silent on this matter. It is imperative that they persuade the Shah through whatever means possible to join the ranks of the Muslims and to refrain from committing further treason against the Quran and its followers. Publicise the crimes of this bloodthirsty afreet more, so that its hidden face may be better revealed. And if the Jews of Iran are busy securing help for Israel (which they are and most certainly they receive help from the Shah), it is incumbent on the nation of Iran to prevent this and to start a relief fund for the fighters who spend their days in fire and blood, and to stop at nothing in their efforts to help. I personally have repeatedly pointed out the danger of Israel and its agents, at the head of whom is the Shah of Iran. As long as the nation of Islam does not pull this germ of corruption out by its roots, its future will be bleak, and as long as Iran is in the grip of this heinous family, she will never look upon the face of freedom.

I ask of God the Exalted to assist the Muslims and render helpless Israel and its black agents.

Ruhullah al-Musawi al-Khomeini

Imam's message dated 14 September 1973 (23 Shahrivar 1352 AHS). Sahifeh-ye Imam, vol. 3, pp. 5-7.

I am afraid that Israel will implement its plans

We were witness to how the Iranian government, on the orders of the Shah, officially recognised Israel at a time when the Muslims were at war with these infidels, and how the *ulama* opposed this act. We were witness to the aid given to Israel by this black-hearted man while Israel was making Muslims homeless and shedding their blood. Oil, arms and other aid, the funds for which were secured through the blood and toil of the Iranian nation, were put at their disposal...

Because I consider the Lebanese situation important and follow it devotedly, I fear that, just as Iran was made into an American colony through the cunning of the evil agents of the embassy, the same thing will also happen in Lebanon and Israel will implement its plans in the region with complete peace of mind. You must keep watch on the operations of the Iranian embassy with the utmost vigilance, and prevent their tricks from succeeding.

Imam's reply to a letter, 4 November 1977 (13 Aban 1356 AHS). *Sahifeh-ye Imam*, vol. 3, p. 262.

The Shah recognised Israel from the beginning

In fact this wretch (the Shah) recognised Israel twenty years ago. I was in Qum at the time. He gave his recognition to a government of infidels - and Jewish infidels at that - thereby affronting Islam, the Quran, the Muslim governments and the entire Muslim people. The name of Israel was not openly mentioned at first, but later it was. Indeed, this person was a servant from the very beginning, as he himself later made clear.

Imam's speech dated 18 February 1978 (29 Bahman 1356 AHS). Sahifeh-ye Imam, vol. 3, pp. 357-8.

The reason for the opposition to the Shah

Question: Is the Shah's pro-Israeli policy one of the reasons for your opposition to the regime?

Reply: Yes, for Israel has occupied the land of a Muslim people and has perpetrated numerous crimes. The Shah's action of maintaining political relations with Israel and giving it economic aid goes against the interests of Islam and Muslims.

Imam's interview with the Le Monde newspaper, 6 May 1978 (16 Ordibehesht 1357 AHS). *Sahifeh-ye Imam*, vol. 3, p. 387.

In the name of nationalising resources, the Shah handed them over to the Zionists

On the other front however, the regime has handed wherever and whatever is of value over to large American, Zionist or British companies; and they have done so in the name of nationalisation. They have handed over our forests, pastures, water sources, rivers, subterranean waters and so on... It is said that the Umran Plain, situated on the outskirts of Qazvin, is the best place for cultivation. They have forced the people there to migrate elsewhere and have handed this land over to the Jews, the Zionists. Yes, they have given it to the Jews who are now using it to their own ends, American and Zionist companies reaping the benefits. These pieces of land, which are second to none, are now theirs to farm and cultivate.

Imam's speech dated 31 May 1978 (10 Khordad 1357 AHS). *Sahifeh-ye Imam*, vol. 3, pp. 427-8.

The Shah's support for Israel: the reason for the people's uprising

Question: What is your opinion of the Palestinian people's struggle? Taking into consideration the fact that more than half of Israel's oil is supplied by Iran, what measures should be taken by Iran on this matter?

Reply: One of the reasons for the uprising of the Muslim people of Iran against the Shah is the unsparing support he gives the usurper Israel. He provides Israel's oil and has turned Iran into a market for Israeli goods; in addition he offers other kinds of support expressed in the spirit of his words if not in the letter, while at the same time he merely condemns Israel in an attempt to deceive world opinion. Neither the Muslim nation of Iran nor any Muslim, nor, in principle, any freedom-seeker, officially recognises Israel, and we will always be the supporters of our Palestinian and Arab brothers.

Imam's interviews with the Middle East News Bulletin, 17 November 1978 (26 Aban 1357 AHS). *Sahifeh-ye Imam*, vol. 5, p. 137.

Israel, the Shah's advocate

Now, however, he (the Shah) imports everything from abroad. And whatever is brought into the country comes either from Israel... Israel the enemy of Islam! God only knows what treason this man has committed against Islam. Israel is the enemy of Islam, it is currently at war with the Muslims. From the very beginning this regime gave it official recognition. Twenty-five or thirty years ago when it was actually at war with the Muslims, these people officially recognised Israel! Then however, they did not make this known to the public. And today, as the end draws nigh, you can all see how one of Muhammad-Rida Khan's strongest advocates, one of the keenest proponents for the continuation of his rule, is Israel. For the Israelis argue that if he goes they will lose their supply of oil, because this regime is supplying Israel with its oil. In other words, they give the oil of a Muslim land to the enemy of Muslims to help it wage war against the Muslims! This is the kind of traitor this wretch is! He sends our oil to them in their tankers, he gets it to them by their own means, to the Israelis who with this oil wage war against the Muslims and who have usurped the Muslims' land, destroying everything they have. Look what they have done to Palestine, look how they have usurped Bayt al-Muqaddas (Jerusalem). This is just one of the treacherous acts this man has committed against Islam and the Muslims. Within Iran itself he has betrayed the Muslims for the sake of the Israelis. As I have been told, the best land of Iran has been given to the Israelis. The best land of Iran has been handed over to these Israeli Jews for them to work on and reap the benefit of.

Imam's remarks dated 25 November 1978 (4 Azar 1357 AHS). *Sahifeh-ye Imam*, vol. 5, p. 113.

The Shah's long-standing co-operation with Israel

Question: We know that by establishing close relations with Iran and by assisting the Iranian regime, international Zionism has always managed to keep Iran apart from the Arabs in their struggle against Israel. What is your view on this?

Reply: One of the reasons why we have been placed in a position of opposition to the Shah is the help he gives Israel. I have repeatedly stated that the Shah has co-operated with Israel from its inception, and when the war between Israel and the Muslims reached its zenith, the Shah unlawfully gave the oil of the Muslims to Israel. This matter is itself amongst the reasons why I oppose the Shah.

The Muslim nation of Iran has never supported Israel and because of this it has been exposed to the oppression and aggression of the Shah's regime.

Imam's interview with Amal, 7 December 1978 (16 Azar 1357 AHS). *Sahifeh-ye Imam*, vol. 5, pp. 183-4.

The media groups of the Shah's regime: defenders of Israel

Question: As you know, the Islamic revolution in Palestine began on 1 January 1956, and after the defeat of 1967, became more powerful and widespread. Did this news reach the people of Iran, and if so, through what means?

Reply: Yes, the news reached them through the same means as it reaches people in other countries. However, the Shah's regime tried to report the news of the Muslims' war with the infidel in a way that was favourable to the infidel, as it has always done, and as usual it presented the Arabs as a handful of people who do not fully understand matters. The regime is one of the biggest supporters of Israel. The Iranian radio, indeed all the means of communication collectively, whether those controlled by the regime or those which operated under pressure from the regime, worked to the advantage of Israel. We were the ones who from the very beginning opposed all the programmes and still do.

Imam's interview with a reporter from the Palestinian Wafa news agency, 15 December 1978 (24 Azar 1357 AHS). *Sahifeh-ye Imam*, vol. 5, pp. 233-4.

The supply of oil to Israel during the period of the national strikes

Apparently some of the *ulama* from Qum went to Abadan to study the situation there, and it was said that these 600,000 barrels of oil which are being exported are being sent to Israel. Some of the workers did not go on strike, and now 600,000 barrels are being sent abroad out of a total of some ten million barrels that were exported previously. The regime deceived these workers by telling them that this oil was to be used for the running of the country! They said it was for us! And so the poor workers carried on working. However, now it is clear, from what is being said, that this oil is going to Israel. It is illegal, it is sinful (*haram*), for this group of people, who have disregarded the strike by others and have been deceived by the government into believing the oil is for domestic consumption, to refuse to join the strike when they know that this oil is destined for Israel, the enemy of the Quran and Islam. They will have to answer to God and the nation. All of them (the oil workers) should go on strike, so that not even one drop of oil leaves the country. The nation of Iran is ready to suffer from the cold as long as Israel, which is harming Islam so, which is killing the Muslims so, doesn't have its oil...

Imam's remarks dated 16 December 1978 (25 Azar 1357 AHS). *Sahifeh-ye Imam*, vol. 5, pp. 244-5.

Israel, a partner in the Shah's crimes

Question: If you cut your relations with Israel for being a country which oppresses the people, do you not think that for the same reason you will cut relations with some of the Western governments too?

Reply: We oppose any country that carries out oppression whether it be in the West or the East. Israel has usurped the rights of the Arab people and we will stand in opposition to it. Israel is the biggest supporter of the Shah and is responsible for setting up SAVAK. For this reason, Israel is a partner in the crimes of SAVAK and the Shah.

Imam's interview with an American university professor, 28 December 1978 (7 Dey 1357 AHS). *Sahifeh-ye Imam*, vol. 5, p. 288.

Israeli soldiers in the service of the Shah's regime

I have been told that these massacres which have taken place were carried out by soldiers from Israel, but I do not have concrete proof of this. A few days ago someone - I can't remember his name - came here and told me that when he and a few others were travelling to Abadan, they stopped along the way to ask for directions and saw a soldier standing nearby. They called him over to them and realised that he didn't understand Persian, so one of the group spoke to him in Arabic and they learned that he was an Arab from Israel! The man himself admitted that he had been brought to Iran from Israel. A truck stood nearby full of his colleagues.

These people have used Israeli soldiers to kill the people of our nation.

Imam's remarks dated 14 January 1979 (24 Dey 1357 AHS). *Sahifeh-ye Imam*, vol. 5, p. 449.

Israeli torturers in the service of the Shah

We were ruled by beasts who, in line with their oppressive and tyrannical nature, destroyed our youths as they languished in their prisons, torturing and killing them in the most horrendous of manners. Torturers were even brought in from Israel to teach the techniques of torture. ?

Imam's address to a gathering of foreign ambassadors and diplomats, 11 February 1981 (22 Bahman 1359 AHS). *Sahifeh-ye Imam*, vol. 14, pp. 71-2.

Imam's Stance on Israel before the Culmination of the Islamic Revolution

(Before 1979 [1357 AHS])

The Bahais: agents of Israel

The gentlemen should realise that many sensitive posts are in the hands of this sect (the *Bahai* sect) who are in fact agents of Israel. The danger Islam and Iran faces from Israel is very close; a pact with Israel in opposition to the Muslim governments has either been made or is in the process of being made. It is necessary that the learned *ulama* and respected preachers make the other classes aware of this so that we can prevent it in time. Today is not the day to adopt the method of our pious forefathers; we shall lose everything by keeping silent and not getting involved.

Imam's reply to the *ulama* of Yazd dated April/May 1963 (Ordibehesht 1342 AHS). *Sahifeh-ye Imam*, vol. 1, pp. 183-4.

Declaration of disgust with the Shah's agreement with Israel

I declare to the heads of the Muslim states, whether Arab or non-Arab: the *ulama* of Islam, the religious leaders and pious people of Iran, together with its noble army, are the brothers of the Muslim states and share their losses and their gains. They abhor and are disgusted with the treaty with Israel, the enemy of Islam and Iran. I say this quite clearly; if they wish, let the agents of Israel come put an end to my life.

Imam's message dated 2 May 1963 (12 Ordibehesht 1342 AHS). *Sahifeh-ye Imam*, vol. 1, p. 194.

A historic warning

Today the Muslims, and in particular the learned *ulama*, have a great responsibility before God the Blessed and Exalted. By our silence, we expose future generations until the end of time to the danger of deviation and unbelief, and we are responsible. The danger we face from Israel and its heinous agents threatens Islam and Iran with extinction. I do not value a few days of life in shame and disgrace, and I expect the learned *ulama* and other classes of Muslims to come together and save the Quran and Islam from the danger which faces them.

Imam's reply to the *ulama* of Hamadan dated 6 May 1963 (16 Ordibehesht 1342 AHS). *Sahifeh-ye Imam*, vol. 1, p. 224.

Palestine is usurped and you fight over rivers

I ask the Muslim governments, why do you fight over rivers?[20] The land of Palestine has been usurped. O you hopeless ones, you should be throwing the Jews out of Palestine, instead you are fighting each other! Palestine has been usurped and you are squabbling over a river! While you dispute over a river, the Israelis have established a government in Palestine. They have driven those misfortunate Arabs out, and now a million or more of them are sleeping in deserts, hungry and bereft. They have become completely homeless and wretched.

Shouldn't the Muslim governments raise any objections?

Shouldn't they say something?

Should you enter into an alliance with a government which has thrown one million Muslims out of their homeland and made them homeless?

If you have not formed an alliance with them, well announce that you haven't in your newspapers; allow that which I am saying now to be published. If you refuse to do so, then obviously you have aligned yourselves with them, you have aligned yourselves with the Jews, with Israel!

You see what the agents of Israel do in this country.

Imam's speech, dated 9 September 1964 (18 Shahrivar 1343 AHS). *Sahifeh-ye Imam*, vol. 1, pp. 391-2.

Announcement of the repudiation of the compromise between the Shah and Israel

I declare to all the Muslim governments and the Muslims of the world wherever they are that the dear Shiite nation abhors Israel and its agents and detests and is disgusted with those governments which co-operate with Israel. It is not the nation of Iran which is presently making terms with the detested Israel, the nation of Iran is not guilty of this great sin, it is these governments which are doing this and which are in no way supported by the nation.

Imam Khomeini's warning to the nation about the danger facing Islam, dated 7 April 1964 (18 Farvardin 1343 AHS). *Sahifeh-ye Imam*, vol. 1, p. 264.

It is the duty of the Islamic leaders to put aside these petty differences

Today it is the duty of the heads of Islamic countries, the kings and the presidents of Islamic countries to put aside these petty differences which occasionally arise among them. There are no Arabs and non-Arabs, Turks and Persians; there is only Islam and unity under Islam. They should adopt the same method of struggle that the Prophet of Islam used in his struggle; they should follow the way of Islam. If they guard their ideological unity, if they put aside these occasional petty differences, if all the Muslims join together, then, according to estimations, there will be a community of seven hundred million. But seven hundred million people divided are not as great as one million united. Seven hundred million divided people are of no use, thousands of millions of divided people cannot do anything either. However, if these seven hundred million, if only four hundred million of them, two hundred million of them, were to unite together, join hands in brotherhood together, protect each other's borders, protect their own boundaries, if they were to unite in the Islamic community which is common to us all, in the religion of monotheism which is common to us all, in the Islamic interests that we share, then the Jews would no longer covet Palestine and India would no longer have designs on Kashmir.

That is why they don't let you unite. The hands that want to take your resources away from you, that want to take your wealth free of charge, that want to plunder both your underground resources and those that lie above the ground, they won't let Iraq and Iran, Iran and Egypt, Turkey and Iran unite together. They won't let them join forces. It is the duty of the leaders to sit down together and reach a mutual understanding. They should protect their own borders, each one should preserve their boundaries and territorial integrity then join forces against that foreign enemy who causes you so much harm. There is a group of thieving Jews in Palestine who have kept more than a million Muslims dispersed for ten years, more than ten years, and have occupied Islamic lands. All the Muslim leaders do is mourn over their plight. But if they unite, how can this bunch of thieving Jews take Palestine from you and drive the Muslims out of Palestine while you look on helplessly?

Imam's remarks, dated 14 November 1965 (23 Aban 1344 AHS). *Sahifeh-ye Imam*, vol. 2, p. 23.

The boycott and repulsion of Israel

In the Name of God, the Compassionate, the Merciful

I have repeatedly invited the Muslim governments to unity and brotherhood in order to confront the foreigners and their supporters who want to create discord amongst the Muslims and the Muslim governments and keep our dear countries weak and captives of imperialism and thus exploit their spiritual and material resources. I have repeatedly cautioned the governments, and in particular the Iranian government, against Israel and its dangerous agents. This source of corruption, which has been placed in the heart of the Islamic countries with the support of the great powers and whose corrupt roots threaten the Islamic countries every day, must be deracinated through the efforts of the Islamic countries and the great nations of Islam.

Israel has embarked on an armed attack against the Islamic countries and it is incumbent upon the governments and nations of Islam to eradicate it. Helping Israel, whether through the sale of arms and explosives or through the sale of oil is forbidden and is contrary to Islam. Having relations with Israel or its agents, whether they be commercial or political, is forbidden and is contrary to Islam. Muslims should refrain from using Israeli goods. I ask God the Exalted for the victory of Islam and the Muslims.

May peace and blessings be upon those who follow the guidance. ?

Ruhullah al-Musawi al-Khomeini

Imam's message to the Muslim governments and nations, dated 8 June 1967 (18 Khordad 1346 AHS). *Sahifeh-ye Imam*, vol. 2, p. 144.

Imam's Interview with Representatives from al-Fath about Assisting the al-Fath Guerrillas

The necessity of supporting and allocating religious funds to the Palestinian combatants

First question: Your Holiness, the leader of the combatants, what is your respected opinion on the giving of religious funds such as *zakat*[21] and sahm-i imam[22] to the brave combatants who, under the command of the Fath movement, are on the front lines of the battle with the enemy and are fighting on the battlefield of honour?

Reply: In the Name of God, the Compassionate, the Merciful. Most certainly it is proper and indeed obligatory that some of the religious funds such as *zakat* and other alms be allocated in a sufficient amount to these combatants who are fighting in the way of God; these combatants who fight on the line of battle and make sacrifices in order to destroy the atheist and anti-human Zionist movement, who strive to revive and restitute the lost glory and honour of Islam and who battle to respect the illustrious history of Islam. It is incumbent on every Muslim who believes in God and the day of retribution to use all the power at his disposal in this path and eventually attain one of these good things: martyrdom or victory. It is your duty to go to the front line and take vengeance for the blood shed and thus erase the mark of shame. Obtain aid and assistance from God's domain and secure the shining victory which is close. Then give glad tidings to the believers for God is the supporter of every courageous and truth-seeking decision: And another (favour will He bestow), which ye do love - help from God and a speedy victory. So give glad tidings to the believers. (Quran 61:13). And God is the supporter of this intent.

It is incumbent on us to use all the powers and means at our disposal to help our brothers, the great men of the Fath movement and their fighting forces al-Assifa, who, with the help of God the Almighty, will achieve the ultimate victory, and the other noble, self-sacrificing fighters who struggle in the way of God. And God guarantees success.

Second question: After the kindling of the fire of holy revolution in the land of Palestine and the attainment of many revolutionary achievements under the leadership of Fath, what is Your Excellency's opinion of our brothers who are resisting in the entrenchments and in the occupied lands?

Reply: In the Name of God, the Compassionate, the Merciful. My first and last opinion about our steadfast and militant brothers is that they should tirelessly continue in their battle because life is belief and struggle in the way of that belief. A matter about which there is no room for doubt, according to Islamic thought, is that death is better than this humiliating life. Therefore, in our present situation there is no other way but to continue to struggle with all the forces and means at our disposal, until, through the greatness of Islam, we attain glory and honour for ourselves and for future generations throughout history. "Against them make ready your strength, to the utmost of your power, including steeds of war to strike terror into the hearts of the enemies of God and your enemies." (Quran 8:60). "O ye who believe, if ye will aid (the cause of) God, he will aid you and plant your feet firmly." (Quran 47:7). "So lose not heart, nor fall into despair, for ye must gain mastery if ye are true in faith." (Quran 3:139). "And slacken not in following up the enemy, if ye are suffering hardships, they are suffering similar hardships; but ye have hope from God, while they have none." (Quran 4:104). So then, oh ye people of Fath, turn to God for help and hasten to the imminent victory and give glad tidings to the believers.

Third question: Would you please give your respected opinion on the culminating armed struggle taking place in the holy land of Palestine and the barbaric measures taken by the Zionists against the Arab and Muslim nation so that our Muslim people in all the countries will muster their material and spiritual forces and eventually take part in the holy war.

Reply: In the Name of God, the Compassionate, the Merciful. As I pointed out earlier, under the circumstances facing Islam and the Muslims at the moment, this is a matter of duty. After submitting to the holy laws of Islam, I know of no matter which is more obligatory for the Muslims than rising up in defence at the cost of one's life and property for the sake of Islam. When you see the blood of your innocent brothers and sisters flowing in the holy lands of Palestine, and when you witness our lands being destroyed at the hands of the destructive Zionists, under these circumstances there is no way other than to continue the holy war and it is the duty of every Muslim to render material and morale support. And God is the supporter of this intent.

Fourth question: At present, when the hands of the Zionists have infiltrated all the vital affairs of the Muslim country of Iran, what, in Your Excellency's opinion, is the best method the Muslim nation in Iran can adopt to sever the hands of Zionism?

Reply: In the Name of God, the Compassionate, the Merciful. The best way is for the Muslim people of Iran to strive with all the means at their disposal to stop doing business completely with Zionists in Iran and elsewhere. They should break their spirit and render them helpless materially; they should restrict their opportunities and embark on an economic struggle against them. They should fight against them in other areas too so that eventually they will be forced to sever all their relations with Iran and with the Muslim people there. Consequently, the Iranian nation can then place all its material and spiritual resources at the disposal of these freedom fighters. These painful circumstances make it necessary for all Muslims to use all their forces to free the occupied lands and wreak vengeance on the occupiers. And God guarantees success.

There is no room for doubt on one point, and that is this is the duty of each individual Muslim, even those Muslims in the farthest reaches of the Islamic world, just as it is the duty of the Muslim people of Palestine. The Muslims are like a hand which is held up in front of anything that is against them and all share the same responsibilities. Disunion and racism have no place here and nothing places one Islamic nation above another except piety and devoutness. "Verily the most honoured of you in the sight of God is he who is the most righteous," (Quran 49:13). "For us God sufficeth, and He is the best disposer of affairs," (Quran 3:173).

Imam's interview with representatives from al-Fath about assisting the al-Fath guerrillas. September/October 1968 (Mehr 1347 AHS). *Sahifeh-ye Imam*, vol. 2, pp. 204-6.

This source of corruption must be repulsed in whatever way possible

I have also pointed this out before that the usurper government of Israel, with the aims that it has, poses a great danger to Islam and the Muslim countries. There is reason to fear that if the Muslims give them (the Israelis) a respite, they will lose their opportunity and stopping them will be impossible. Since the potential danger is to the very foundations of Islam, it is incumbent on the Muslim governments in particular and Muslims in general to repulse this source of corruption in whatever way possible and not to neglect helping the defenders. It is permitted for them to use money from the *zakat* funds and other alms to carry out this vitally important task. I ask God the Most High to prepare the motives for the rousing and awakening of the Muslims and to repel the evil of the enemies of Islam from the Muslim lands.

Imam's reply to a letter from a group of freedom-fighters, dated August 28, 1968 (Shahrivar 6, 1347 AHS). *Sahifeh-ye Imam*, vol. 2, pp. 199-200.

Boycott of Israel

You have no knowledge of the dreams they have for these countries. I have repeatedly brought the danger posed by the government of Israel and its agents to the attention of the nation and have told them they must adopt a policy of passive resistance towards them and avoid doing business with them.

Imam's telegram, July / August 1970 (Mordad 1349 AHS). *Sahifeh-ye Imam*, vol. 2, p. 286.

Calling on the Muslims to defend the Palestinian fighters

And then, at the head of all these disasters there is Palestine. Difference of opinions and the mercenary nature of some of the leaders of Islamic countries have not given the seven hundred million Muslims of the world the chance nor the possibility, despite their wealth, minerals and other natural resources, to sever the hands of imperialism and Zionism and to limit foreign influence. Selfishness, servitude and the surrender by some Arab governments to direct foreign influence have prevented the tens of millions of Arabs from freeing Palestine from Israeli occupation and usurpation.

Everyone must know that the goal of the great powers in creating Israel does not end with the occupation of Palestine. They are planning to make all the Arab countries share in Palestine's fate, God forbid. Today, we are spectators of the Palestinian combatants' struggle in their holy war (*jihad*) to place the destiny of Palestine into the hands of the Palestinians; we are onlookers as these freedom fighters take their lives in their hands and bravely rise up in holy war against occupation and aggression and to free Palestine and the occupied lands; we are spectators of that which the hands of the imperialist appointees did to these freedom fighters yesterday in Jordan and what they are doing to them today in Lebanon; we are spectators of the propaganda that is instigated by the imperialist appointees and the machinations that are carried out by them, in various ways, all with the aim of distancing the Muslim groups from the Palestinian combatants and of throwing the battle out of the strategic areas - for it would have given them a prime opportunity to deal a serious blow to the forces of Israel and Zionism, this usurping enemy.

Under such circumstances, do the Muslims and the heads of the Islamic states not have a duty and a responsibility before God? Morally and rationally are they not obliged to help? Is it right that the Palestinian freedom fighters be massacred by imperialist appointees in areas under imperialist sway while others remain silent in the face of this crime and even collaborate and conspire together to throw this freedom-bestowing *jihad* out of its most suitable and strategic zone? Do not the Arab governments and the Muslim residents of this region know that with the annihilation of this *jihad*, the other Arab countries will not be safe and secure from the malevolence of this perverse enemy?

Today, in order to safeguard their own independence, it is necessary for all Muslims in general and the Arab regimes and governments in particular to devotedly aid and support this group of fighters and not to spare any effort in supplying them with arms and provisions. The self-sacrificing fighters must continue resolutely and earnestly, by relying on God and holding fast to the teachings of the Quran, to reach their holy aim. They should not despair because of the indifference or apathy of some elements nor let this deal a blow to their zeal for freedom. It should be emphasised that relations between these fighters and the people of the areas where they are active must be based on Islamic brotherhood and good conduct.

I ask all aware, vigilant and far-sighted Muslims, especially God's pure servants and the learned *ulama*, to beseech God during these blessed days to help the Muslims free themselves from the perverse rule of imperialism. In the gatherings of the holy month of Ramadan, and other great Islamic gatherings such as Friday Prayers and *hajj* strive to make the truth known to all Muslims and invite the people to follow the (teachings of the) Quran which call for everyone to unite. Join hands to liberate Palestine and resolve the destructive problems with which the entire Islamic world is grappling. I ask God, the Most Great, to sever the hands of foreigners from Muslim lands. And He is the listener and the acceptor.

Imam's message calling for support for Palestine, 10 November 1972 (19 Aban 1351 AHS). *Sahifeh-ye Imam*, vol. 2, pp. 479-80.

Close ranks in order to destroy Israel

In the Name of God, the Compassionate, the Merciful

"And slay them wherever ye catch them, and turn them out from where they have turned you out," (Quran 2:191). "And fight them on until there is no more tumult or oppression," (Quran 2:193).

Now that the usurping government of Israel has begun to excite more disturbances, to encroach further on Arab lands, to stretch out usurping hands against the ones on the side of right and fan the flames of war for the umpteenth time, and now that our Muslim brothers have taken their lives in their hands and are fighting on the fields of battle, the fields of honour, to root out this source of corruption and to free Palestine, it is incumbent on all governments of Islamic countries, and especially the Arab governments, to mobilise all their forces and with trust in God the Exalted and reliance on His everlasting power come to the aid of the self-sacrificing men who are fighting on the front lines and are looking optimistically to the Islamic nation for help. They should waste no time and join in this holy war to liberate Palestine and revive the glory, honour and greatness of Islam. They should refrain from destructive and weakening disagreements and discord, extend the hand of brotherhood to one another, close ranks and organise themselves. They should not be afraid of the frail power of the defenders of Zionism and Israel, nor deluded or subdued by the vain promises and idle threats of the great powers. They should avoid apathy and procrastination as this will lead to ignoble defeat and dangerous consequences.

The heads of the Islamic countries should be aware that this germ of corruption which has been planted in the heart of the Islamic countries has not been put there merely to suppress the Arab nation, rather it is dangerous and harmful to the Middle East region as a whole. The plan is for the domination and supremacy of Zionism over the Islamic world and the further colonisation of the rich lands and abundant resources of the Islamic countries. Only through self-sacrifice, perseverance and the unity of the Muslim governments can freedom from the evil of this black incubus of colonialism be found. If one government fails to act as it should in this vital matter which now faces Islam, then it is incumbent upon the other Muslim governments to persuade it to co-operate through reproaches, threats and the severing of relations. It is the duty of the governments of Islamic oil-producing countries to use their oil and the other means they have at their disposal as weapons against Israel and the imperialists and to refuse to sell their oil to governments supporting Israel.

Imam's message, 7 November 1973 (16 Aban 1352 AHS). *Sahifeh-ye Imam*, vol. 3, pp. 1-2.

Giving Israeli agents control is an act of treason against the country

The creation of military, communication and espionage bases for foreigners contravenes the Constitution. Giving foreigners and their vile agents, amongst them Israel, control of the best lands in the country and stopping the nation from using them constitute a breach of constitutional law and an act of treason against the country. ?

Imam's reply to a group of people seeking advice about boycotting the Rastakhiz party, dated 12 March 1975 (21 Isfand 1353 AHS), vol. 3, p. 74.

SECTION THREE

IMAM AND THE ISLAMIC REVOLUTION, BASTIONS OF RESISTANCE TO ISRAEL

Imam and the islamic revolution, bastions of resistance to israel

Elucidating the Reasons for the Weakness of the Muslims

(Division in the Ranks and the Weakness of the Governments)

If the rulers of the Muslim countries joined together like the fingers of one hand

If the Muslims had acted in accordance with this command: "Prepare against them whatever force you can muster and horses tethered" (Quran, 8:60), and, after forming a government, made the necessary extensive preparations to be in a state of full readiness for war, a handful of Jews would never have dared to occupy our lands, and to burn and destroy the al-Aqsa mosque without the people's being capable of making an immediate response. All this has resulted from the failure of the Muslims to rise up and execute God's law and set up a righteous and respectable government. If the rulers of the Muslim countries truly represented the believers and enacted God's ordinances, they would set aside their petty differences, abandon their subversive and divisive activities, and join together like the fingers of one hand. Then a handful of wretched Jews (the agents of America, Britain and other foreign powers) would never have been able to accomplish what they have, no matter how much support they enjoyed from America and Britain. All this has happened because of the incompetence of those who rule over the Muslims.

Islamic Government, pp. 46-47.

It is the disputes among the heads of Muslim states that have allowed the problem of Palestine to arise

If the heads of Muslim states were to abandon their mutual disputes in order to acquaint themselves with the lofty goals of Islam and to orient their policies in accordance with Islam, they would no longer be the abject captives of imperialism. It is those disputes among the heads of Muslim states that have allowed the problem of Palestine to arise and that do not permit it to be solved. If the 700 million Muslims, with the vast countries that they inhabit, had the political maturity to unite and organise themselves in a single front, it would not be possible for the big imperialist powers to penetrate their countries, let along a handful of Jews who are the servants of imperialism.

Imam's message dated 8 February 1971 (19 Bahman 1349 AHS). *Sahifeh-ye Imam*, vol. 2, p. 333.

The lack of reliance on Islam has caused these catastrophes

If the Muslim states and peoples had relied on Islam instead of relying on the Eastern or Western bloc and had paid attention to the luminous and liberating teachings of the Noble Quran and then practised those teachings, they would not be enslaved today by the Zionist aggressors, nor terrorised by American Phantoms, nor at the mercy of the satanic cunning of the Soviet Union. It is the gulf between the Muslim states and the Noble Quran that has plunged our people into this dark and catastrophic situation and placed the destiny of the Muslim peoples and countries in the hands of the treacherous policies of imperialism of the right and the left.

Imam's message to students, dated 13 July 1972 (22 Tir 1351 AHS). *Sahifeh-ye Imam*, vol. 2, pp. 456-7.

The mercenary nature of some of the leaders

And then, at the head of all these disasters there is Palestine. Difference of opinions and the mercenary nature of some of the leaders of Islamic countries have not given the seven hundred million Muslims of the world the chance nor the possibility, despite their wealth, minerals and other natural resources to sever the hands of imperialism and Zionism and to limit foreign influence. Selfishness, servitude and the surrender by some Arab governments to direct foreign influence, have prevented the tens of millions of Arabs from freeing Palestine from Israeli occupation and usurpation.

Imam's message calling for support for Palestine, 10 November 1972 (19 Aban 1351 AHS). *Sahifeh-ye Imam*, vol. 2, p. 479.

Divergence, loss of countenance or the mission of some of the leaders have brought about the sovereignty of imperialism

As I have warned so many times, if the nation of Islam does not awaken and become aware of its duties, if the *ulama* of Islam do not acquire a sense of responsibility and do not rise up, if the hands of the foreigners' agents are allowed to keep true Islam - which produces the unity and movement of all Muslim denominations against the foreigners and guarantees the supremacy and independence of the Muslim nations and Islamic countries - hidden in this way behind the black curtain of imperialism, and if the flames of disagreement and divergence are kindled amongst the Muslims, then blacker and more catastrophic days than these lie ahead for the Islamic community, and the very foundations of Islam and the laws of the Quran face a destructive danger. The overt and covert assaults of the enemies of Islam and the international attacks against the Holy Quran and the freedom-bestowing laws of Islam are being vigorously pursued from every direction. Many governments of the Islamic countries, as a result either of their loss of countenance or the mission given to them, are the executers of the enemies' fatal and treacherous plans. Whether those who speak of Islam and establish the so-called "Islamic" Conference or those who abolish religion in Islamic countries and knock Islam from its official status, all of them, knowingly or unknowingly, are moving along one path, the path of implementing the malicious, imperialistic aims of the enemies of Islam who want to see this catastrophic situation of the Islamic community perpetuated; who want Israel to prevail over the lives, possessions and lands of the Islamic nation; who want imperialist supremacy and rule preserved in the Islamic world for ever and the destructive expansionist programme of Zionism reach the stage of implementation in the Islamic countries; who want to see the nation of Islam and the governments of the Islamic countries remain always abject and humble, the captives of international aggression; who want to see them stretch out a begging hand and turn a pleading eye to the criminal imperialists and never enjoy independence, freedom, peace and security.

Imam's reply to students dated 15 March 1973 (24 Isfand 1351 AHS). *Sahifeh-ye Imam*, vol. 2, p. 506.

Lack of maturity on the part of the governments is a source of regret

Many more Muslim countries are also beset by unending difficulties. There is Lebanon which has been reduced to a heap of dust. What damage to life and property have the Muslims there, especially the Shiites, not suffered? The foreigners and their treacherous agents fan the flames of ravaging wars and deprive the people of their possessions. Then there is the situation in Palestine and the problems there which increase daily. That which is a source of great regret is the lack of maturity on the part of the governments and the leaders of the people who rise up in disagreement with one another because of the foreigners.

Imam's message on the occasion of the auspicious *Id al-Fitr*[23], dated November, 1977 (Aban 1355 AHS). *Sahifeh-ye Imam*, vol. 3, p. 172.

Most of the Muslim governments busy themselves with unproductive talks

The deplorable situation in Lebanon and the tragedies inflicted upon our innocent brothers in faith in the southern region of that country have caused us great suffering and pain. Presently, tens of thousands from the well-equipped and criminal army of Israel - this germ of corruption - are in control of the lands of southern Lebanon, the base of our brothers in faith, equipped with arms, artillery, tanks and aeroplanes. They are driving the innocent inhabitants of this area out of their homes, destroying their houses and burning their crops, while the Muslim governments remain largely indifferent in the face of these crimes even occasionally assisting in them or busying themselves with unproductive talks, leaving the brave Palestinian freedom fighters, who are courageously resisting Israel, to battle alone. Perhaps this shows that there is a plot devised by the superpowers. At present our brothers and their defenceless children are burning in the flames and are facing many dangers.

Imam's message on the deplorable situation in Lebanon, dated 22 March 1978 (2 Farvardin 1357 AHS). *Sahifeh-ye Imam*, vol. 3, p. 372.

If they join forces, America cannot do anything

These differences have arisen either because of the acts of betrayal committed by the leaders of these countries, of these Islamic countries, or because of their ignorance and unawareness whereupon they have failed to reach any mutual understanding or to combine like the roaring waves of the sea in order to smash whatever confronts them.

Indeed, you can see for yourselves how in Palestine a certain number of Zionists, a limited number of Jews, have intimidated the Arab countries, with a total population exceeding 100 million, such that some of them have surrendered to them whilst others, although not surrendering, can't actually do anything about the situation. How many years is it now since Israel usurped this land which belongs to the Palestinians? Yet throughout all this time this vast Arab population and all of these Arab countries haven't been able to free Palestine. They say that America is supporting her (Israel) and they can therefore do nothing. But this is not so, it is you (the Arabs) who are feckless! Yes, they are feckless.

If this one-hundred-million-strong Arab population were to join forces, then even America wouldn't be able to stand in their way and neither would the European countries. No country would be able to stand in their way. But the fact is that they are not united.

Yes indeed, what the foreign powers do is to ensure that these Arab nations are prevented from joining forces. If at any time they suspect that these Arab governments plan to unite, what they do is to act so as to foil these plans. Hence, for example, they take the Egyptian President to America where they sign a treaty with him or whatever. They thus lead him along a path which is not open to others, whilst they lead another Arab leader along a different path which, again, is not open to anyone else. It is because of our lack of understanding and our inability as Muslims to do something that we are all under foreign domination and that America, Russia and other countries like them are taking away whatever is of worth in the East.

Imam's message dated 31 October 1978 (9 Aban 1357 AHS). Sahifeh-ye Imam, vol. 4, pp. 216-8.

The governments could not preserve independence and unity

My opinion of the Arab governments is not a good one. The Arab governments have not been able to preserve their independence nor create unity amongst themselves in order to destroy Israel. Differences among them along with the treason of some of the Arab heads of state have resulted in the Zionists being here and establishing themselves here, and unfortunately in the Egyptian president recently doing what he did.[24] Of course, possibly some of the governments are, relatively speaking, not that bad, but on the whole they could not bring about unity amongst themselves through which to free themselves both from the imperialists and their henchmen, amongst them Israel. However, as far as the Arab nations are concerned, they are our brothers and we treat them as such.

Imam's interview with an Egyptian reporter dated 12 November 1978 (21 Aban 1357 AHS). *Sahifeh-ye Imam*, vol. 4, p. 431.

If the Muslims were men of action, they wouldn't be so helpless before Israel

I must say that the enemies of Islam, those countries which hold sway over the Islamic countries and the Muslims, comprise men of action, not words, while the Muslims, after the early period of Islam, have been men of words, not action. They were deft at reciting poetry, adept at preaching sermons, when they discussed problems they did so expertly, but they did not exceed the bounds of words, they did not reach the stage of action. If they had done, then it would be hard to believe that more than a hundred million Arabs could be so helpless before Israel, and with everything they possessed, along with the West's dependence in many areas on the Islamic countries, they could fall under its sway, particularly when one considers their huge populations and their many resources. This is down to nothing other than the fact that we have now lost that spirit which existed in the early age of Islam and was the cause of supremacy.

Imam's remarks to a gathering of ambassadors of Islamic countries dated 10 July 1979 (19 Tir 1358 AHS). *Sahifeh-ye Imam*, vol. 9, pp. 38-9.

The source of the Muslims' problems

Many of the calamities which befall the Muslims stem from the Muslim governments, these Muslim governments who should speak with one voice, who should share the same views, who are all of one and the same religion and the adherents of the same book. They all see how their differences have benefited others, they know what the affliction is but they don't seek a cure. Rather, every day their differences increase and the gulf between them widens. This is what the big powers want, for us to be disunited, even become enemies, become occupied with one another's affairs so that they can take advantage. The Muslims should think of a basic solution to their problems and the Muslim governments should do likewise. They shouldn't think only of remaining in power in their countries and of living a prosperous life, they should cure this affliction of disunion for there is no other solution; no assembly, no conference and no league will be effective. I ask God the Blessed and Exalted to awaken Muslims in general and the Muslim governments in particular and help them to overcome their problems, and for Islam to be materialised in the Islamic countries the way it truly is, the way it was in the early age of Islam.

Another problem the Muslims have is that of the (relationship between the) government and the nation. To the best of my knowledge, and as you yourselves are also aware, the governments are ones which are not in agreement with their people, they treat the people as an enemy would treat an enemy, the nation turns its back on the government and the government tries to impose itself upon the nation, for this reason the nations do not support their governments, rather they treat them as an enemy would treat an enemy and this is the cause of the weakness of these governments.

Imam's remarks to a gathering of ambassadors of Islamic countries dated 10 July 1979 (19 Tir 1358 AHS). *Sahifeh-ye Imam*, vol. 9, p. 40.

The enigma of disunion

There is something which puzzles me and it is that all the Muslim governments and nations know what the problem is, they know that the hands of foreigners are involved in disuniting them, they see that this disunity will weaken and destroy them, they see how the frail government of Israel has stood against the Muslims, and they know that if united and each one of them threw a bucket of water over Israel it would be washed away, yet still they are helpless before it. I am puzzled as to why, when they know this, they do not turn to the sure remedy which is unity and alliance? Why do they not neutralise the plots which the imperialists use to undermine them? At what time will this puzzle be solved and who is to be the one to solve it? Who should neutralise these plots other than the Muslim governments and the Muslim nations? If you have the answer to this puzzle and have solved it, then tell us too.

Imam's remarks dated 16 August 1979 (25 Mordad 1358 AHS). *Sahifeh-ye Imam*, vol. 9, pp. 250-1.

The two most important problems facing the Muslims

We realise and the Muslims realise, although it is important that the Muslim governments realise too, that that which befalls us and has befallen us in the past stems from two problems: one is the problem which the governments face and which sadly until now they have not been able to solve and that is the differences which exist among them and the fact that they know all the difficulties of the Muslims spring from these differences.

For nearly twenty years now I have told them to do something about this problem. I have spoken and written about this matter and I have called on the heads of governments to unite, however, unfortunately hitherto to no avail. And the second problem is that which the governments have with the people, for they have treated their people in such a way that now they do not enjoy their support. Because of this lack of concord, when a problem arises for the governments which must be solved with the help of the people, the people either aggravate the situation further or at the very least remain indifferent. And I have said, perhaps repeatedly, that it is a good idea for the governments to learn a lesson from the experiences of our former and present governments. If a problem arose for the former government under the *taghuti*[25] regime, the nation either aggravated it further or was indifferent towards it.

Imam's remarks at a gathering of some members of the Islamic Council and the Palestine Resistance Organisation, 15 September 1979 (24 Shahrivar 1358 AHS). *Sahifeh-ye Imam*, vol. 9, pp. 491-2.

All the difficulties are a result of the carelessness of the heads of state

All these difficulties which have arisen for our brothers in Quds throughout this long period have been the result of the carelessness of the Arab leaders. For more than twenty years now in my sermons and speeches I have advised the heads of state to put aside these petty regional differences, to think as one, to unite for the sake of Islam and to advance the aims of Islam. It shames me to say that a small number of people can come and, in the face of an Arab population of more than one hundred million and an approximate seven hundred or eight hundred million Muslim population, commit such deeds. The fact that America is behind them is no excuse, for America was behind the Shah too. When a nation came together for a cause, neither the satanic might of the Shah could resist it nor the support of the superpowers. If the Arab community brings together all its forces and, more importantly, if the leaders of this community unite, then without a doubt neither America nor the other powers can do anything to them.

Imam's rema at a meeting with Abu Jihad, 14 October 1979 (22 Mehr 1358 AHS). Sahifeh-ye Imam, vol. 10, pp. 201-2.

Servitude of the governments

The problem for the Muslims is their governments. It is these governments that have brought the Muslims to this state of affairs. Nations are not the Muslims' problem; nations, with the innate character they possess, can solve the problems, but the problem is with the governments. When you look at all the Muslim countries, you can find very few places where their problems have not been created by their governments. It is these governments which, as a result of their relations with the superpowers and their servitude to the superpowers of the left and right, have created problems for us and for all the Muslims. If this problem is removed, the Muslims will attain their aspirations. The solution lies in the hands of the nations.

Imam's remarks at a gathering of participants in the Congress for the Freedom of Quds, 9 August 1980 (18 Mordad 1359 AHS). *Sahifeh-ye Imam*, vol. 13, pp. 73-4.

Why do the Arab governments take a slap in the face from Zionism?

Why are the Muslims unaware of this power? Why are the Muslim governments unaware of this power of Islam? Why have the Arab governments, throughout these long years, taken a slap in the face from Zionism? Why should they be in the control of foreign powers? Sadly there are differences among them and this is the problem for the Muslims.

Imam's remarks dated 20 October 1980 (28 Mehr 1359 AHS). *Sahifeh-ye Imam*, vol. 13, p. 241.

We shouldn't complain too much about America!

We shouldn't complain too much about America, even though it is the source of corruption, but we should complain and cry out about the Islamic countries and the Muslim governments. Islam strongly communicates the need for coming together and having unity of purpose, not only that, it actually brings it into practice too. There are days commemorated in

Islam whereby unity is strengthened by their very existence and by the motives behind them, days such as Ashura and Arbain. The Noble Quran has insisted upon this point that the people, the Muslims, should not be disunited, they should be like the fingers of one hand and hold fast to the rope of God. America's doctrine, however, is that it must sow dissension among the Muslims, exploit them, strip them of their dignity, plunder their wealth and resources and keep them a consumer society, this in order to pursue its foul aims. We don't expect anything else from America. But as far as the Muslims are concerned, that is the Muslim leaders, these we do have a complaint about, and we must cry out because of them, for they present themselves as supporters of Islam, yet they act against the text of the Noble Quran, against the *sunnah* (traditions) of the great Prophet of God and against the interests of the countries under their control. The problem for the Muslims is these governments which are governing over them and these differences which are created by them. If it weren't for this plan of America's[26] and its second plan drawn up by Fahd,[27] along with the other plans which will be formed later, Israel would not have dared to annex the Golan Heights. These plans have created dissension and have opened the way for Israel.

Imam's remarks dated 16 December 1981 (25 Azar 1360 AHS). *Sahifeh-ye Imam*, vol. 15, pp. 370-1.

The treason of some leaders

The problem lies in the inattentiveness of the governments who give away their resources, proffer their wealth, and in return bring the gift of obsequiousness for themselves and their people. The problem for all the Muslims and Islam lies in this inattentiveness or the treason of some of the heads of state. If the nations are sitting back waiting for these governments to restrain Israel for them and restrain the other powers who want to rob them of their wealth and drag them into abjection, then they are waiting in vain. You can see how they have sowed dissension among the Arabs with this plan, well now they want to create differences among our Muslim governments with this one piece of propaganda: they (the Iranians) buy weapons from Israel, they are playing terrorist games and have done such and such in Bahrain. This is all part of the plan for Muslims that they have drawn up which today opens the way even further for dissension and widens the gulf between the governments daily. And it has begun to produce results. This annexation of the Golan Heights by the usurper Israel is just a taste of things to come. Israel, with the backing it has from America, pays no heed to these American-installed organisations, however much they may protest, it carries on doing what it wants to do.

Imam's remarks dated 16 December 1981 (25 Azar 1360 AHS). *Sahifeh-ye Imam*, vol. 15, p. 371.

Why do those who claim to care about the noble cities of Mecca and Medina support this?

That which afflicts Islam today is that the ears which should listen to the problems of the Muslims have become deaf, the tongues which should speak in the interest of the Muslims have become dumb, and the eyes which should see the calamities that have befallen the Muslims have become blind. What should we say to these deaf, dumb and blind people. Don't the governments of the region view the Lebanese problem as a disaster? Don't they see it as being a disaster for Islam? Don't they see it as being a disaster for the Muslims of the world? Isn't the attack by Israel on Lebanon and the numerous killings perpetrated there a disaster? Do they not constitute a disaster for Islam, a disaster for the Muslims? Does the statement that this attack took place with the approval of America go in one ear and out the other? If they are not deaf, then why do they not hear these cries and moans of our dear ones in Lebanon? If they are not blind, then why do they not see these killings which are taking place every day in Lebanon and Iran? Why do they not see the dear youths being killed at the warfronts and the women, children and old men being killed away from the warfronts in the towns and cities? If they see these things and view them as a catastrophe, then why is nobody speaking out? If they care about the state of Islam, if they care about the Noble Quran, if they care about the noble cities, then why today, when these religious guideposts are being trampled upon, when Islam, the Quran and the noble cities (of Islam) are being threatened, do they not speak out? Why do they still proffer help (to the enemies of Islam)? What has happened to them that these calamities take place in their presence, such crimes are committed in their presence and yet not only do they remain silent on the matter but they pledge their support too. Once again they want to endorse the Camp David agreement; once again they want to endorse the Fahd plan; once again they want to officially recognise Israel. To whom should we turn with these tragedies? To these governments who have closed their eyes and ears to the matter and have faint-heartedly surrendered themselves to America? Or to these innocent nations who are writhing under the yoke of their repression?

Imam Khomeini's remarks dated 13 June 1982 (23 Khordad 1361 AHS). *Sahifeh-ye Imam*, vol. 16, pp. 281-2.

To whom can we turn with our complaints about these governments?

To whom can we turn with our complaints about these governments other than to God the Blessed and Exalted? Where should we begin with our complaints about those who call for a holy war against Iran? They call for a holy war against Iran which has risen up and means to stand up to all the powers and to carry Islam into effect globally, yet they remain silent when it comes to Israel which has risen in battle against Islam, which states clearly that the lands from the Nile to the Euphrates belong to it and views the noble cities as its own. To whom can we turn with these problems? With whom should we discuss these tragedies? Whom should we petition about this lethal silence, this silence which endorses the criminals, this silence which encourages the oppressors, to whom can we turn for help to break this silence? Are you few in number? Is your wealth little? Is your oil insignificant? Are your lands few in number? Do you not possess important centres which are of strategic value? All the means are there, only one thing is missing: faith. There is no faith.

Imam Khomeini's remarks at a gathering of representatives from some of the world's freedom movements, 13 June 1982 (23 Khordad 1361 AHS). *Sahifeh-ye Imam*, vol. 16, p. 198.

The governments bear the humiliation Israel brings upon them in order to rule the people

In the Name of God, the Compassionate, the Merciful

We are from God and to Him is our return

As we commemorate Quds Day for the year 1982 (1361 AHS), we are going through the saddest and most painful of days and we are leaving behind us the most regrettable and disastrous of times. Our sadness and pain are not only on account of the innocent, defenceless people who have been martyred in the oppressed country of Lebanon; nor do our distress and feeling that a disaster has occurred stem merely from the extensive attack that the criminal Israel carried out on the Arab inhabitants and Muslims of Beirut using cluster and fire bombs, causing the martyrdom and injury of thousands of innocent and defenceless men and women, young and old alike, and children; nor are we grieved simply because of the malicious plans of America, the supercriminal, to destroy the foundation of Islam in Iran and other countries; nor because of the material and psychological help that Egypt and Jordan and their colleagues give to the two unrestrained criminals, Begin and Saddam, who have brutal and criminal natures and whose material life and existence depend on infringing upon the rights of the nations and the weak of the earth and who pride themselves on tyrannising and suppressing the oppressed nations; nor on account of the ruthless aggression of the Aflaqite Saddam and the Baath party of Iraq against the Islamic country of Iran, the murder of thousands of children, old men and women, and the razing of the verdurous, populous Arab- and Persian-inhabited cities of Iran - for this infidel party cannot bear Islam thus its plan is to overthrow Islam and its supporters. No, our affliction, distress, sadness and pain stem from the fact that the Muslims are scourged by these governments who have sold themselves and lost themselves to the superpower America and who blindly follow the commands of the enemies of Islam and Muslims.

They (these governments) use excuses to try to justify their opposition to the Islamic Republic and for supplying arms to Saddam - to a man who sees Islam as his enemy - along with the other military, material and psychological help they give him. They bring up this matter of us being Persians and them being Arabs, which totally contradicts Islamic precepts and those of the Noble Quran, and over their propaganda loudspeakers and in their media, which is in the service of the superpowers, they use the big lie that Israel is supporting Iran as an excuse for helping Saddam.

What excuse do they have for their lethal silence today when Israel has attacked an Arab Muslim country and is shedding the blood of Muslims there?

What excuse can they come up with before God the Avenger and the Islamic nations for the help they give to Israel and its criminal master?

What excuse do they have for following up the demeaning Camp David proposal and the Fahd plan?

What excuse do they have for compromising with these congenital and professional bloodthirsty criminals?

Is today's America any different from the America of yesterday with which they (the Arab governments) falsely accused us of compromising? Or is this Israel any different from the Israel which they said was arming the Islamic republic and then used this false claim as a pretext to rush to the aid of Saddam and demonstrate animosity towards us as they hurried to save the Aflaq Baath party?

Oh God, the Muslims of the region have to contend with such rulers just as their lord Ali ibn abi Talib had to contend with the hypocrites - who put on a show of being good and pious - at whose hands during this period he was sent to meet You, thus being relieved of his burdens.

Oh God, today Islam is beset by hypocrites more criminal than those people at Nahrawan (the Kharijites), hypocrites who, in the name of Islam, crush Islam and co-operate with the enemies of Islam to, in effect, plunder the oppressed, deprived nations and fetter the freedom-seekers of those nations.

Oh God, these ignorant men of power carry upon their shoulders the burden of the knowledge that they bear the humiliation Israel brings upon them so they can rule over the Muslim nations for a few days.

Oh God, these ignorant governments, with all the means at their disposal for victory over the superpowers, endorse the crimes of America and Israel and work day and night to strengthen the foundations of unbelief.

Imam's message dated 16 July 1982 (25 Tir 1361 AHS). *Sahifeh-ye Imam*, vol. 16, pp. 328-9.

Some governments turn to America for protection from Israel!

It is the duty of the nations, with the arrival of Quds Day and the anniversary of the martyrdom of that great man in the history of mankind (Imam Ali [pbuh]), in their gatherings and marches to earnestly demand that their governments rise up against America and Israel using their military might and their oil weapon. And if they (the governments) pay no heed to this demand and instead support the criminal Israel which threatens the whole region, even the noble cities, and the depth of whose aspirations are now apparent, they must force them into action through pressure, strikes and threats. In a situation when Islam and its holy sites are under threat of aggression, no Muslim can remain indifferent. That which the governments of the region are doing at this time, when Israel is encroaching extensively on Muslim lands and is killing innocent, defenceless Muslims, is nothing other than uttering empty, conciliatory words. And more disastrous than this is that they turn to America, the criminal kingpin, for protection against Israel, in effect like turning to a dragon out of fear of a snake, and even though they have the means with which to fight them, they are not prepared even to utter a hostile word against them or threaten them. In such a situation, everyone should prepare himself for obliteration and throughout his life consent to any form of humiliation.

Imam's message dated 16 July 1982 (25 Tir 1361 AHS). *Sahifeh-ye Imam*, vol. 16, p. 330.

The self-love of some leaders

Self-love is what makes these leaders of Muslim countries indifferent to the crimes perpetrated by these powers and their dependants. If they didn't possess this self-love and this love of position and power, then they wouldn't sit by watching as these tragedies took place, as these unjust acts were perpetrated against Iran and Lebanon where the situation is even worse. All of them are afraid that their power, which I must say is imaginary and worth nothing, will be taken from them. For this reason, they humble themselves so before America and even worse and more disastrous than this, before Israel. Presently, all the commotion which is being made in most of these Islamic countries is in order to get Israel officially recognised and to consolidate the Camp David agreement. If it weren't for love of these few days of presidency, for these few days of rule, who would have imagined that Israel could do such things with Muslim lands and could humiliate the Muslims so presumptuously before everyone.

Imam's remarks dated 31 August 1982 (9 Shahrivar 1361 AHS). *Sahifeh-ye Imam*, vol. 16, p. 272.

Oh God awaken these governments

Oh God the Blessed and Exalted, make these nations pay attention to these matters and awaken these governments in Islamic countries from their slumber. They think that Israel, Israel, whose very basis lies on its grabbing Arab lands, is their protector that is why they help it, or they think America is their protector, America which only wants your oil, wants to gain from you and wants you to be a market for it.

Imam's remarks dated 18 September 1983 (27 Shahrivar 1362 AHS). *Sahifeh-ye Imam*, vol. 18, pp. 108-9.

Regret is expressed over the sleep of ignorance of some of the governments

Is it not regrettable that in the face of this catastrophe, the heads of Arab countries are presently either sitting back and not saying anything, thus opening the way for (the implementation of) this malicious plan, or, in order to please America or safeguard their transient positions, are supporting Israel? In order to perform my Islamic duty, I have at every opportunity carried the cry from the heart of the region's deprived and oppressed to the world, including the governments of the Islamic countries, and henceforth whenever the opportunity presents itself, I will, God willing, continue to do so. Perhaps my words will have an effect on the governments of these countries, some of whom busy themselves in the pursuit of hedonism while others persist in quarrelling and wrangling with their brothers or are so afraid of America that they have surrendered themselves to it. Perhaps they will be roused from this sleep of ignorance to an Islamic awakening, perhaps they will come to their senses, act like human beings and bring an end to this disastrous situation of theirs, and like Iran the brave reject all the superpowers. Our Lebanese brothers are presently in the clutches of Israel and the bloodthirsty Lebanese government, and even worse, of the aggressor America. Every day a group of them are either martyred or made homeless, yet most of the governments in the region are busy making compromise with Israel or supporting the Lebanese government.

Imam's message dated 22 September 1983 (31 Shahrivar 1362 AHS). *Sahifeh-ye Imam*, vol. 18, pp. 122-3.

Foolishness turns some of the Muslim leaders against one another

Unfortunately, they use the foolishness of some of the leaders to turn all of them against one another. They force this one to attack Iran, causing the Iraqi nation to suffer so much loss and pain. They bring so much hardship upon them for the sake of a stupid person whom they told: "Go, be the commander of Qadisiyyah[28]." On one side they turn the Palestinians against one another - as you witness in the battle which is taking place between them - and on the other they create differences between the Muslim governments. Why should it be this way? If these Muslim governments truly awaken from their slumber, if they realise what power they hold in their hands, what resources they possess, resources which are their (the superpowers') lifeblood, they would establish relations with one another, friendly relations. We are all the time shouting out: "Come, let us be friends," even though they keep saying: "No, Iran wants to destroy every country in the world." Why should Iran want to do such a thing. Iran wants to put things right, she wants all the Muslim governments to come together, to be as brothers. Unfortunately, they don't understand this. I hope that the nations at least will gradually awaken and that this matter will be rectified by the people themselves. ?

Imam's remarks dated 20 December 1983 (29 Azar 1362 AHS). *Sahifeh-ye Imam*, vol. 18, p. 189

The Divulgence of Plots and Treacherous Plans

Camp David: a plot to legitimise Israeli aggression

Question: Do you oppose the Camp David agreement as the other Muslim leaders do?

Reply: The Camp David agreement[29] and others of that nature are but plots to grant legitimacy to Israel's aggression and have resulted in the situation being turned in favour of Israel and to the detriment of the Arabs and Palestinians. Such a state of affairs will not be accepted by the people of the region.

Imam's interview with Associated Press News Agency dated 7 November 1978 (16 Aban 1357 AHS). *Sahifeh-ye Imam*, vol. 4, p. 341.

Camp David is condemned

Question: How do you appraise the Camp David accords and Sadat's backpeddalling on Bayt al-Muqaddas?

Reply: I condemn it absolutely.

Imam's interview with the Libyan news agency, 17 November 1978 (26 Aban 1357 AHS). *Sahifeh-ye Imam*, vol. 5, pp. 1-2.

Camp David is to the detriment of all the countries in the region

Question: What effect have the Camp David accords and Sadat's treason had on the revolution in Iran?

Reply: The Camp David agreement, and indeed any move which strengthens Israel's position, is basically not only to the detriment of the Palestinians and Arabs, but also to the detriment of all the countries in the region and will as a consequence bolster all the reactionary forces of the region.

Imam's interview with the Libyan newspaper Al-Safir, dated 23 November 1978 (2 Azar 1357 AHS). *Sahifeh-ye Imam*, vol. 3, p. 238.

Camp David is a political game

Question: What is your opinion of Camp David? What do you see as the solution to the Palestinian problem?

Reply: Camp David is nothing other than a trick, a political game meant to perpetuate Israel's aggression against the Muslims. For more than 15 years, in my directives and speeches, I have condemned Israel and defended the Palestinian people and (their right to) their land. Israel is a usurper and must leave Palestine, the sooner the better. The only solution is for the Palestinian brothers to destroy this corrupt entity as quickly as possible and pluck the roots of imperialism out of the region so that peace can return once again to the region.

Imam's interview with the magazine Africa Tomorrow, dated 5 December 1978 (14 Azar 1357 AHS). *Sahifeh-ye Imam*, vol. 5, p. 173.

Camp David is an act of treason against Islam and the Muslims

Iran sees itself as being in step with its Muslim brothers in Arab countries and as sharing in their decisions. Iran considers Sadat's peace agreement with Israel to be an act of treason against Islam, the Muslims and the Arab brothers and endorses the political stance of those countries which oppose the agreement.

Imam's message dated 25 March 1979 (5 Farvardin 1358 AHS). *Sahifeh-ye Imam*, vol. 6, p. 361.

The Camp David plan demonstrates Sadat's dependence

I have, for more than 15 years now, been pointing out the danger of the usurper Israel and have informed the Arab governments and people about this fact. Now, with the imperialist plan for peace between Egypt and Israel, this danger has become greater, closer and more serious. By accepting this peace, Sadat has revealed further his dependence on the imperialist government of America. One cannot expect anything else from a friend of the former Shah of Iran.

Imam's message dated 25 March 1979 (5 Farvardin 1358 AHS). *Sahifeh-ye Imam*, vol. 6, p. 361.

The Camp David plan will disunite Muslims

From about 20 years ago until the present, I have spoken of this problem and have advised the Arab governments and other Muslims to work together on this matter. If the Arab governments, whose populations and groups are many in numbers, had united on this issue, then these disasters which have taken place for Palestine and Quds would not have occurred. Unfortunately, however, the Arab governments did not heed my words of advice and did not turn their attention to the differences which existed among them, differences which the hands of foreigners created and which still exist today, indeed which increase with each passing day. Among these are the differences which the agreement between Egypt and Israel, brought about by the hands of foreigners, caused. This agreement aggravated the differences among the Muslims and the Muslim governments and because the latter are not politically mature, they could not solve this problem and thus they gave in on such a grave issue, on such an act of treason. Subsequently, the differences among the Muslims and the Muslim governments became greater. This is a cause of great sorrow for us.

Imam's remarks at a meeting with the Somalian ambassador dated 7 May 1979 (17 Ordibehesht 1358 AHS). *Sahifeh-ye Imam*, vol. 7, p. 183.

The decree for severing ties with Egypt because of the Camp David agreement

In view of the treacherous treaty between Egypt and Israel, and the Egyptian government's unquestioning obedience to America and Zionism, the provisional government of the Islamic republic of Iran announces the severance of diplomatic ties with the Egyptian government.

Imam's decree concerning the severance of ties with Egypt dated 1 May 1979 (11 Ordibehesht 1358 AHS). *Sahifeh-ye Imam*, vol. 7, p. 152.

The hands of Sadat the traitor must be severed from the land of Egypt

The Egyptian nation must sever the hands of this traitor (Sadat) from their country and erase the shame of submission to America and Zionism from (the face of) the nation.

Imam's reply to a message from Qaddafy, the Libyan leader, dated 7 May 1979 (17 Ordibehesht 1358 AHS). *Sahifeh-ye Imam*, vol. 7, p. 154.

The plot of Egypt, Israel and America

The Islamic countries must adopt an inimical stand against the occupying regime in Israel, which has caused most of the problems they now face, and must uphold the aspirations of the dear Palestinian and Lebanese people with all their might. The Islamic countries must defend those organisations world-wide which seek to implement freedom. We thoroughly condemn the plot of Egypt, America and Israel to suppress the great movement of the militant people of Palestine.

Leaders and representatives of countries gathered in beloved Algeria, come let us unite and sever the hands of the criminals of the left and right - at whose head stands America - uproot Israel and entrust the rights of the people of Palestine to their own hands. I ask God the Exalted to awaken the Muslims and grant the Islamic countries unity and greatness.

Imam's message dated 30 October 1979 (8 Aban 1358 AHS). *Sahifeh-ye Imam*, vol. 10, p. 276.

Regret is expressed over union with the enemies of Islam

Yes, Mr. Sadat is obedient, he is obedient to America. Like the Shah of ours, he has succumbed completely. How much longer do I have to go on expressing regret that someone who calls himself the head of an Islamic country sits at a table with two people who are both the enemies of Islam - the Israeli regime is the enemy of Islam and Carter is their brother - and enters into an agreement against Islam while we sit back and listen, while the Egyptian nation sits back and listens and while you writers sit back and listen. How regretful this is. How much longer do I have to deplore this situation, this union they have formed with the enemies of Islam, with people who have trained their guns on the Muslims. They sit together at one table and come to an agreement against the Muslims, and worse than that, the Muslims sit back and watch, the Muslim governments sit back and watch and the nations sit back and watch.

Imam's interview with Hasanein Heikal, 19 December 1979 (28 Azar 1358 AHS). *Sahifeh-ye Imam*, vol. 11, pp. 252-3.

The sowing of dissension by the servants of America

At a time when criminal Israel is unleashing a comprehensive onslaught against the Muslims in beloved Palestine and Lebanon, and is laying its criminal plans to transfer its capital to Bayt al-Muqaddas; when it plans to intensify and extend its crimes against the Muslims it has driven from their homelands and brutally kill them in even greater numbers; at a time when the Muslims stand in greater need than ever of unity, Sadat, the traitor and servant of America, the friend and brother of Begin and the dead, deposed Shah, and Saddam, another humble servant of America, are trying to sow dissension among the Muslims and will not hesitate to commit any crime their criminal masters enjoin upon them in order to achieve their goal. America is engaged in continuous attacks on Iran, sending spies in the hope of defeating our Islamic revolution and conspiring with Sadat to diffuse (by way of Iraq) lies and false propaganda concerning the leaders of the Islamic government. The Muslims must beware of the treason to Islam and the Muslims in which these agents of America engage.

Imam's message dated 12 September 1980 (21 Shahrivar 1359 AHS). *Sahifeh-ye Imam*, vol. 13, pp. 180-1.

Instead of finding a solution to the Palestinian problem, they set Shiites and Sunnis against one another

We don't expect anything else of Saddam other than to say such absurd things at the Taif[30] conference. We don't expect anything else of some of the heads of state who have fallen into their hands (the superpowers) and those heads who supported the Shah in his time and helped him in his crimes and who today help Saddam in his. They act as their inhuman nature dictates. Instead of thinking about (the situation of) Islam, the Islamic countries, Palestine and our Islamic movement when they sit down together, they are interested only in devising plans against an Islamic country which wants to put Islam into practice in all its affairs and wants to implement the laws of Islam throughout the land, and in coming up with various plots to make the different groups fall upon one another and to turn Sunni and Shiite brothers against each other.

Imam's remarks dated 31 January 1981 (15 Bahman 1359 AHS). *Sahifeh-ye Imam*, vol. 14, p. 43.

What did the Taif conference achieve?

Don't these so-called Islamists see that Islam is being trampled under the boots of the superpowers and their dependants in all the Islamic countries? Don't they know what is going on in the south of Lebanon, in Palestine, Iran, Iraq and in the other Islamic countries? Don't they know what they have done to the people there, what young, innocent children they have made fatherless and homeless? Was the Taif conference not aware of these things? The participants came together at this conference in the name of Islam, but there was not even a whiff of Islam to be had there, only exorbitant expense and aristocratic living; no attention was paid to Islam and to taking care of the affairs of Muslims. Have they not heard the saying of the Prophet that he who rises in the morning and shows no concern for the affairs of Muslims is himself not a Muslim? "Whoever rises in the morning and does not strive to help in the affairs of the Muslims is not a Muslim." Did they strive to help in the affairs of the Muslims of the world? These heads of state who came together at the Taif conference in an area, in a country where the Messenger of God, the Prophet of Islam, had lived and where he propagated his message, what did they say about Islam? What concern did they show for the Muslims and their affairs? What did they achieve? Based on the wording of the honourable tradition, can we count them as being amongst the Muslims?

Imam's remarks dated 18 February 1981 (29 Bahman 1359 AHS). *Sahifeh-ye Imam*, vol. 14, pp. 119-20.

It is incumbent upon us to condemn the plan of Sadat and Fahd

From the beginning of the struggles, issues relating to Lebanon and Palestine have been among our main aims and have not been separate from those of Iran. In general, a Muslim should not only take one Muslim group into consideration...

Since the region is on the verge of a general Islamic uprising, America is resorting to certain plans in an attempt to prevent the defenceless people of the region from taking control of their own destinies, and, unfortunately, there are some governments which aid the US in this regard. The plans of Sadat and Fahd constitute one such aid. Even if we assumed that America had proposed a one hundred percent Islamic and humane plan, we would still not believe that it would take steps for peace and our interests. Even if America and Israel were to recite the profession of faith "*La ilaha illallah*" (there is no god but God), we would not accept it, for they want only to deceive us. They speak of peace but seek to create warfare in the region. Do you expect us to remain indifferent towards America, Israel and the other superpowers who want to devour the region? No, we will compromise with none of these superpowers or powers. We are Muslims and intend to live as Muslims. We prefer a poor life if it means that we are free and independent. We do not want this progress and civilisation which calls for us to stretch out our hands to foreigners. We want a civilisation which stands firmly on the foundations of dignity and humanity, and it is on this basis that we want peace preserved. The superpowers wish to control the humanity of human beings and you and I are duty bound to resist, to refuse compromise and reject such plans as those of Sadat and Fahd, as indeed is any Muslim. It is incumbent on us to condemn such plans which are not to the benefit of the deprived. I can assure you that the issues which concern us are not separate from those which concern you, but as you know only too well, America and its local agents do not leave us alone for a moment, consequently, if we are not able to give you the help you deserve, it is because we are preoccupied with these criminals. We consider Lebanon to be a part of us. The Shiites of Lebanon and Iran and all Muslims of the world are one, and I hope that we can preserve our unity.

Imam's remarks at a gathering of members of Amal, 28 October 1981 (6 Aban 1360 AHS). *Sahifeh-ye Imam*, vol. 15, pp. 293-4.

The Camp David plan may also possibly take Mecca and Medina out of Muslim hands

Regarding regional issues, these plans which America, the Zionists and some of their lackeys have devised are the most important topic of conversation at the moment. They are plans which the Muslim governments, the Arab governments that is, want to draw up and impose on everyone.

This plan has no positive points about it. Those who think otherwise have either paid scant attention to the issue, or have other ideas. There are no positive points in such plans.

Our country, our nation, gave so many martyrs and so many were maimed and crippled - a large number of whom are here today (may God heal them) - for the sake of Islam. We do not regard Islam as being confined to Iran. Islam is Islam everywhere. It is the same Islam in Egypt, Sudan, Iraq, the Hijaz, Syria and other places. We cannot separate our fate from that of other Muslims. All these damages that have been inflicted upon us, all the martyrs we have given, all the people who have been maimed and crippled, all those who became homeless, all this we sustained for the sake of Islam. It is because Iran is an Islamic country that we go through so much for it. We cannot consider the Arabs or the destiny of the Arabs, nor that of the other (Muslim) countries, as being separate from ours. Everywhere it is Islam, and all Muslims - and we are included in their number - are duty bound to protect Islam wherever it is. We are duty bound to guide these Islamic countries which today are contemplating accepting this extremely pernicious plan and want to approve it, to the best of our ability. We must remind the Muslim peoples and Islamic countries of the facts. I hereby give warning of the danger posed to Islam by this plan. Those who have proposed it are either ignorant or under the influence of America and Zionism. This is also true of those who regard this plan as having positive points. If there were not one negative point in it apart from that calling for Israel to be officially recognised - one of the clauses of this proposed plan is that Israel be officially recognised and be given guarantees - even if all the points mentioned in it were positive apart from this one clause, it alone would be enough to negate any positive point.

The meaning of giving such guarantees to Israel is that the Muslims would have to ensure the security of this Israel which for many long years has usurped Muslim lands; has carried out mass killings in Palestine, Lebanon and other places; has made Muslims homeless; has endangered the properties and lives of Muslims, and has subjected them to its corrupt goals! It means that were someone to attack this usurper, this usurping, criminal government, all Muslims and all governments in the region would be obliged to oppose him in order to protect Israel. Israel, which has sucked the blood of the Muslims, which has done all that it has to Palestine and Quds, which has given Lebanon the appearance it has today, which has murdered Muslims and plundered their possessions, from now on all of us would be obliged to be its protectors, to safeguard it, in order to recompense it! From now on we would be obliged to officially recognise those who, from the first day they entered Palestine and Quds, have done nothing but usurp! The Arab countries would have to officially recognise this corrupt regime, this nefarious, infidel regime and recompense it after all those crimes it has committed.

As some would have it, one of the positive points in this plan is the clause which calls for Israel to withdraw to borders which existed before the war of whenever, but this too is one of its negative points. For it means that providing it withdraws from a few areas, it will keep all the lands it occupied up until that period. It is like us reaching a settlement with Iraq that a part of Khuzistan remains ours while another part becomes theirs.

This is one of the negative points of the plan. Indeed, all its other points serve to benefit Israel and to bring about Israeli domination over the Arabs.

I hereby warn the Islamic nations, in particular the Arab nations, and also the Islamic and Arab armies, that approving this plan behind closed doors without allowing the people to have a say in the matter will result in nothing but your enslavement by Israel, in making you the slaves of Israel till the end of your lives and placing you blind and powerless at the mercy of Israel and America. There is no greater shame for the Islamic and Arab nations than to submit to this vicious, corrupt plan which is one hundred percent against Islam. It is a disgrace for the Arabs to accept the dominion of Israel. I caution you all that if this plan is approved, tomorrow Israel will take Mecca and Medina out of your hands. The nations should be vigilant; they should awaken their governments and make them oppose this infidel, immoral plan. While this plan is being put together, America is showing its teeth and claws in an attempt to make them (the Arabs) accept it. It has sent its commandos and troops to the region and has carried out manoeuvres, bringing its performers to put on a show (of power) to frighten the inhabitants of the region. If the governments are afraid of such moves, the people should be full of spirit and brook no fear. It would be better for us all to die than to live in disgrace under the control of Zionism and America.

And this is a huge step taken on the orders of America to humble the Arabs and Muslims. Shame upon those Arabs who, for the sake of a short duration in power over a country and because of the profits they gain, submit themselves to such humiliation. And shame on us all if we sit back in silence. Even if the governments, those that are heedless of the facts or those that intentionally mean to commit treason against Islam, the Arab nation and the Muslims, approve of this plan, still it will have no value.

Imam's remarks dated 17 November 1981 (26 Aban 1360 AHS). *Sahifeh-ye Imam*, vol. 15, pp. 317-8.

Conciliatory plans pave the way for Israel's aggression

If it weren't for this plan of America's[31] and its second plan drawn up by Fahd[32], along with the plans that will be proposed at a later date, Israel would not have dared annex the Golan Heights. These plans have created dissension and have opened the way for Israel.

Imam's remarks dated 16 December 1981 (25 Azar 1360 AHS). *Sahifeh-ye Imam*, vol. 15, p. 370.

The different plans aimed at turning attention from the main enemy

Today, Saddam the traitor understands only too well that he will not be saved from this trap they have laid for him, and he and the atheist Iraqi Baath party face no other fate than downfall and destruction.

On account of this, he has, today, despite all his boasting, his absurd arrogation of the title commander of Qadisiyyah, his beating on a hollow drum for revolution and his claim to bear irreconcilable enmity towards Israel, sought refuge in the arms of governments devoted to America, the friend and colleague of Israel. He has stretched out the hand of humility and medicity to the enemies of the Arabs and Islam, first (to try) to save himself from this fatal situation that he has made for himself, and secondly to turn attention from the main enemy of Islam and the usurper of Muslim lands, and by returning Husni Mubarak to the Arab fold, enforce the shameful Camp David accord or implement the Fahd plan which will bring shame to the Arab nations and, more importantly, to Islam.

I warn the Arab governments of the region that by submitting to such plans they will, in addition to accepting their own bondage at the hands of America - and even more shameful than that at the hands of Israel - evoke the eternal enmity of the nation, government and powerful armed forces of Iran. If you don't return to the lap of Islam, tomorrow will be too late. Don't let the tricksters of America and the boasters Husni, Hasan, Husayn and Qabus[33], who truly are in need of a custodian and who foolishly use the youth of their countries and the arms and munitions of their armies against Iran instead of using them in the way of freeing themselves from the clutches of Israel, trick you into provoking contention with an Islamic country which sent the now annihilated Shah - with all that diabolical power and support he had from the great and the small Satans - and Saddam, who is more of a criminal than the annihilated Shah was, to hell.

Imam's message dated 27 May 1988 (6 Khordad 1361 AHS). *Sahifeh-ye Imam*, vol. 16, pp. 231-2.

Recognising Israel would be a tragedy for the Muslims

The Iranian nation, like the other Muslims of the world, will be responsible before God for the problems and dangers which are being created for Islam. And one of the greatest dangers today comes from the Camp David accord and the Fahd plan[34] which will strengthen Israel and let it intensify its crimes. All of us, particularly the Saudi Arabian government, are responsible before Islam, the Noble Quran and the future generations. And I fear that the day will come when the Muslim governments and nations realise that, at the hands of the criminal America, Israel has, God forbid, achieved its unjust and criminal aims and the Muslims will not be able to do anything about it.

I consider support for the plan for the independence and recognition of Israel to be tragic for the Muslims and explosive for the Muslim governments, while opposition to it I view as a great Islamic duty. I seek refuge in God Almighty from these plans which are being drawn up for Islam by pseudo-Muslims.

Imam's message dated 5 June 1982 (15 Khordad 1361 AHS). *Sahifeh-ye Imam*, vol. 16, pp. 254-5.

Some of the Muslim governments seek shelter with the wolf!

Today, the dear nation of Iran, relying on divine power, advances despite the ignorant ones who thought that because of their inhuman crimes and the martyring of the nation's esteemed personalities the people would leave the scene, and who could not and cannot understand the secret of their presence (on the scene). We hope that by defeating America's recent plot for preserving Saddam and the Aflaqite party, our brave forces will, with the final defeat of the Iraqi government, pave the way for an advance towards Bayt al-Muqaddas, just as it is hoped that we will not witness indifference from the countries of the region whose every possession is now in danger of destruction after the recent attack by Israel on the Islamic country of Lebanon and the murder and plundering perpetrated there.

The Muslim nations should realise that with this lethal silence of some of the regional governments and this unquestioning submission of theirs to America and Israel, today beloved Lebanon is being put into the gullet of these world-devourers and their vassals, and the same will happen to the other dear countries in the near future. If today the regional governments stood against these criminals using the oil weapon and guns, the problem of Israel, and subsequently of America and any other rapacious power, would be solved. We express our severe disapproval of some of the Muslim governments who have stretched out their hands to America, which is the original criminal and the main plotter, in an attempt to seek their deliverance from something which is nothing other than a man-eating wolf, and we condemn them absolutely. Indeed, if it were not for this problem of the war with Iraq, this plot to distract us from the existing problems that face us, and the plan to defeat us on two fronts, the brave nation and revolutionary government of Iran would adopt another course of action.

For the umpteenth time we turn to the Muslim governments, particularly the regional governments, and ask them, indeed advise them most categorically to rise up to preserve the dignity, lives, honour and wealth of the Islamic nations; to unite with us, the Syrian government and the Palestinians and present a single front to defend the glory and honour of Islam and the Arabs; and to sever for evermore the hands of these criminals from their rich countries. Do not miss the opportunity, for tomorrow will be too late.

Imam's message dated 27 June 1982 (6 Tir 1361 AHS). *Sahifeh-ye Imam*, vol. 16, pp. 313-4.

If Israel is officially recognised, it will become the ruler of them all

Today, Israel is gradually gaining sovereignty over these Islamic countries, and if this indifference, this aid and this procrastination in order to get Israel officially recognised is efficacious, then Israel will become the ruler of them all, and just as now it has been able to humiliate and abase them before itself on the orders of America, so too, according to the plan of America, this affair will continue, will spread, and will become rooted everywhere.

Imam's remarks of 31 August 1982 (9 Shahrivar 1361 AHS). *Sahifeh-ye Imam*, vol. 16, pp. 395-6.

Guaranteeing Israel's existence at the Fez summit

Do you know what went on at the Fez summit?[35] And what Israel did after it? Many things have been said about Fez and I will not repeat them here. One thing I will say, however, and that concerns the seventh clause which some claim does not officially give recognition to Israel. Is this the case? Or does it indeed recognise Israel, even going further than simply recognising it? When the Islamic countries come together and ask the Security Council to guarantee peace and secure borders among all countries of the region, is Israel considered as one of these countries or not? If it is, then was it considered the exception at this Fez summit or not? No it wasn't, it was included as one of the regional countries. Well, when you say that Israel, like the Hijaz, like Lebanon and like all the other places, should have its security guaranteed, such that if one of them tries to attack another, the Security Council will stop them, this means that if one of the regional countries tries to deal a blow to Israel or take some kind of action against it, the Security Council must, at the behest of these men who came together at Fez, stop it. This constitutes not only recognising Israel, but guaranteeing its existence...

Then what did Israel do afterwards? In the Israeli parliament it was subsequently said that this plan is not worth looking at, is not worth reading. And then just in these past two days, Israel perpetrated this crime, a crime which according to some of these gentlemen was described by America as butchery. Just imagine what must have happened there for America, the head of all butchers, to describe it as butchery. What happened to those innocent people of Lebanon, of Beirut, and other places like them. What did they do to deserve this? The gentlemen guaranteed the security of Israel, but it paid no heed to them.

I want to say just one thing and that is if Israel, throughout the whole of its life, has ever uttered a word of truth it is that this agreement is not worth even looking at. Why? Because those who signed it are worth nothing, if they were, would Israel have said such a thing? If such an insult is hurled at someone, if your ordinary man in the street is told by someone that essentially what he is saying is not worth listening to or his written word is not worth reading, he will be the enemy of that person until the end of his days. These gentlemen have sided with people who have insulted them in this manner, have humiliated them in this way and following that have set Beirut, Lebanon and the south of Lebanon alight the way they have...

At the same time as Israel has humiliated you so, the police in the Hijaz, out of support for America, out of support for Israel, have arrested our youth, our old men, our women and our children, and returned them to Iran. What had they done wrong? Are they not Muslims? What did they say? They said 'Death to America! Death to Russia! and Death to Israel!' They said death to these three, so does that mean they are not Muslims?! Did they not go there to worship God?! What did they do wrong? All they did was shout for Islam. They came to say death to Israel. What's so important about Israel anyway? Is it our friend? Is it friendship when it tells you that you are not worth listening to? Is this how a friend acts? Or is this more like the action of an overlord? America has never said such things to you. America with all its might has never said such a thing, it has never said that the proposals of a group of people who all lay claim to something or other are not even worth listening to. America has never said such a thing to you, yet you accept this from Israel. Well now you must expect humiliation in this world and the next.

Imam's remarks dated 19 September 1982 (28 Shahrivar 1361 AHS). *Sahifeh-ye Imam*, vol. 16, pp. 429-32.

The governments that claim to be Islamic work for the gratification of America and Israel

With the arrival of the Feast of Sacrifices (Id al-Qurban), when, under normal circumstances, I would congratulate all the Muslims of the world, in particular the pilgrims to the sacred House of God, those going towards the site of the great sacrifice of the father of the prophets, Hadrat Abraham, the friend of God (may the peace and blessings of God be upon him and his descendants), this year, unfortunately, because of the disasters which have been brought upon the Muslims, instead of congratulating them I must offer them my condolences. Condolences not only for the violation by the Great Satan, America the criminal, of the Muslims' sanctuary, nor just for the attack by the terrorist and criminal leaders of Israel on the beloved Islamic country of Lebanon, nor even for the crimes of the Aflaqite Saddam, this spineless servant of America and Israel, perpetrated against the Arab and non-Arab Muslims in the south and west of Iran, nor for the rejoicing of the heads of the countries of Egypt, Jordan, Sudan, Morocco and others over the victory won by the enemies of Islam and mankind over the innocent people of Lebanon and Beirut and the killing of thousands of young and old people, of children, of innocent men and women - even though these are all calamities and call for condolences. No, I must offer them my condolences for an even greater disaster and more significant catastrophe which makes all others pale into insignificance beside it, and that is that a handful of contemptible Zionist terrorists could carry out an assault on Muslims in the most odious of manners in the face of the rest of the Muslim world, which has such huge material and spiritual resources at its disposal and which, with a little bit of browbeating, could even drive America, let alone Israel, out of the Arab regions.

It is not only the plight of a group of innocent people who have been driven out of their land and are now homeless and shelterless which grieves us, for the great disaster is that these crimes were carried out by Israel in full view of the governments which claim to be Islamic. And the great catastrophe is that these governments which claim to be Islamic work for the gratification of America and Israel and implement the Camp David plan, or others of a similar nature, to the letter, and in the wake of this terrible crime, they formally recognise Israel or its dominion. The tragedy for the Muslims is that when these terrible events occur, some of the so-called Muslim governments prevent the tyrannised from even moaning about the tyrant.

Imam's message on the auspicious occasion of the Feast of Sacrifices (Id al-Qurban), dated 20 September 1982 (29 Shahrivar 1361 AHS). *Sahifeh-ye Imam*, vol. 16, pp. 435-6.

The subjugating Camp David plan is a stigmatising brand of shame and abjectness

If the Muslims of the world come to understand the motives of the prophets, upon whom be peace, the main one of which is in the last book designed to produce true human beings, the Noble Quran, this book of guidance which shone from the origin of light "God is the light of the heavens and earth" (24:35) lighting up the lamp in the niche of the effulgent heart of the Seal of the Prophets, peace and blessings of God be upon him and his descendants, so that the hearts of mankind may be delivered from the veils of darkness and light and the world illuminated with light upon light, and if they join the ocean of light, they will never be enslaved by Satan and his offspring. They will never accept the brand of shame and abjectness on their foreheads for the sake of a few days of chimerical rule or presidency, and will not leap up and down in joy over the subjugating Camp David plan and others like it in order to ingratiate themselves with the Great Satan.

Beware oh droplets estranged from the ocean of the Quran and Islam! Come to your senses and join this divine ocean, seek light from the absolute light so that it can turn the avaricious eyes of the world devourers away from you and sever their hands of usurpation and aggression so that you can acquire an honourable life and attain human values. Free yourselves from this shameful life in which a handful of Israeli hucksters can rule over you and trample on innocent Muslims in your presence. Oh God, awaken us sleepers and bring the leaders of the Islamic countries to their senses so that they rule the Muslims according to Islamic criteria and crush the ill-omened idols and the *taghut*s.

Imam's message dated 20 September 1982 (29 Shahrivar 1361 AHS). *Sahifeh-ye Imam*, vol. 16, pp. 439-40.

Egypt's reward for kissing the hand of America

It is not surprising that America and its devotees knock on any door in order to get Egypt returned to the Arab fold. What is both surprising and regrettable is the attitude of the Arab leaders who, after those lengthy preparations, all that propaganda, the meetings both behind the scenes and those which are public knowledge, the amazing hullabaloo and all those formalities, sat down together then rose from their seats concluding that all the problems of Islam and the Muslims would be rectified with the return of Egypt, who has an agreement with Israel, to the Arab fold. One day they ostracise Egypt because of its agreement with the Zionists, then the next they welcome it back for consolidating Israel's position and recognising it. Yesterday they ostracised Egypt for turning its back on Arab demands, then today they welcome it back for kissing America's hand. Yesterday they ostracised Egypt because it betrayed the aspirations of Palestine, and today they welcome it back so they can collectively support that act of betrayal. And more regrettable and shameful than this is that Egypt, with complete indifference, did not accept any of their conditions for its return. One of the top officials from Cairo even said: 'The Arab heads of state should admit their mistake'! The Lebanese question, the Afghanistan issue and other problems besetting the Arab nations are not matters on which the so-called heads of the Islamic countries should waste their precious time!

How can the innocent and respected Arab and non-Arab nations, indeed how can the Muslims tolerate such shame and allow them to be their rulers? Hasn't the time arrived for the Islamic nations to rise up and make their leaders either yield to the superiority of Islam or be treated in the same manner as was the Shah of Iran?

Imam's message dated 11 February 1983 (22 Bahman 1362 AHS). *Sahifeh-ye Imam*, vol. 18, pp. 271-2.

The plot for preventing the continuation of the intifadah

They have all joined hands together to prevent the Palestinian nation from continuing with this course of action upon which it has embarked. They are shedding crocodile tears for Palestine and are saying 'It's a pity what is happening to

Palestine. It is a good idea for them (the Palestinians) to accommodate (the Israelis) until things are put right.' The Palestinian nation should realise that if it takes a step backwards on the present issue, the situation will revert to what it was. At present the Palestinians are on the verge of crushing the Jews (the Zionists) and I hope they achieve this. The words of those who believe they are doing good or those who mean to deceive, those who say there should be a short cease-fire, a five-month cease-fire, and other such talk of which you are all aware, are all aimed at stopping Palestine from continuing what it has started. They want to quieten it and suppress it once again.

Imam's remarks dated 10 February 1988 (21 Bahman 1366 AHS). *Sahifeh-ye Imam*, vol. 20, p. 449.

The tergiversating pseudo-revolutionaries have turned to America and Israel

The Muslim nations should devote thought to the deliverance of Palestine and should repeatedly announce to the world their repulsion for and aversion to the conciliatory and reconciliatory policies of the ignoble leaders who have sold themselves and who, in the name of Palestine, have destroyed the aspirations of the people and Muslims in usurped lands. They should prevent these traitors from sullying the dignity, respect and honour of the brave Palestinian nation at the negotiating table and in their meetings, for these tergiversating pseudo-revolutionaries of little dignity have, in the name of freeing Quds, turned to America and Israel.

Imam's message dated 28 July 1988 (6 Mordad 1366 AHS). *Sahifeh-ye Imam*, vol. 20, p. 302.

The servant of the sanctuary gives Israel assurances

The Muslims do not know where to turn with this pain they are suffering. The house of Saud, the servants of the sanctuary, give Israel assurances that they will not use their weapons against it, and in order to prove what they say, they sever relations with Iran. Really, how warm and close do relations between the heads of the Islamic countries and the Zionists have to be before the pretence of doing battle with Israel is taken off the agenda in conferences and meetings of the heads of Islamic states. If they had even an ounce of self-respect and ardent zeal for Islam and the Arab cause, they would never be prepared to sell themselves and their countries out by carrying out such a vile political transaction.

Imam's message on the anniversary of the bloody killings in Mecca, 20 July 1989 (29 Tir 1367 AHS). *Sahifeh-ye Imam*, vol. 21, p. 77.

The Rejection of Israel's Existence and the Call for Unity and Support for the Struggle against Israel

Permission is given to use religious funds to back the Palestinian and Lebanese struggle

It is necessary that the benevolent Muslims, in particular the honourable people of Iran who are in the forefront of charity giving, set about as soon as possible this crucial task of saving the defenceless refugees. They should rush to their aid with whatever means possible, and with a sense of responsibility before God the Almighty they should not refrain from giving them any kind of honourable assistance. If so desired, they are permitted to use up to a third of the monies from the blessed share of the Imam (*Sahm-i Imam*[36]), upon whom be peace, to help the refugees and those affected by the war.

Imam's message marking events in Lebanon, 22 March 1978 (2 Farvardin 1357 AHS). *Sahifeh-ye Imam*, vol. 3, p. 371.

Israel is a great disaster for the Muslims

One of the great disasters to have struck the Muslims is the aggressor Israel, which is presently in a state of war with the Muslims and is busy advancing on Lebanese soil while receiving help from the Shah. The Muslim governments are mainly indifferent to this vital issue, heedless of the fact that if Israel is successful in its advances, God forbid, it will treat the other countries in exactly the same manner. These disasters which have befallen us stem from America and its henchmen.

Imam's message dated 24 March 1978 (4 Farvardin 1357 AHS). *Sahifeh-ye Imam*, vol. 3, p. 375.

I will persist in my aims to unite the Muslims against Israel

Question: Do you wish Iran to close ranks with the Arab countries against Israel?

Reply: I have always and persistently expressed my desire that the Muslims of the world unite in a struggle against their enemies, Israel being one of them. Unfortunately, however, the different regimes that have come to power in the Muslim countries have not heard my calls. I hope that finally these calls will be heard. As for myself, I will persist with this course of action.

Question: The last series of military attacks by Israel resulted in the occupation of another Arab land, that is the south of Lebanon, where the people are Shiites. What are you going to do about this?

Reply: The people of south Lebanon must return to their homes through whatever means it takes. It is their duty to struggle for the restoration of their land before the Israelis settle their own people there.

Imam's interview with Le Monde, 6 May 1978 (16 Ordibehesht 1357 AHS). *Sahifeh-ye Imam*, vol. 3, p. 387.

Twenty years of exhorting unity

For approximately twenty years now I have been exhorting the Arab countries to come together and drive out this corrupting element. If Israel gains power, it will not be content with Bayt al-Muqaddas. Unfortunately, however, my advice has had no effect on them. I ask of God to awaken the Muslims.

Imam's remarks dated 7 May 1978 (17 Ordibehesht 1357 AHS). *Sahifeh-ye Imam*, vol. 7, p. 171.

We have always been at one with you

Mr Abu Ammar[37]:

We have always opposed the Shah, Israel and their supporters on the issue of Palestine, while agreeing with you on this matter and making the nations aware of Israel's tyranny. Now that the Iranian people are being trampled beneath the boots of the Shah's executioners, are besieged by tanks, guns and machine guns, and Israeli soldiers are helping by positioning themselves in the streets of Tehran to kill the defenceless people of Iran, be at one with our innocent people and make our voices reach the world through your propaganda machinery.

Imam's reply to Yassir Arafat, 19 September 1978 (28 Shahrivar 1357 AHS). *Sahifeh-ye Imam*, vol. 3, p. 495.

We support the Arab countries which oppose Israel

Question: What is your position on the Arabs?

Reply: We extend our hands to the Arab countries who are continuing with their struggle against Israel, and indeed have always supported them against Israel. It is hoped that the Arab nations will defend the struggles of the Iranian nation.

Imam's interview with a representative of the Arabic language Al-Qaumi al-Arabi magazine, 11 November 1978 (20 Aban 1357 AHS). *Sahifeh-ye Imam*, vol. 4, pp. 417-8.

We will stand in the same line of battle as our Palestinian brothers

Question: What is the view of His Holiness, the Ayatullah, on the Palestinian movement and the Palestinian people on the whole and in particular on Bayt al-Muqaddas? What relations exist between you and the Palestine Liberation Organisation?

Reply: For many years now, we have always spoken of Israel and the fact that it is a usurper. Our intention has always been to stand by our Palestinian brothers, and whenever we gain power, we will join them in defending their rights like brothers standing as equals in the same line of battle as them. Bayt al-Muqaddas must be returned to the Muslims, the Israelis are usurpers. Unfortunately, I cannot understand why, despite their large populations and all the kinds of vast material means they have at their disposal, the Arab governments cannot regain their rights and their lands and defend their homeland. This is because of the differences that exist among them. I hope they will put an end to these differences and will pay attention to Islamic issues, so that, God willing, they will tear this cancerous element out from their lands.

Imam's interview with the Lebanese Al-Nahar daily, 11 November 1978 (20 Aban 1357 AHS). *Sahifeh-ye Imam*, vol. 4, pp. 420-1.

Twenty years of support for Palestine

Under the present circumstances, the Shah's regime supports Israel. For nearly twenty years now I have, in my declarations and speeches, opposed this policy and have declared my support for the rightful struggles of the Arab and Palestinian people.

Imam's interview with the German Third World daily, 15 November 1978 (24 Aban 1357 AHS). *Sahifeh-ye Imam*, vol. 4, p. 475.

No freedom seeker officially recognises Israel

Neither the Muslim people of Iran, nor indeed any Muslim, and in general no freedom seeker officially recognise Israel, and we will always support our Palestinian and Arab brothers.

Imam's interview with the Middle East News Bulletin, 17 November 1978 (26 Aban 1357 AHS). *Sahifeh-ye Imam*, vol. 5, p. 137.

Quds must be returned to the Muslims

Question: What is your view on the fate of Quds?

Reply: Quds belongs to the Muslims and must be returned to them.

Imam's interview with the Lebanese newspaper Al-Safir, 23 November 1978 (2 Azar 1357 AHS). *Sahifeh-ye Imam*, vol. 5, p. 80.

Be united and rely on Islam so that they do not aspire to dominate you

Question: Do you have a message for the Arab people?

Reply: My message for the Arab and Muslim brothers is this: put your differences aside and offer each other the hand of brotherhood, be in step and unite with all the Muslim brothers, even the non-Arab brothers. Make Islam your only point of reliance. Only by having uncountable material resources and, more importantly, by possessing divine and spiritual resources which are to be found in Islam, can you become a power over which the superpowers will never aspire to dominate and will not subject to attacks from the left and the right in this manner and plunder everything you have.

Imam's interview with the Lebanese newspaper Al-Safir, 23 November 1978 (2 Azar 1357 AHS). *Sahifeh-ye Imam*, vol. 5, p. 80.

We will throw the Israeli advisers out

We will throw these American military men out of Iran, we will throw these military advisers out of Iran along with those from Israel and those others who are swallowing up the people's land and destroying the Muslims' resources. God willing, we will throw them out, and it will be the hand of God which will do this.

Imam's remarks, 19 November 1978 (28 Aban 1357 AHS). *Sahifeh-ye Imam*, vol. 5, p. 40.

We will have no relations with Israel

Question: If the Shah goes and the government Your Holiness envisages is established in power, what changes will appear in the relations between your government and Israel?

Reply: We will reject Israel and will have no relations with it. It is a usurping government and our enemy.

Question: Does that mean that Israel will not be supplied with oil from Iran?

Reply: It will not.

Imam's interview with an American reporter, 1 December 1978 (10 Azar 1357 AHS). *Sahifeh-ye Imam*, vol. 5, p. 146.

We support the oppressed Palestinians

Question: Is it true that you support the aims of the Palestine Liberation Front?

Reply: We support the oppressed. We support whoever is oppressed wherever they may be, and the Palestinians are oppressed, the Israelis oppress them. For this reason, we support them.

Imam's interview with an American reporter, 1 December 1978 (10 Azar 1357 AHS). *Sahifeh-ye Imam*, vol. 5, p. 146.

Freeing Quds from the malice of Israel is the duty of all Muslims

Question: In their defence against Israel's continual aggression, Amal has given a lot of martyrs. What advice do you have for the people of south Lebanon?

Reply: Everyone should unite and stand in a united front against these aggressors. They should act and chop off their usurping hand. This is the duty of all Muslims in general, to free Quds and put an end to the malice of this germ of corruption in Islamic lands.

Imam's interview with Amal, 7 December 1978 (16 Azar 1357 AHS). *Sahifeh-ye Imam*, vol. 5, p. 183.

Selling the wealth of the Muslims to Israel is forbidden

It is prohibited for anyone to scatter to the winds the wealth of the Muslims, that wealth which belongs to a nation, or sell it to the enemies of Islam such as Israel who is presently at war with the Muslims. It is said that most of Israel's oil is supplied by Iran, and in exchange, so it is said, many of our number killed were murdered by Israeli soldiers.

Imam's remarks dated 9 December 1978 (18 Azar 1357 AHS). *Sahifeh-ye Imam*, vol. 5, p. 192.

Under no circumstances will we officially recognise Israel

Israel has been rejected by us and never will we supply it with oil, nor will we, under any circumstances, officially recognise it.

Imam's interview with the American CBS channel, 11 December 1978 (20 Azar 1357 AHS). *Sahifeh-ye Imam*, vol. 5, p. 204.

The Iranian nation has always supported Palestine

Question: Would you say that you have links with all the freedom movements in the different Arab countries, each one of which fights for independence (like the people of Palestine), autonomy, political, economic and ideological freedom in its own special way and its own particular circumstances?

Reply: The sacred Islamic movement taking place in Iran has no organised links with groups outside the country. However, we hope that because the Iranian people always supported the struggle of all freedom-fighters, in particular that of the Palestinian brothers against the aggressor Israel, and because for more than fifteen years in my directives and speeches I have always endorsed their movement and assisted them as far as possible, they, and indeed all freedom-fighters throughout the world, will today support the justice-seeking struggles of the Iranian nation. We hope that this will happen as soon as possible and to the greatest degree possible.

Imam's interview with the Italian Communist Party newspaper Unita, 14 December 1978 (23 Azar 1357 AHS). *Sahifeh-ye Imam*, vol. 5, p. 228.

Palestine is like one of our limbs

Question: In 1948, Palestine was seized unlawfully and, with the co-operation of the big imperialist governments, Zionist dreams were realised. How did this tragedy affect the people of Iran at that time and what reaction did it provoke?

Reply: Actually it must be said that the usurpation of Palestine by the aggressor Israel with the co-operation of the big imperialist governments was a tragedy for all Muslims including those in Iran. It was a very painful tragedy in which it must be said the imperialist governments of the time were the main aggressors for they were the ones who devised this plot against the Muslims in this region. Indeed, the Islamic countries have suffered many disasters at the hands of the superpowers and this was just one of those huge disasters, only this time it was perpetrated by the Zionists.

Because of the people's deep Islamic sentiment, the loss of Palestine for the Iranian nation - and that does not include the Shah and his government - was like losing one of its own limbs. For this reason, and despite the co-operation of the Shah and his puppet governments with Israel, the Iranian nation has always offered its deepest and sincere sympathies to the Palestinian fighters.

For more than fifteen years I have repeatedly protested against the co-operation of the Shah and his government with Israel, and so many Iranians, clergymen and laymen alike, have gone to prison and been tortured for protesting about Israel's aggressions. We have always defended Palestine to the best of our ability as part of our Islamic duty, and, God willing, we will always carry out this divine duty alongside other Muslims.

Question: Could you talk about the kind of relations that exist between you and the Palestine resistance? It is well known that open relations exist between the Shah and Israel in different areas and in particular that the Shah helps Israel to a great extent by supplying its oil. Could you elaborate on what your relations with Israel will be after Iran has been freed from the Shah's rule?

Reply: As I pointed out before, we will always, to the best of our abilities and with all our might, help our Palestinian brothers to bring an end to Israeli aggression and free Islamic lands from the hands of the usurper Israel. We will never assist Israel even in the smallest degree.

Imam's interview with a journalist from the Palestinian Vefa news agency, 15 December 1978 (24 Azar 1357 AHS). *Sahifeh-ye Imam*, vol. 5, pp. 232-5.

We will not allow even the slightest bit of negligence

Because of his actions against the interests of the Muslims, the Arab countries and the Palestinian brothers, Sadat has been ostracised by the Arab and Islamic world. According to Islam, the Muslims and indeed all international criteria, Israel is a usurper and an aggressor, and we will not allow even the slightest bit of negligence or weakness in putting an end to its aggressions. At appropriate times, I have supported Yassir Arafat's measures and attempts to obtain rights for the Palestinians and have Islamic lands returned to the Muslims.

Interview dated 31 December 1978 (10 Dey 1357 AHS). *Sahifeh-ye Imam*, vol. 5, pp. 298-9.

Israel is a usurper

Question: Will the Ayatullah and the new government change Iran's policy on Israel and South Africa? Will the sale of Iranian oil depend on the past and present political stance of the purchasing country on Iran?

Reply: Israel is a usurper and no kind of relation will exist between Iran and a handful of usurpers. Who on earth would be prepared to sell oil to a racist, criminal country?

Interview with foreign journalists, 4 January 1979 (14 Dey 1357 AHS). *Sahifeh-ye Imam*, vol. 5, p. 323.

We will not give oil to Israel

Question: When you return to Iran, what decision will you make on the issue of oil supplies to Israel and South Africa?

Reply: Israel is at war with the Muslims and is the usurper of our brothers' lands, we will not supply it with oil. Other countries, however, which have dealt with us in a just manner, will benefit from our oil.

Imam's interview with a reporter from the BBC, 5 January 1979 (15 Dey 1357 AHS). *Sahifeh-ye Imam*, vol. 5, p. 340.

We will not have relations with Israel the usurper

Question: In the field of foreign policy, what position will Your Holiness adopt on countries such as the United States, Russia and Israel?

Reply: We will not have relations with Israel because it is a usurper and is at war with the Muslims. However, as regards America and Russia, if they do not interfere in our internal affairs and seek proper relations with us, we will establish relations with them.

Imam's interview with French television's Channel 2, 8 January 1979 (18 Dey 1357 AHS). *Sahifeh-ye Imam*, vol. 5, p. 371.

Even if Israel repents, we will not have relations with it

Question: If those governments which throughout the present revolution in Iran have openly supported the Shah express their regret, would you continue relations with them?

Reply: Yes, apart from Israel. Israel is the exception, as is South Africa and any country which supports racism.

Question: In your comments you have said that Israel is the enemy of Islam. Is then it possible that an Islamic government will declare war on this country.

Reply: It depends on the circumstances at the time.

Imam's interview 23 January 1979 (3 Bahman 1357 AHS). *Sahifeh-ye Imam*, vol. 5, p. 506.

There is no valid reason for Israel's existence

Question: What is your view on relations with Israel and the collaboration of the army with the Arab army against Israel?

Reply: The Arab countries will not need us in a war against Israel. They must not allow the entity Israel to become more deep rooted. We will cut off all relations with Israel because there is no valid reason for its existence.

Imam's interview with the German magazine Der Spiegel. Kayhan newspaper, 5 February 1979 (16 Bahman 1357 AHS).

A warning to Arafat: the superpowers are not a reliable refuge!

In the Name of God, the Compassionate, the Merciful

Even though the material strength of our revolution is little, its spiritual power is what has caused its progress. So it was that our people with only their fists and blood prevailed over a great satanic power which was supported by the superpowers equipped with all kinds of satanic paraphernalia, and over those powers which before this victory supported the Shah and expressed loyalty to him. It was the power of the people's faith that caused them to be victorious over all of these with only their fists and blood. And in addition to the power of faith which existed, the true secret of this victory, indeed something which was a consequence of this power of faith, was the people's ideological unity.

Because this was an Islamic and human revolution, it spread like wildfire throughout all the regions of Iran, from the remote villages to the major cities, and through all sections of society. It was because of this ideological unity that these satanic powers were unable to resist it and one stronghold after another was relinquished. Of course, we still have many problems to face; they plundered our country, they turned our country upside down and perverted all signs of civilisation. In the name of a great civilisation they put our educational system in a state of backwardness; in the name of progress they completely destroyed our agrarian economy; and in the name of freedom they suppressed the freedoms of all our newspapers and propaganda organs. We have inherited a country which is in a terrible mess. Everything in it is ruined and must be built anew. However, through God's grace, because the affair is a divine one and I feel that it is God's intention that the weak will be victorious, all sections of the nation are united to overcome these difficulties of ours, and, God willing, through the efforts of our people we will solve our problems.

I ask of God the Blessed and Exalted that our brethren nation of Palestine will overcome their difficulties. We are their brothers. From this movement's inception more than fifteen years ago, I have always, in my writings and speeches, spoken of Palestine and called attention to the crimes that Israel has perpetrated there. God willing, after we are freed from these fetters then to the same degree that we stood with you at that time and are now standing with you, I hope that we will confront the problems together like brothers. I beseech God the Blessed and Exalted to exalt Islam and the Muslims and to return Quds to our brothers.

Yassir Arafat addressing Imam: It was my misfortune, or good fortune, to have been born there; it is my homeland. Fate decreed that I be born there, but that does not mean I alone am responsible for freeing Bayt al-Muqaddas. You are all responsible. After this great victory in Iran, your responsibility is greater than mine, even though I was born there. I have nothing to offer in the way of freeing Quds apart from my blood, but you, with this great victory and the means at your disposal, have a great flood at your command; you must do something so that you can all pray in Quds. God willing.

Imam: God willing.

Yassir Arafat: An earthquake is now in the offing and may have even arrived. "When thou threwest a spear, it was not thy act but God's." (Quran 8:17). In reply to Dayan and Begin, I told them they could go and choose a patron and rely on America, but I too could find support and indeed have done so:

I rely on the Iranian nation under the leadership of His Holiness the Grand Ayatullah Musawi al-Khomeini.

Imam: The Shah too relied on America, Britain, China, Israel and the others, but these refuges are powerless. That refuge which is not powerless, but powerful, is God. God is our refuge. I advise you, my own people and your people, to always turn to God, not to these powers. Do not rely on material things but on the spiritual. The power of God is greater than all these powers, thus it was that we saw a nation which was weak and empty-handed prevail over all the powers, and, God willing, will continue to do so. When we are with God, we are not afraid of anything, for if we are slain in the way of God, we are blessed, and if we slay in the way of God, we are also blessed.

Yassir Arafat: Last year, a large force from the Israeli military was sent to the south of Lebanon to crush the Palestinian people and the Muslim people of south Lebanon. The fighters gathered to resist these large military units did not exceed 2,000. Facing them were 65,000 Israeli soldiers, either reserve forces behind the front line or forces on the battlefield who believed that they would destroy them in two hours. We found ourselves in a very difficult situation. At the height of the difficulties, I turned to God and said: 'Oh God, if these people, this group of people are killed, there will be none of your worshippers left in this region', then victory arrived. That man, Mr. Brzezinski, had said goodbye to the Liberation organisation, believing it to be lost, but we saw that God granted us a great victory, a victory in southern Lebanon. A year had not passed since that victory - and our victory in southern Lebanon was a small, simple victory - when we achieved the greatest of victories here "Truth has now arrived and falsehood perished, for falsehood is by its nature bound to perish." (Quran 17:81).

We struck terror into the hearts of our enemies. When Begin says that a dark period has begun for the Israelis, it has great meaning. This is the cause of their fear. When Kissinger says: 'the greatest event since the Second World War has occurred', he is referring to the victory of the revolution in Iran. How is the victory of the Islamic revolution in Iran dangerous for America? If America does not adopt the measures in Iran that it took in Vietnam, the revolutionary movement in Iran will be maintained until it reaches Israel. This is what Kissinger said yesterday. From his comments we can see just how dangerous it is for American interests in the region, and from the mouth of our enemy we can understand the truth of our situation.

When I went to Baghdad, I told the heads of the Arab countries there, the Arab rulers, that the very least I had heard from them was: 'What do you have to do in Iran? What business do you have with Grand Ayatullah Khomeini?' This was the least of their remarks. Others told us our interests would best be served with the Shah in power. 'Keep the Shah and your interests may even be furthered,' they said. In the last meeting with the leaders of the Persian Gulf states in the Persian Gulf, just a few days before your victory here, they said information had reached them to the effect that Bakhtiar would be victorious and the Americans could keep him in Iran.

Imam Khomeini: All the estimations that the big governments made turned out wrong because this was a divine affair.

Yassir Arafat: "And the unbelievers plotted and planned, and God too planned; and the best of planners is God." (Quran 3:54).

Imam: They continue to make these appraisals and will do so in the future, but they will all turn out to be wrong.

Yassir Arafat: They say an earthquake has taken place, we say an explosion of light has occurred. We say the time has come when our people and our region will be free and independent. Many problems lie before us, but nevertheless I am optimistic about the future. A greater *jihad* and even more exhausting struggles lie ahead of you, rebuilding a society is more difficult than fighting and achieving victory. The Shah has ruined this place.

Imam: We place our hopes in God and do not despair of Him. God willing, we will overcome our problems, but we don't believe we will overcome them through material means, victory is attained through spiritual means. As long as our people put their trust in God the Blessed and Exalted, they will progress, and if, God forbid, there is any deviation, then it will be the end for us all.

Yassir Arafat: I don't think that the conspiracies of the enemies have ended. When we look at the flood of events, we are certain that the enemy will not let such a fortress collapse as easily as this.

Imam: The enemy doesn't want this to happen, but God will act against him, if He so wills.

Yassir Arafat: Even though I may smile now, the smile is only on my lips. My heart is bleeding because of the killings that have occurred in Iran.

Imam: God willing, your heart will be gladdened.

Yassir Arafat: God is my witness that in my life I have not been as happy as I was when you achieved victory.

Imam Khomeini: May God protect the Muslims, God willing.

Yassir Arafat: In Lebanon, shooting bullets into the air in celebration is not allowed. It has been forbidden for more than a year now, the commander-in-chief of the Palestine Liberation forces having given the command that no one must waste any bullets no matter what the occasion. Yet with all of Lebanon engulfed in flames, Abu Ammar himself broke this law for the first time by shooting five bullets into the air in celebration. The villages in the south of Lebanon, the Shiite-inhabited regions, these Shiite villages will undoubtedly be pounded in air raids now, for Begin is grieved about events in Iran. May God protect the south of Lebanon from the Israeli bomb attacks. May He protect the forces of the Arab governments. God willing, may He protect His Holiness the Grand Ayatullah and his people.

Imam: I hope that God will protect them.

Arafat: It is true that Israel has friends, but we too have brothers and friends.

Imam Khomeini: We place our trust in God the Blessed and Exalted.

Yassir Arafat: The last week was the start of a new period.

Imam: God willing.

Imam's remarks in a meeting with the Palestine Council, 18 February 1979 (29 Bahman 1357 AHS). Sahifeh-ye Imam, vol. 6, pp. 159-62.

Unity and relying on God are the requisites for victory

I ask God the Blessed and Exalted that just as our people triumphed through ideological unity and reliance on God the Blessed and Exalted, freeing themselves from the yoke of this dynasty and the people who supported and promoted them, so too may God Almighty free our Palestinian brothers. The important thing is that they have ideological unity and rely on God the Blessed and Exalted.

The secret of our victory was ideological unity, reliance on God the Blessed and Exalted and the power of faith. The power of our nation's faith was such that martyrdom was seen as a blessing. The people sought martyrdom, they had no fear of death, and thus it was that their fists prevailed over the tanks. The other nations, the Palestinian nation, must find ideological unity and place their reliance in God the Blessed and Exalted. Wherever this secret of victory materialises, victory will ensue. Our dear Palestinian people must be united and rely on God the Blessed and Exalted, they must turn their attention to the clergy, to spiritual matters and to God the Blessed and Exalted so that they will be victorious. I ask God the Blessed and Exalted to grant victory to all the oppressed nations.

For many years now, perhaps twenty years, I have repeatedly aired my views on Palestine and Israel, and I will say again: We condemn Israel. Israel is a usurper. The land it has taken it has taken unlawfully. Quds must be freed and Israel driven out. The Arab governments must unite and drive Israel out of their lands and sever the hands of the colonisers. I ask God the Blessed and Exalted to grant that we achieve these aspirations and we can meet in Quds.

Imam's remarks at a meeting with a group of Palestinians and Bishop Cappucci, 2 April 1979 (13 Farvardin 1358 AHS). Sahifeh-ye Imam, vol. 6, pp. 413-4.

Uprising of the people, the path to freeing Palestine

Do not wait for your governments to do something for you. For more than 15 years now, I have been exhorting the Arab governments to unite together and free Quds, but my words had no effect at all because they are not concerned about this problem... not one of them is concerned about the people, the people must think about themselves. If we were expected to sit and wait until the governments did something for us, we would still have that same state of backwardness that we had and the former Shah would still be ruling over us. It was through the power of faith that our people acquired that we opposed the superpowers and, praise be to God, were victorious and severed their hands. If you want to overcome your problems, if you want to free Quds, if you want to free Palestine, if you want to free Egypt and the other Arab countries from the hands of these agents, from the hands of the foreigners, then the people must rise up. The people must do this, they cannot sit by and wait for the governments to do something about these problems, for they only act when it is profitable for them. The people must rise up, they must realise that the secret of victory is to wish for martyrdom and place no value on material life, on the worldly, animalistic life. This is the secret that can take the people forward, this is the secret that the Quran has revealed.

Imam's remarks, 6 April 1979 (17 Farvardin 1358 AHS). Sahifeh-ye Imam, vol. 6, pp. 444-5.

Unite and deracinate this germ of corruption

Unfortunately, the differences that are evident in the region, particularly the Arab region, have made it possible for Israel with its small population to resist the Arabs with their large population and the vast means they have at their disposal. This germ of corruption covets the whole region, if it is not stopped it will not be content with just Palestine and the al-Aqsa mosque, it wants to conquer everywhere. It is up to the Muslims and the Muslim governments to unite and deracinate this germ of corruption and not allow those who support it to continue doing so.

I beseech God the Blessed and Exalted to enhance the power of Islam, to exalt Islam and the Muslims and bring them unity.

Imam's remarks dated 21 April 1979 (1 Ordibehesht 1358 AHS). Sahifeh-ye Imam, vol. 7, p. 59.

The people must awaken

For many years now I have continuously spoken about Israel and its crimes in my sermons and writings, and have brought to the notice of the Muslims that Israel is a cancerous tumour in a corner of the Islamic countries which will not be satisfied with Quds and the other places. No, they (the Zionists) intend to move on. They are the followers of America's policy and America does not simply aspire after one place, just as all the superpowers wish to bring all the countries under their control if they can... the Muslims must awaken. Today is not the day for the Muslims to be sitting in a corner, each living his own particular life, this cannot be. At a time when it is the policy of the superpowers to swallow up every place, the Muslims must awaken. I hold out no hope for most of the governments, but the people must awaken and come together under the banner of Islam and the command of the Quran. God be praised, the Muslims number about a billion, their countries are rich and their people are meritorious. However, those who seek to rule over these countries (the imperialists) have, through the distorted propaganda they have circulated over the past few hundred years and the influence they have achieved in the universities and the centres which educate the sons of Muslims, made the Muslims lose hope in themselves, they have made them lose themselves. The Muslims must strive to find their greatness.

*Imam's remarks at a gathering of Shiite representatives from southern Lebanon, 21 May 1979 (31 Ordibehesht 1358 AHS). *****Sahifeh-ye Imam*****, vol. 12, pp. 278-9.*

We are by your side fighting Israel

Brothers, after offering you greetings and wishes for good health and peace, I would like to say that the situation in Lebanon and the disasters which are being brought upon our brothers have not escaped our attention. We are deeply grieved by these inhuman actions being carried out against Muslim countries, particularly against the people of Lebanon and our brothers, by the Zionists with the help of America. We hope that God the Blessed and Exalted, who is the supporter of the weak and oppressed, will help you and all our brothers. We are fighting Israel and America by your side and hope that the forces of Truth will defeat the satanic and tyrannical forces. Your troubles and suffering are not new to Islam and the Muslims, the forces of tyranny have always opposed Islam and fought with the Muslims. I ask for your victory and the success of all the Muslims.

Imam's message to the Shiites of Lebanon, 6 June 1979 (16 Khordad 1358 AHS). *Sahifeh-ye Imam*, vol. 8, p. 65.

Prayers for the Palestinian and Lebanese brothers

Now all the Muslims and the oppressed, particularly (those in) beloved Iran and (the) usurped (lands of) Lebanon and

Palestine, are facing a sensitive period. Iran confronts agitators connected to the regime along with renegades and international Zionism, while Lebanon and Palestine stand against Israel the enemy of Islam and the Muslims and the man-eating corrupter. At present, our Muslim brothers in Palestine and Lebanon are bedevilled by the inhuman aggressions of Israel, and if, God forbid, Israel is victorious on that front, its aggressions will spread to other countries. It is required that in the gatherings during the holy month, prayers are offered for the Palestinian and Lebanese brothers.

Imam's remarks dated 21 August 1979 (3 Mordad 1358 AHS). *Sahifeh-ye Imam*, vol. 9, p. 212.

Advice to make revelations about Israel in public gatherings

I have repeatedly warned the brothers in Islam in all countries, and particularly the Arab brothers and the great Arab nation who are the vanguard of Islam, of the great danger the foreigners, especially Zionism, pose to them. In the month of Ramadan, which is a month of Islamic assemblies, it is necessary that the believers pull back the curtain on the plots of this world-devouring monster in their public gatherings and reveal the dangers posed by this enemy of mankind.

Imam's remarks dated 25 July 1979 (3 Mordad 1357 AHS). *Sahifeh-ye Imam*, vol. 9, p. 214.

If the Muslims come together, Israel will be destroyed

If the Muslims were united and each one of them threw a bucket of water over Israel it would be washed away, yet still they are helpless before it. I am puzzled as to why, when they know this, they do not turn to the sure remedy which is unity and alliance? Why do they not neutralise the plots which the imperialists use to undermine them? At what time will this puzzle be solved and who is to be the one to solve it? Who should neutralise these plots other than the Muslim governments and the Muslim nations?

Imam's remarks dated 16 August 1979 (25 Mordad 1358 AHS). *Sahifeh-ye Imam*, vol. 9, pp. 250-1.

The need for the Muslims to unite in order to rectify the basic mistake

With the deepest of regret I must state that the governments and nations of Islam, in particular the Arab governments and nations, made a mistake. The mistake that all the Muslims made, particularly the Arab nations and governments, was to give Israel a respite. The personal interests of the governments prevented them from stifling Israel's voice at the very start and stopping it from gaining power. Unfortunately, their interests prevented them from heeding our exhortations, which we have been voicing loudly over the past

20 years, or a little less, along with our call to unite against Israel. They gave it a respite until the affair reached the stage it has. Now its aggressive hands have reached out and set southern Lebanon aflame, and it means to extend the borders of Palestine even further.

We have said repeatedly that Israel, this germ of corruption, will not be satisfied with Quds, will not content itself with Bayt al-Muqaddas. If it is given further reprieve, all the Muslim governments will be placed in danger. The past mistake must be rectified through the Muslims' unity and through the formation of a 'Party of the Oppressed' to stand against the imperious ones at whose head are the criminal America and its most corrupt servant Israel.

This was the mistake of the Muslim governments and the Arabs in particular; they must rectify this mistake and repent before God the Blessed and Exalted.

Imam's remarks dated 18 August 1979 (27 Mordad 1358 AHS). *Sahifeh-ye Imam*, vol. 9, p. 256.

It is incumbent upon every Muslim to arm himself against Israel

Dear sisters and brothers, in whatever country you may live, defend your Islamic and national honour! Defend fearlessly and unhesitatingly the peoples and countries of Islam against their enemies: America, international Zionism and all the superpowers of the East and West. Loudly proclaim the crimes of the enemies of Islam.

My Muslim brothers and sisters! You are aware that the superpowers of the East and West are plundering all our material and other resources, and have placed us in a situation of political, economic, cultural and military dependence. Come to your senses; rediscover your Islamic identity. Endure oppression no longer and vigilantly expose the sinister plans of the international bandits, headed by America.

Today, the first *qiblah* of the Muslims has fallen into the grasp of Israel, that cancerous growth in the Middle East. Today, it is suppressing and slaughtering our dear Palestinian and Lebanese brothers with all its might. Today, with all the diabolical means at its disposal, Israel is casting dissension among the Muslims. It is incumbent upon every Muslim to arm himself against Israel. Today, our African Muslim countries are writhing beneath the yoke of America and other foreign powers and their agents.

Imam's remarks dated 29 September 1979 (7 Mehr 1358 AHS). *Sahifeh-ye Imam*, vol. 10, p. 112-3.

We must unite and deracinate Israel

The Islamic countries must adopt an inimical stand against the occupying regime in Israel, which has caused most of the problems they now face, and must uphold the aspirations of the dear Palestinian and Lebanese people with all their might. We thoroughly condemn the plot of Egypt, America and Israel to suppress the great movement of the people of Palestine. Leaders and representatives of countries gathered in beloved Algeria, come let us unite and sever the hands of the criminals of the left and right - at whose head stands America - uproot Israel and entrust the rights of the people of Palestine to their own hands. I ask God the Exalted to awaken the Muslims and grant the Islamic countries unity and greatness.

Imam's remarks dated 30 October 1979 (8 Aban 1358 AHS). *Sahifeh-ye Imam*, vol. 10, p. 276.

Why do one billion people sit back and watch?

How can Israel, with such a small number of people, come and prevail over these countries which possess everything and have all kinds of powers, the way it has? Why should it be this way? Is it not because the nations are divided and stand apart from their governments, and the governments are disunited, that a population of one billion Muslims, with all the means they have at their disposal, are sitting by and watching as Israel perpetrates these crimes in Lebanon and Palestine? Is this what they should be, merely onlookers? The voice of our brothers there is raised so loudly yet we merely listen and sit back as spectators. When are we going to discover our own power?

Imam's remarks dated 1 November 1979 (10 Aban 1358 AHS). *Sahifeh-ye Imam*, vol. 10, pp. 291-2.

Oh endless sea of humanity, rise up and defend the centre of revelation

Oh Muslims of the world! Oh you Muslims who have risen up! Oh endless sea of humanity! Rise up and defend your national and Islamic existence. Israel has taken Bayt al-Muqaddas from the Muslims and has met only tolerance from the (Muslim) governments. Apparently America and its corrupt appendage Israel now intend to seize the holy mosque and the mosque of the Prophet. Still the Muslims sit back, indifferent onlookers. Rise up and defend Islam and the centre of revelation. Do not be afraid of this ballyhoo, for today Islam needs you and you are responsible before God Almighty. Trust in God Almighty and march forth united.

As followers of the great religion of Islam, we support all the weak and oppressed and back you as we do any organisation in the world which has risen to save its own country. We completely support the struggle of the Palestinian brothers and the people of southern Lebanon against the usurper Israel. By the will of God Almighty we will be victorious over the enemy of mankind and Islam. It is hoped that God's help and the victory of the Muslims are close.

Imam's message dated 25 November 1979 (4 Azar 1358 AHS). *Sahifeh-ye Imam*, vol. 11, p. 91.

I hope we can remove the problems in Palestine's path

****In the Name of God, the Compassionate, the Merciful****

Mr. Yassir Arafat, chairman of the Palestine Liberation Organisation executive committee.

I received your kind message while in hospital. I thank you for the concern you have shown over my illness. It is hoped that by the grace of God this indisposition will be remedied and we will be able to carry out the heavy responsibility we bear with greater strength and remove the difficulties that the enemies of Islam, namely the occupier Israel and the agents of Zionism, have created in our way, one after the other from the path of the Muslims of the world particularly the Palestinian brothers. Perhaps we can bring about even greater victories for them.

I ask God Almighty to grant success to all struggling in this path.

Imam Khomeini's reply to Yassir Arafat's telegram dated 31 January 1980 (11 Bahman 1358 AHS). *Sahifeh-ye Imam*, vol. 12, p. 113.

Let us all rise up and destroy Israel

We will defend the defenceless people of Lebanon and Palestine against Israel. Israel, this germ of corruption, has always been a base for America. For nearly 20 years I have pointed out the danger posed by Israel. We must all rise up and destroy Israel and replace it with the brave nation of Palestine.

Imam's remarks dated 11 February 1980 (22 Bahman 1358 AHS). *Sahifeh-ye Imam*, vol. 12, p. 126.

Support for the courageous people of Palestine

We are at war with international communism no less than we are struggling against the global plunderers of the West, headed by America, Zionism and Israel... Once again, I declare my support for all movements and groups that are fighting to gain liberation from the clutches of the superpowers of the left and the right. I declare my support for the courageous people of Palestine and beloved Lebanon.

Imam's message dated 21 March 1980 (1 Farvardin 1359). *Sahifeh-ye Imam*, vol. 12, pp. 176-7.

If the Muslims had been united, the Quds problem would not have arisen

In any case, if the Muslims were united, then they would be faced with no issues such as Quds, Afghanistan or other issues which have arisen and will arise for Muslims in other places (in the future).

Imam's remarks dated 6 August 1980 (15 Mordad 1359 AHS). *Sahifeh-ye Imam*, vol. 13, p. 65.

The people must arise, let us not seek shelter in the lap of these wolves

If the Muslims become conscious of the fact that we are from God and we must be for God, they will experience no harm and Israel will no longer force its way forward. We must determine to drive Israel out of these Arab lands, not simply be satisfied with telling it not to establish anything in Bayt al-Muqaddas. No, and we must not be deceived by America and these councils which have been created, nor by the dramas they direct with the aim of devouring us. We must not be deceived by them. Each person must rise up himself. The Muslims must themselves rise up against these. They must not expect their governments to do this for them, for they won't do anything. The people themselves must act. You should not seek shelter in the arms of one expecting it to protect you from the other. No, for they are all wolves and they will devour all of you. You must protect yourselves. Turn your attention to God and Islam, rise up for God and for Islam, march forward for God and for Islam, then, God willing, you will be victorious.

Imam's remarks dated 6 August 1980 (15 Mordad 1359 AHS). *Sahifeh-ye Imam*, vol. 13, p. 71.

To solve the Palestinian issue, the people must return to the early age of Islam

Until the time that we return to Islam, the Islam of the Prophet of God, our problems will remain. Until that happens, we can solve neither the Palestinian problem nor the problems besetting Afghanistan and other places. The nations must turn to the earliest age of Islam, if their governments do so with them there is no problem, otherwise the nations should detach themselves from their governments and do to them what the nation of Iran did to its government, so that the problems can be solved. Otherwise, we can commemorate Quds Day as much as we like, we can shout, the gentlemen can gather and talk, but shouting and talking will not stop them. Certainly sometimes it may, but we don't even talk.

Imam's remarks dated 9 August 1980 (18 Mordad 1359 AHS). *Sahifeh-ye Imam*, vol. 13, p. 77.

All together beneath the banner of Islam

The Muslim population is approximately one billion, so why then, when we have a population of one billion, should the Zionists be able to take our Quds and place the other governments under their control? If these governments were to unite, they would form one huge government. Each one would still rule its own area, but all would be together under the banner of Islam.

Imam's remarks dated 5 March 1981 (15 Esfand 1359 AHS). *Sahifeh-ye Imam*, vol. 14, p. 156.

Has not the time arrived to tear open the heart of Israel using weapons

Oh Muslims of the world! Oh oppressed people under the sway of oppressors! Beware! Rise up and offer the hand of unity to one another. Defend Islam and your destiny and fear not the hue and cry of the superpowers, for this century, by the will of God the all powerful, is the century of victory of the oppressed over the imperious and haughty and of truth over falsehood. The world must know that Iran has found the way towards God and it will continue in an irreconcilable struggle against America, the global plunderer and the bitter enemy of the deprived of the world, until its interests have been severed.

Not only will events in Iran not set us back even for a moment, but they will make our people more determined to destroy American interests. We have begun our decisive and unceasing struggle against America and we hope that our children, free from the yoke of the oppressors, will hoist the flag of divine unity (tauhid) in the world. We are sure that if we continue to closely pursue our duty, which is to fight against the criminal America, our children will taste the sweetness of victory.

Is it not a disgrace for the Muslims of the world, with all of this human, material and spiritual capital they have at their disposal and with such a progressive religion and divine backing, to surrender to the control of the arrogant powers and the sea and land robbers of this century?

Has not the time arrived to put aside carnal desires, to offer one another the hand of friendship and brotherhood and drive the enemies of humanity from the scene, bringing an end to their heinous, tyranny-laden existence?

Has not the time arrived for the brave and militant nation of Palestine to strongly condemn the political games of those who claim to be fighting against Israel and, using weapons, tear open the heart of Israel, this staunch enemy of Islam and the Muslims?

What excuse will the Muslims have to give God Almighty who has called on them to hold fast to the rope of God and shun division and dispute?

Do they not consider it their duty to support the nation and government of Iran who through holy *jihad* have pulled down the banner of blasphemy and raised the great and noble flag of Islam?

Do the court-affiliated preachers consider crushing the Islamic revolution of Iran to be more imperative than opposing America and Israel?

We call upon our brothers in Islam in the lands of the East and West to act in unison with the Islamic Republic of Iran for a single purpose, namely, with help from God the Exalted, to rid the Islamic countries and the deprived lands of the evil of these criminals and this policy of plundering, thus giving a positive response to God Almighty's call in this vital matter.

We ask the pilgrims to the sacred House of God to pray for the victory of Islam while at the noble stations and to convey the message of the Iranian nation and the call of 'Oh Muslims' of this oppressed nation to their countries.

I most humbly beseech Almighty God to grant us all the blessing of unity and familiarity with Islamic duties.

Imam's message dated 6 September 1981 (15 Shahrivar 1360 AHS). *Sahifeh-ye Imam*, vol. 15, pp. 146-7.

The Egyptian army must not bring this shame upon itself

Today, the Egyptian nation has the power in its hands. It is not certain that the army is with the government, except for those elements that are in the pay of America. The Egyptian army must be careful not to bring shame upon itself by supporting this government which has announced that it is dependent on America and Israel and has openly asserted that it will suppress anyone who breathes a word about Islam. Do not give Israel the opportunity to once again tomorrow enter your country and lord over you, or for America and Israel to take your destiny into their hands.

Imam's remarks dated 9 October 1981 (17 Mehr 1360 AHS). *Sahifeh-ye Imam*, vol. 15, p. 246.

The way out

The Muslims should not sit back waiting for their governments to act for them and save Islam from the hands of Zionism. They should not sit back waiting for the international organisations to do something for them. The people themselves must rise up against Israel. The nations must rise up and force their governments to stand against Israel, and not be content simply with condemnation. Those who have a friendship agreement with Israel also condemn it, although their condemnation is in reality a farce. If the Muslims are sitting back waiting for America or its agents to do something for them, then this process will be held up for an eternity. One method which was chosen many years ago to encourage and strengthen the unity of the Muslims, the aware Muslims, was to bring them together in gatherings to commemorate festivals, among them the birthday of the Most Noble Messenger or other birthdays and other religious occasions.

Imam's remarks dated 16 December 1981 (25 Azar 1360 AHS). *Sahifeh-ye Imam*, vol. 15, pp. 371-2.

If you unite together Israel would not have the nerve to do anything

It is regretful that other countries do not follow the example set by Iran. Why don't they follow Iran's example and unite and work together with their people and with one another to stop Israel from prevailing over them? You saw how Israel took the Golan Heights paying no heed to any of you, and how it declared that no power could make it change its mind. Why instead of inviting everyone to make a united front against Israel, against an Israel which is the enemy of Islam, the enemy of humanity, which is your enemy, the enemy of the Arabs and which bears animosity towards you all, must you create such a state of disunion amongst yourselves? Why do you create divided communities amongst yourselves? Why do governmental groups create divisions? Why do you form different fronts? This front forming goes against Islam, goes against the Noble Quran. The Noble Quran calls the Muslims to unity and you call them to disunion and confrontation with one another. You must let reason be your leader and Islam be your guide. All of you submit yourselves to Islam and act according to the rules of reason. Reason and Islam say that you should unite, for if you do, no country can commit an aggression against you and Israel will not dare stay in these countries, in these lands, it has usurped. Now that differences exist among you, Israel shouts out that no power can stop it, for it has America behind it. But our people have God backing them.

What happened to make you start forming fronts? You know that forming fronts has no advantage for you, indeed it is to your detriment.

Islam wants you to unite, it wants you to come together as one, it wants you to hold fast to the rope of God. Why do you not hold fast to the rope of God together? Why do you each turn to one direction, either the East or the West? Come, stop doing such things, unite together and be as brothers to one another. Just as God the Blessed and Exalted has stated that the believers are brothers, be as brothers to one another. Reject the opponents of Islam and be certain that if you unite, you will be victorious and no power of the East or West will be able to rule over you.

I ask God the Blessed and Exalted to grant unity to the Muslims and awareness of the laws of Islam and the interests of the Muslims to the Muslim leaders.

Imam's remarks dated 28 December 1981 (7 Dey 1360 AHS). *Sahifeh-ye Imam*, vol. 15, pp. 381-2.

Drive out this germ of corruption with ideological unity

Another problem concerns the Muslims, it concerns the Muslim countries and must be solved by them. You all know, as does everyone that the difficulties of the Muslims have been brought upon them by these great powers and that which can solve these problems is the Muslims' ideological unity. The Muslim governments and people should hold hands together and attack Zionism, this staunch enemy of Islam, which has attacked Islam and intends to take the Muslims' countries off them one after the other. But instead of uniting together and driving this germ of corruption and cancerous growth out of Muslim lands, cleansing them (of Zionists), they are all either sitting back simply talking, or sometimes even discussing things which are to their interests. All that worries some of these countries is the fact that Iran wants to establish Islamic rule. Every day they make such a song and dance about Iran, claiming different things along the lines that, for example, it is colluding with Israel, while from the very beginning it has shouted out: we must free Palestine, we must free Quds.

Imam's remarks dated 24 January 1982 (4 Bahman 1360 AHS). *Sahifeh-ye Imam*, vol. 15, pp. 433-4.

The presumptuousness of Israel is a result of the division amongst the Muslims

If there were not this division amongst the Muslims, would it have been possible for Israel with such a small population to be so presumptuous and trample over the dignity of all the Muslims the way it has? If these differences did not exist among the Islamic countries, among the Muslim governments, could America rule over them and plunder their resources?

Imam's remarks dated 10 January 1982 (20 Dey 1360 AHS). *Sahifeh-ye Imam*, vol. 15, p. 399.

The command of the Quran, battle with Israel

Oh Muslim nations! Oh oppressed nations of all Islamic countries! Dear nations who have been placed under the rule of individuals who hand over your wealth to America while you yourselves live in hardship and abjectness! Awaken and rise up! Oh oppressed of the world, rise up and stand against the superpowers! For if you stand against them, they cannot do anything. You saw how the Muslim nation of Iran united and rose up empty-handed, unarmed against those great satanic powers of Muhammad-Rida and the superpowers who lined up behind him, pushing them all aside. They drove this corrupt government and this illegal and corrupt monarchy from the scene with the power of their faith and the cry of *Allahu akbar* (God is the Greater), sending them to hell. And as you see today, even though they had no financial, physical or military resources, only the power of their faith, in their place they established an Islamic government, a government which supports the weak and oppressed of the world.

If you assist God the Blessed and Exalted, he will assist you. "Oh ye who believe! If ye will aid (the cause of) God, He will aid you, and plant your feet firmly." (Quran 47:7). To assist God, you must assist his religion, his servants and the oppressed. If you stand against the oppressors and demand justice for the oppressed, if you stand against the superpowers like America which comes from the other side of the world and seeks to rule over us, to bring us all under its sway and destroy our resources, then God will help you. Unfortunately, the governments consent to their actions more than they (the superpowers) expect or even want them to.

Islam is today suppressed, the Quran has been abandoned. The laws of the Quran have been abandoned. The call to prayer rings out from the minarets and you perform your prayers (*namaz*), but you pay no heed to most of the political laws of Islam, and the Quran remains in its state of abeyance. Of course reading the Quran and its presence in all affairs of man's life is necessary, but it is not enough. The Quran must be acted upon in all affairs of our life. When the Quran states: "And hold fast all together to the rope which God stretches out for you, and be not divided among yourselves" (Quran 3:103), and "Fall into no disputes, lest ye lose heart and your power depart" (Quran 8:46) these are progressive political decrees which if acted upon will bring you world supremacy. We have all abandoned this Quran and have paid no heed to this problem. The Quran should be involved in all affairs (of man's life). It should be read, it should occupy the thoughts of all of us, everywhere, all of the time. The Quran should be involved in all aspects of man's affairs, not simply involved in some and not others. Amongst its political directives is the command to fight against those who are waging war against the Muslims, and today

Israel is standing against the Muslims and wages war against them, America is standing against the Muslims and wages war against them, and Saddam, America's mercenary, is standing against the Muslims and wages war against them. God has commanded you to fight against those who have risen up against the Muslims or against a group of Muslims.

Imam's remarks dated 10 February 1982 (21 Bahman 1360 AHS). *Sahifeh-ye Imam*, vol. 16, pp. 31-4.

The hand of brotherhood for the expulsion of Israel

As I and the officials of the Islamic Republic have announced time and again, the nation and government of the Islamic Republic of Iran submit to the holy laws of the Quran and Islam and, in accordance with the command of the noble Quran, consider themselves to be the brothers in faith of all the Islamic nations in the various countries whatever their cultural and geographical position. They seek peace and a peaceful existence with all the governments and nations, and as long as a government does not violate their country's borders and adheres to the commands of Islam, they regard it as a brotherly government. They want the countries and nations to unite together, to rise up with one voice against the aggressors, whoever they may be, to deliver themselves from the clutches of the world devourers, and in accordance with the command of Islam, defend their rights against infringement, their borders against violation, and teach the aggressors a lesson. It is in this way that, by the grace of God Almighty, no power will be able to stop them in this holy defence. I exhort the governments to cease in this vindictiveness and muscle flexing and extend the hand of brotherhood to the Iranian nation and government so that together we can drive the usurper Israel out of the Islamic countries and occupied lands. Abandon this racism and these ideas about superiority of language which Islam has condemned and rejected, so that happiness in this world and the next can be yours and no power can confront you.

Imam's message dated 11 February 1982 (22 Bahman 1360 AHS). *Sahifeh-ye Imam*, vol. 16, p. 41.

The Iranian nation's long-standing wish

Today, Iran stands firmly by what it said from the very first day: we do not seek war with any country, Islamic or non-Islamic, and we desire peace and harmony for all. Hitherto, we have been engaged in defence which is for everyone a divine precept and a human right; we have never had the intention to attack other countries, nor do we have. We want the Islamic countries to stand together in an Islamic pact to defend the rights of the Muslims and the Islamic countries against aggressors and bellicose elements like the aggressor Israel. And if this long-standing wish of the nation and government of Iran is realised, no power, however great, can attack the Islamic countries or one of them, or bring their power and might to bear on them.

Imam's message dated 1 April 1982 (12 Farvardin 1361 AHS). *Sahifeh-ye Imam*, vol. 16, p. 142.

Defending the uprising of the oppressed in the occupied lands

It is right to speak as one with the oppressed people who have risen up in the occupied lands of Palestine and actively support their demonstrations and uprising against the injustices of Israel, so that in the same way as Iran with its demonstrations and Islamic revolution brought down the tyrannical imperial regime, they too can triumph over this man-eating fiend and atheist usurper. It is hoped that the oppressed in the occupied centres continue with their demonstrations and anti-Zionist activities until they achieve victory.

Imam's message dated 1 April 1982 (12 Farvardin 1361 AHS). *Sahifeh-ye Imam*, vol. 16, p. 143.

Now that the Muslims of Palestine are roaring out, with what excuse can one remain indifferent?

In the Name of God, the Compassionate, the Merciful

The Quds problem is not a personal one, nor is it a problem peculiar to just one country or to Muslims of the world in the present age. Rather it is a matter which has concerned the monotheists of the world and the believers from the day the foundations of the al-Aqsa mosque were laid to the present, and will continue to concern them in the future.

How painful it is for the Muslims of the world in the present era that, even with all the material and spiritual means they have at their disposal, such presumptuous actions can still be carried out before their very eyes against God Almighty and His exalted messengers and by a bunch of criminal riffraff at that. And how shameful it is for the Muslim governments who, with the lifeblood of the world superpowers in their hands, sit back and watch as America, the super criminal of history, establishes a corrupt, worthless element in their midst and, with only a paltry few, unlawfully seizes their holy place of worship and their first *qiblah* from them, and with the utmost insolence puts on a show of strength before them all. How heinous silence is in the face of this great tragedy of history, and how wonderful it would have been had the loud speakers of the al-Aqsa mosque sounded from the very day that Israel, this malicious element, set to perpetrating this great crime.

Now that the revolutionary and brave Muslims of Palestine are, with great determination, roaring out from the place of ascension of the last messenger (peace be upon him and his descendants) with a divine call to the Muslims to rise up and unite in a movement against global unbelief, what excuse does one have before God Almighty and the aware human conscience for remaining indifferent to this Islamic ordinance? Now that the walls of the Quds mosque are stained with the blood of the beloved Palestinian youth, their legitimate demand for justice having been answered with machine-gun fire from a handful of villains, is it not shameful if the zealous Muslims do not respond to their appeal and do not proclaim their sympathy for them? Let it be that their shouts of sympathy stir the governments to use the great power of Islam, to sever the hand of America - the word devourer, this criminal in history who, from the other side of the ocean in support of tyrants, clasps the unclean hand of the Israelis - and to save themselves and the oppressed nations of the world.

It is hoped that God the Beneficent will confer His favour on mankind and fulfil His promise as revealed in the Quran soon, and the weak and oppressed of the earth will triumph over the proud and arrogant ones.

Blessings upon Quds and the al-Aqsa mosque.

Blessings upon the people who have risen up against Israel the criminal and the Muslims and oppressed of the world.

Ruhullah al-Musawi al-Khomeini

Imam's message on the occasion of the uprising of the Palestinian people in the occupied territories, dated 14 April 1982 (25 Farvardin 1361 AHS). *Sahifeh-ye Imam*, vol. 16, pp. 167-8.

Israel, the common enemy

Iran does not intend to give up on the Muslim governments, it still hopes that Islam will be successful and that these governments will themselves conform to Islam. We have common ground. Repulse our common enemy, which today is Israel and America and the like, who wants to destroy our dignity (and resources) and once again bring tyranny upon us. When you have done this, then each country can have their own government in their own land.

Imam's remarks dated 3 June 1982 (13 Khordad 1361 AHS). *Sahifeh-ye Imam*, vol. 16, p. 251.

Use force to throw Israel out, then there can be a cease-fire

We say that unlike you, we are not bellicose and we speak the truth, the fact that we are defending ourselves (against you) is proof of this[38]. You call yourselves peace-seekers, your peace seeking is like that hitherto demonstrated by Israel. Even now Israel says 'Come, let us make peace', but what does it mean? It has entered Lebanon and taken its towns and now it calls for a cease-fire. The day they force Israel out of their towns will be the day there is a cease-fire. It is on that day they can say 'very well, now let us talk of a cease-fire, let us sit down and see who the culprit is'.

There should not be peace at any price; it should be made clear who is to be held accountable. Can Israel just come, perpetrate whatever crime it desires then turn around and say 'very well, we've finished what we set out to do, you go about your daily affairs while the places we have taken will remain in our hands'? Is this what a cease-fire is all about?

Imam's remarks dated 13 June 1982 (22 Khordad 1361 AHS). *Sahifeh-ye Imam*, vol. 16, pp. 276-7.

Nations must stand

So long as the Islamic countries, the Islamic nations, do not take what happened in Iran as their model and spill out into the streets demanding that their governments confront Israel, then do not expect these blind and deaf people to come to their senses. The nations must stand up and demand that their region's armies and governments help these Palestinians and Syrians who have been subjected to oppression, until this cancerous tumour is destroyed. If they don't, if they simply act as observers, watching to see what happens, if they are indifferent and bring the excuse that it is the governments who should act, then they will not be able to offer God a credible excuse. Iran is evidence for all countries. Perhaps in the hereafter, God the Blessed and Exalted will cite Iran as evidence for those who tolerated oppression, surrendered to oppressors and did not rise up. If they believe in God and the day of resurrection, they must prepare an answer for God the Blessed and Exalted. On that day, America and Israel will not be able to come to their aid. And if they do not believe, still they must provide an answer for the oppressed nations of the world and for the future generations who may, God forbid, fall into the trap because of the policy their predecessors had adopted. If religious values count for nothing to them, then let them consider the values of their own system, their national and human values and not succumb to abjectness for the sake of a few days of rule, abjectness under the heel of Israel at that!

The Muslims must rise up. God has said: "I admonish you to do one thing: to arise for God, it may be in pairs or it may be individually." (Quran 34:46). Thus, you cannot use the excuse that you are alone, for we must rise up whether alone or in a group. We must rise up together. We are all duty bound to rise up for God, to rise up to protect the Islamic countries against these two cancerous tumours, one of which is the corrupt Baath party of Iraq and the other Israel, and both of which issue from America.

Imam's remarks dated 13 June 1982 (23 Khordad 1361 AHS). *Sahifeh-ye Imam*, vol. 16, pp. 285-6.

Advice to the Palestinian leaders

I advise the Palestinian leaders to stop their shuttling to and fro, and with reliance on God the Exalted, the people of Palestine and their own weapons fight Israel to the death. For these comings and goings will cause the combatant nations to lose faith in you. Rest assured that neither the East will be of use to you nor the West. With faith in God and reliance on weapons, wage war against Israel and be as the nation and armed forces of Iran who, without relying on other powers or the superpowers and with faith in God the Exalted and His eternal power, will not lay down their arms until their legitimate demands have been met.

Imam's message dated 16 July 1982 (25 Tir 1361 AHS). *Sahifeh-ye Imam*, vol. 16, p. 331.

The turn will come of those who remain silent in the face of Israel's crimes

Israel is now standing against all the Islamic countries and telling them not to do a damn thing. Is this not deplorable? Those who run affairs are not human that they allow Israel to stand against them and tell them to stop poking their noses into its business. It took Beirut, perpetrating all those crimes, it threw the liberation organisation into confusion forcing everyone to scatter. Know that the turn will come of those of you who have remained silent in the face of these crimes and do not take a stand against them, Israel will come after you too.

Imam's remarks dated 22 August 1982 (31 Mordad 1361 AHS). *Sahifeh-ye Imam*, vol. 16, p. 374.

Those who want to officially recognise Israel should be afraid of our people

Observe how deplorable the situation is when Israel can bring such suffering upon the women, children and old people of Lebanon right before the very eyes of these governments who call themselves Islamic. It has killed so many people, made many more homeless and is now busy with its activities there. How deplorable it is that such things have taken place in the presence of these governments. Now unfortunately, they are on the point of accepting these plans that America is proposing, these conspiracies that it is plotting, for all its plans are anti-human and anti-Islamic. They intend to accept the proposals America made previously, such as those at Camp David and others of that ilk which followed, and all agree that the Muslims should now recognise Israel, which has perpetrated so many crimes, as a responsible, independent government. How painful this is for any decent human being.

I state categorically here and now that if these governments in the Persian Gulf region and other areas approve such an action, as they did the American plan and subsequent plans that have been laid, and recognise Israel, our people, our army, our revolutionary guards, Islam and God the Blessed and Exalted will not forgive them. They should fear the day when this nation, this army and these revolutionary guards feel that they have the duty, the religious duty, to teach these people who have approved the Camp David accords or similar agreements for the independence and recognition of Israel a lesson. What happened in Lebanon and Iran, the attacks on Iran and Lebanon were carried out in accordance with an American plan. Because it realised it had lost Iran, America laid the plan and contrived to create problems for Iran. (It created as many problems as it could, however all to no avail). So then it created the problem of the war and sought to prolong it by not allowing the truth to be acted upon so it could take advantage of the situation. The same was true in Lebanon too. It had a plan to execute there. It brought Israel in to perpetrate those crimes, so that plans which are to America's advantage, and which make all countries even more of a prisoner of America than they already are, could be executed there. How much longer are these Islamic nations and these so-called Islamic governments going to put up with this submissiveness and accept such humiliation? How much longer are they going to ignore the fact that an honourable life is better than a pleasant one which lacks honour? They should come to their senses and give this matter due attention. If they give their approval to the Camp David accords and others like them for recognising Israel, then maybe it will become our religious duty to deal with them in another manner.

Imam's remarks dated 5 September 1982 (14 Shahrivar 1361 AHS). *Sahifeh-ye Imam*, vol. 16, pp. 410-1.

Israel must be erased from the pages of history

You saw how a frail government of (a nation of only) two million people, the government of Israel, confronted a billion Muslims and attacked Lebanon, perpetrating so many crimes that the action was unprecedented in history. Yet we see that the Muslim governments are presently trying to formally recognise it. We say Israel must be erased from the pages of history, Bayt al-Muqaddas belongs to the Muslims and is their first *qiblah*.

Imam's remarks dated 8 September 1982 (17 Shahrivar 1361 AHS). *Sahifeh-ye Imam*, vol. 16, p. 418.

Recognising Israel, a tragedy which makes every self-respecting Muslim shudder

The honourable clergy and the committed writers and speakers must defend Islam and the Islamic revolution of Iran in the presence of Muslims at every appropriate opportunity and show their true visage to the people of the world in order to counter the poisonous propaganda, rumours and lies busily being disseminated by the mass media aligned with America and Israel against Islam and the Islamic Republic of Iran. To prepare the nations, they must highlight the Islamic achievements gained through the unrelenting struggle of the committed nation of Iran in the face of all the problems and hindrances created by the enemies of Islam inside and outside the country. They must raise the curtain on the calumnies trumpeted against this nation over the enemies' propaganda loudspeakers and reveal the plans and machinations devised by America and those dependent on it. They must inform the people of the world about the attacks carried out by the army of the Aflaqite Saddam on the orders of America and with the support of countries dependent on it. They must notify the Muslims of actions taken by some American-controlled rulers against them and Islam, the worst of which is officially recognising Israel followed by the savage attack on the Islamic country of Lebanon and the martyring and injuring of tens of thousands of innocent, defenceless people. Then perhaps the nations, with faith in God the Most High, can prevent this great tragedy in history, this tragedy which will bring shame upon the Muslims in the eyes of the world and the future generations, from taking place. Perhaps then they can save beloved Islam and the Muslims from this great disgrace and free themselves from this humiliation and this undesirable abjection, the thought of which makes every self-respecting Muslim shudder.

Imam's message dated 20 September 1982 (29 Shahrivar 1361 AHS). *Sahifeh-ye Imam*, vol. 16, pp. 439-40.

The Muslims look on

And today we see that in different Muslim lands, Muslims are being subjected to tyranny and oppression. Lebanon is set aflame by America, troops are mobilised there by the US, France and their henchmen for the sake of a handful of innocent Shiites, of innocent Muslims, yet the rest of the

Muslims sit back and look on. The most the (Muslim) governments did was to refrain from celebrating the feast day. Is this enough? This is an action, but the tyranny continues. Our youth in Lebanon and Palestine are still being killed in their dozens, crimes are still being perpetrated in Afghanistan, Iraq and against Iran. Is it enough to say 'we won't celebrate the feast day this year'? Will this make things right? Will this lift the burden of responsibility from the shoulders of these governments? They attack with bayonets, with guns and tanks while the tyrannised are left to stand on their own. Nevertheless they are hitting back. The governments, however, sit back, watching, and the most they can do is announce that the feast day will not be celebrated.

Imam's remarks dated 26 September 1983 (4 Mehr 1362 AHS). *Sahifeh-ye Imam*, vol. 18, p. 131.

The people will not sit back

If these governments join hands together with their people, and their people are ready to do this, and if they surrender to the (will of) their people, then they (the superpowers) would not be able to perpetrate such heinous acts in this region and Israel would not be able to go there (to Lebanon) and do such harm. Unfortunately, however, it is these governments themselves which are paving the way for the great powers. Consider how much wealth there is in this region, wealth which the superpowers are taking from these governments, how much oil alone there is that each day about twenty million barrels of it are taken and swallowed up by different countries. Still these governments sit by. They have poured into their home, for Lebanon is the home of Arabs, they have poured into the home of Arabs and are perpetrating such crimes against them, yet the Arab nation sits back and says nothing. When Iran gets involved they retort: 'But they're Persians.' Well, they (the Lebanese) are Arabs, but you don't care, you don't care if people are 'Persian' or Arab', all you care about is having the high life for a few days. But ask yourselves how long will this last? For how long can a human being sacrifice his reputation, his honour, everything for the sake of the high life? These big powers too, who have made you their agents and who are presently perpetrating these acts in Lebanon against the poor Lebanese people, should also realise that the people will not sit quietly by watching as these acts are perpetrated; eventually what happened in Iran will be repeated elsewhere.

They should start thinking about it from now. The Americans should not suppose that they can tyrannise the people and they will sit by and accept it. The explosion at their base showed them this. The same thing can happen again, however hard they try to prevent it. The people have had enough, the Lebanese people have reached the end of their tether, the Palestinians have had enough and thus they are willing to commit suicide.

Imam's remarks dated 7 December 1983 (16 Azar 1362 AHS). *Sahifeh-ye Imam*, vol. 18, p. 198.

Our crime is defending Palestine

Today everyone knows that from the point of view of the world plunderers and aggressors our real crime is defending Islam and making the Islamic Republic government official instead of the oppressive, imperial regime of the *taghut*. Our crime and our sin is giving life to the traditions of the Prophet (may the peace of God be upon him and his descendants); acting upon the commands of the Most Noble Quran; promulgating the unity of Muslims in general, Shiite and Sunni alike, in the confrontation with the plots of global atheism; supporting the bereft people of Palestine, Afghanistan and Lebanon; closing the Israeli embassy in Iran and declaring war on this cancerous tumour and world Zionism; waging war on racism and defending the deprived people of Africa; and annulling the obsequious contracts made by the vile Pahlavi regime with America the world plunderer.

Imam's message dated 28 July 1987 (6 Mordad 1366 AHS). *Sahifeh-ye Imam*, vol. 20, p. 304.

Defending the true sons of Islamic Palestine

Defending the honour of Muslims, defending the lands of Muslims and defending their resources is an imperative and we must ready ourselves for achieving these divine goals and for defending Muslims. In the present circumstances particularly, where the true sons of Islamic Palestine and Lebanon, that is the Hizbullah and the revolutionary Muslims of the usurped land and Lebanon, let out the cry of 'oh Muslims' as they sacrifice their lives, we should stand against Israel and the aggressors with all the spiritual and material strength at our disposal; we should confront all that bloodshed and savageness; we should intervene and hasten to assist them identifying the compromisers and introducing them to the people as we do so.

Imam's remarks in a meeting with members of the central council of Hizbullah in Lebanon, dated 28 February 1988 (9 Esfand 1366 AHS). *Sahifeh-ye Imam*, vol. 20, p. 462.

Animosity with Israel: a source of pride for us

Our nation, indeed all Islamic nations and oppressed peoples of the world, are proud of the fact that their enemies, who are the enemies of God Almighty, the Most Noble Quran and beloved Islam, are rapacious animals who stop short of no crime or treacherous act in order to achieve their sinister, criminal aims. They recognise neither friend nor foe in their quest to attain leadership and realise their base desires. And at the head of these enemies are America, this terrorist by nature that has set the whole world aflame, and its ally international Zionism, which, in order to realise its designs, will commit crimes about which pens are ashamed to write and tongues to speak. It will stop short of no crime in its attempt to realise this stupid fantasy it has of creating 'greater Israel'. The Islamic nations and the oppressed of the world are proud that their enemies Husayn of Jordan, this criminal huckster, Hasan (of Morocco) and Husni Mubarak share the same stable as felonious Israel, and who in order to serve America and Israel will perpetrate any act of treason against their own people. ?

Imam's last will and testament dated 5 June 1989 (15 Khordad 1368 AHS). *Sahifeh-ye Imam*, vol. 21, p. 403.

Announcement of International Quds Day

In the Name of God, the Compassionate, the Merciful

For many years, I have been notifying the Muslims of the danger posed by the usurper Israel which today has intensified its savage attacks against the Palestinian brothers and sisters, and which, in the south of Lebanon in particular, is continually bombing Palestinian homes in the hope of crushing the Palestinian struggle. I ask all the Muslims of the world and the Muslim governments to join together to sever the hand of this usurper and its supporters. I call on all the Muslims of the world to select as Quds Day the last Friday in the holy month of Ramadan - which is itself a determining period and can also be the determiner of the Palestinian people's fate - and through a ceremony demonstrating the solidarity of Muslims world-wide, announce their support for the legitimate rights of the Muslim people.

I ask God Almighty for the victory of the Muslims over the infidels.

Imam's message announcing Quds Day dated 7 August 1979 (16 Mordad 1358 AHS). *Sahifeh-ye Imam*, vol. 9, p. 243.

Quds Day is the day for the weak and oppressed to confront the oppressors

In the Name of God, the Compassionate, the Merciful

Quds Day is an international day, it is not a day devoted to Quds alone. It is the day for the weak and oppressed to confront the arrogant powers, the day for those nations suffering under the pressure of American oppression and oppression by other powers to confront the superpowers; it is the day when the oppressed should arm themselves against the oppressors and rub their noses in the dirt; it is the day when the hypocrites will be distinguished from the true believers. For the true believers acknowledge this day as Quds Day and do what they must do. The hypocrites, however, those who are secretly affiliated with the superpowers and are friends of Israel, are either indifferent on this day or do not allow the people to hold demonstrations.

Quds Day is the day when the fate of the oppressed nations should be determined. The oppressed nations should announce their existence against the oppressors and just as Iran rose up and rubbed the noses of the oppressors in the dirt, and will continue to do so, so too all the nations should rise up and throw these germs of corruption into the rubbish bin.

Quds Day is the day when the followers of the former regime in Iran and those who conspire for the corrupt regime (Israel) and the superpowers in other regions, particularly in Lebanon, should be put in their place. It is the day when we must strive to rescue Quds and deliver our Lebanese brothers from these pressures. It is the day when we must free all the oppressed from the clutches of the oppressors, the day when the Muslim community, when all the Muslims should announce their existence and warn the superpowers... Quds Day is the day when the superpowers should be warned to stay at home and leave the oppressed alone. Israel, the enemy of mankind, the enemy of humanity, which is creating disturbances every day and is attacking our brothers in south Lebanon, must realise that its masters are no longer accepted in the world and must retreat. They must give up their ambitious designs on Iran, their hands must be severed from all the Islamic countries and their agents in these countries must step down. Quds Day is the day for announcing such things, for announcing such things to the satans who want to push the Islamic nations aside and bring the superpowers into the arena. Quds Day is the day to dash their hopes and warn them that those days are gone.

Quds Day is the day of Islam; it is the day when Islam should be revived, so let us revive it and implement Islamic laws in the Islamic countries. Quds Day is the day when we must warn all the superpowers that they can no longer keep Islam under their control by means of their evil agents. Quds Day is the day to give life to Islam. The Muslims must awaken, they must come to realise the power they have, the material power and the spiritual. What are the Muslims, who form a population of one billion, enjoy divine support and have Islam and their faith behind them, afraid of? The governments of the world should know that Islam will not be defeated; Islam and the teachings of the Quran should prevail in all countries. Religion should be the religion of God and Islam is the religion of God so it should advance on all regions of the world. Quds Day is the day to announce such a matter, the day to announce 'Muslims, advance!' Advance on all the regions of the world. Quds Day is not confined to (matters pertaining to) Palestine alone, it is the day of Islam, the day of Islamic government, the day when the flag of an Islamic Republic should be raised in all (Islamic) countries, the day when the superpowers should be made to realise that they can no longer advance on the Islamic countries.

I see Quds Day as a day of Islam and a day of the Most Noble Messenger (peace be upon him and his descendants). It is the day when we must prepare all our forces and bring the Muslims out of the seclusion they (the foreign powers and their agents) forced them into, so that with all their might and main they can stand up to the foreigners. And with all our strength we are standing against the foreigners and will not allow anyone else to interfere in our country's affairs. The Muslims should not allow anyone else to interfere in the affairs of their country. On Quds Day, the nations should caution those governments which are traitors. Quds Day is the day when we shall discover which individuals and which regimes approve of the conspiracies of international groups and oppose Islam. Those who do not participate oppose Islam and are in agreement with Israel, and those who participate are committed, are in agreement with Islam and oppose the enemies of Islam at the head of whom are America and Israel. It is a day when truth will be distinguished from falsehood, the day when truth and falsehood will be distinct.

I beseech God the Blessed and Exalted to grant victory to Islam over all sections of the population in the world and to the oppressed over all the oppressors. And I beseech God the Blessed and Exalted to deliver our brothers in Palestine, in Lebanon and in southern Lebanon, indeed anywhere in the world they may be, from the hands of the oppressors and plunderers.

Peace and blessings be upon the Messenger of God and the Imams of the Muslims

Imam's message dated 16 August 1979 (25 Mordad 1358 AHS). *Sahifeh-ye Imam*, vol. 9, pp. 252-4.

Quds Day, a precursor to the Party of the Oppressed

Quds Day is an Islamic day and a day for a general Islamic mobilisation. I hope that this event will be the precursor to the creation of a party for the oppressed throughout the world which will go by the name of the party of the oppressed. I hope that all the oppressed will join this party to remove the obstacles that lie in their path; that they will rise up against the oppressors and plunderers of the East and West and no longer allow oppressors to tyrannise the weak of the earth; that they will make a reality Islam's proclamation, Islam's promise which is that the weak will rule over the oppressors and will inherit the earth. Hitherto, the oppressed have been disunited, and nothing will be accomplished by disunity. Now that an example of unity among the oppressed has materialised in the Muslim lands, this must find reality more extensively among all strata of mankind throughout history under the name of the 'Party of the Oppressed' which is the same as the 'Party of God' (Hizbullah). And it is in accordance with the will of God the Blessed and Exalted that the oppressed must inherit the earth.

We invite all the oppressed of the world to join the Party of the Oppressed and solve their problems together with a firm determination and a common will, and through this party, remove any problem which arises anywhere in the world and for any nation.

Imam's remarks dated 18 August 1979 (27 Mordad 1358 AHS). *Sahifeh-ye Imam*, vol. 9, pp. 255-6.

Keep Quds Day Alive

The gentlemen must pay attention, all the Muslims must pay attention, Quds Day is a day to which all the Islamic nations together must direct their attention and keep alive. If a hullabaloo is raised by all the Muslim nations on the last Friday of the holy month (of Ramadan), which is Quds Day, if all the people rise up, if they stage demonstrations and hold marches as they are doing now, this will be the beginning, God willing, of our stopping these corrupt elements and kicking them out of Islamic lands. But we are apathetic, the Muslims are apathetic, the people remain unwilling to take a stand, they seldom rise up or hold demonstrations about this affair. When Israel saw that the nations are at variance with one another, that the Egyptian government is its companion, its brother, and Iraq too is its brother, it advanced step by step. And you can be sure that if you remain apathetic then it will try to reach the Euphrates, for the Zionists claim that all of the land up to the Euphrates belongs to them. You must take a firm stand against them. And if it happens that the Muslim nations take a firm stand against the Zionists but their governments oppose them in this, then they should hit them in the mouth just as the Iranian people hit Muhammad-Rida in the mouth. Muhammad-Rida was stronger than any of the Muslim governments and enjoyed more (international) support than any of them, nevertheless, our nation rose up, made Islam their objective and shouting *Allahu Akbar* (God is the Greater), destroyed this and other powers. Even if all the powers came together, they would still never be able to hurt such a nation.

Imam's remarks dated 6 August 1979 (15 Mordad 1358 AHS). *Sahifeh-ye Imam*, vol. 13, pp. 68-9.

God willing, we will pray in Quds

May God help us succeed in one day going to Quds and praying there. I hope that the Muslims will consider Quds Day an important day and that in all the Islamic countries on Quds Day, the last Friday of the holy month (of Ramadan), they will stage demonstrations, hold meetings, have gatherings and attend the mosques where they will shout out. When a population of one billion shouts out, Israel cannot do anything, it will be afraid of their shouts alone. If all the Muslims who are in the world today, and there are about one billion of them, come out of their homes on Quds Day and shout 'Death to America, Death to Israel and Death to Russia,' the very words will bring about the demise of these countries.

You number one billion, your resources are so abundant that all the governments are dependent on them, and yet they force you to be divided and sow dissension among you while they take your resources telling you not to utter a word. It would be a good idea for the non-Iranian nations to follow the example of the Iranian nation a little, of this dearly beloved and noble nation of ours. And it would be a good idea for them to take a leaf out of the book of those youths who stage demonstrations in America, England and other western countries, braving the police who put them in manacles and chains and shouting out in this condition so that the truth may prevail. We must learn from those youths who shout out for Islam. Yet as it is, the nations remain neutral, and there the youths shout out for Islam while here we argue among ourselves. This is not right.

Imam's remarks dated 6 August 1980 (15 Mordad 1359 AHS). *Sahifeh-ye Imam*, vol. 13, pp. 70-1.

If everyone shouted out on Quds Day, victory would be achieved

If on Quds Day, all the nations would rise up and shout out, that foolish government would not be able to stop them. However, only a small number actually rise up. If on Quds Day all the people of the Islamic countries would rise up and shout out, not only for Quds but for all the Islamic countries, they would be victorious. Do you think we drove Muhammad-Rida out with guns? We drove him out with our cries. With our cries and shouts of *Allahu Akbar* (God is the Greater). Their heads pounded with the cries of *Allahu Akbar* to such an extent, that they gave up and fled the country. The Muslims must shout out, they must not suppose that chanting slogans is useless. No, slogans are effective if everyone chants them. For me to shout out alone would achieve nothing, likewise the shouts of just one district or one city. You observe that the shouts which rise from Iran today are not confined to Tehran, Qum or Ahwaz. One time you see that the Revolutionary Guards give the command for all the people to go onto their rooftops on a certain night and shout *Allahu Akbar*, and all obey.

Imam's remarks dated 9 August 1980 (18 Mordad 1359 AHS). *Sahifeh-ye Imam*, vol. 13, p. 78.

The prayer of unity in Quds

I wish success for you dear people who have come here for Quds Day, as I wish success for all Muslims. God willing, one day all the Muslims will be brothers to one another, all roots of corruption will be deracinated from all Muslims lands, this root of corruption, Israel, will be plucked out of the al-Aqsa mosque and our Islamic country, and by the will of God the Exalted, together we will go to Quds and pray the prayer of unity there.

Imam's remarks dated 9 August 1980 (18 Mordad 1359 AHS). *Sahifeh-ye Imam*, vol. 13, p. 80.

Message for Quds Day: machine-guns relying on faith must be used and political games must be laid aside

The last Friday of the holy month of Ramadan is Quds Day and in the last ten days of the month of Ramadan it is very probable that the Night of Power[39] will fall. It is a night the commemoration of which is a practice sanctioned by God. Its value and station is superior to a thousand months under the hypocrites for it is on that night that the destiny of mankind is determined. It is necessary that Quds Day, which falls in close contiguity to the Night of Power, be commemorated by the Muslims, that it serves as the origin of their awakening and vigilance and delivers them from the indifference they have exhibited throughout history, particularly in the last few decades, so that this day of vigilance and awakening will be more valuable than decades under the superpowers and the hypocrites of the world, and the Muslims of the world will take their destinies into their own powerful hands and determine their own fate themselves.

By staying awake through the night on the Night of Power and praying, the Muslims will free themselves from the shackles which bind them to anything other than God - which means demons whether in jinn or human form - and they will come to worship only God. On Quds Day, which falls in the last days of 'the great month of God' (Ramadan), it would be fitting for all the Muslims of the world to free themselves from the shackles of slavery and servitude to great satans and superpowers, to join the eternal power of God, sever the hands of the criminals of history from the oppressed, deprived countries and break off any covetous ties these criminals may have created.

Oh Muslims and deprived of the world, rise up and take your destiny in your hands. How long are you going to sit by and allow Washington or Moscow to determine your destiny for you?

How much longer must your Quds be trampled under the boots of the usurping Israelis, these worthless people whom America has put there (to see to their interests)?

How much longer must the lands of Quds, Palestine and Lebanon, must the oppressed Muslims of these lands, remain under the rule of criminals while you remain onlookers and some of your perfidious rulers even make it easy for these criminals?

How much longer are about one billion Muslims world-wide - and about a hundred million Arabs - with their vast lands and endless resources going to act merely as witnesses to the plunderings by the East and West and the tyrannies and inhuman massacres perpetrated by them and their petty vassals?

How much longer are they going to put up with the horrific crimes perpetrated against their brothers in Afghanistan and Lebanon and not answer their calls?

For how much longer are they going to ignore the use of arms and military and divine power to confront the enemies of Islam and liberate Quds, choosing instead to waste their time on political actions, conciliatory approaches to the superpowers and giving Israel time to commit its crimes?

How much longer will they stand by and witness the massacres?

Do the leaders of the people not know, have they not seen, that political negotiations with powerful politicians and the criminals of history will not free Quds, Palestine and Lebanon, and that every day the crimes and tyrannies will increase?

In order to liberate Quds, machine-guns relying on faith and the power of Islam must be used, and political games redolent of compromise and keeping the superpowers happy laid aside.

The Muslim nations, particularly the Palestinian and Lebanese nations, must punish those who waste time with political manoeuvres and not tolerate political games which end in nothing but loss and disadvantage for the oppressed nations. How long will these myths about the East and West continue to fascinate the powerful Muslims and the hollow propaganda they trumpet over their loudspeakers frighten them?...

Today, despite the foreign loudspeakers and the propaganda apparatus of America, the Zionists and those who have been hard hit by the revolution, Iran is on its way towards its final constitution. This serves as an example for the Islamic and deprived countries of the world, showing them that they must discover their Islamic power and not fear the hue and cry made by the East and West, by their dependants and their vassals. With faith in God the Exalted and relying on the power of Islam and the power of faith, they should rise up and foreshorten the hands of the criminals from their lands. They should give top priority to the liberation of Palestine and honourable Quds and remove the humiliation of Zionist control, control by the American vassal, from their lands. They must keep Quds Day alive...

It is hoped that by keeping this day alive, indifference will be obliterated, negligence eliminated and the noble nations, through their uprising, will remove from the arena some of those perfidious leaders - who, despite the Muslims and Islam, hand in glove with Israel and following the command of America, continue with their shameful political lives and their criminal existence against the interests of the Muslims - and bury them in the graveyard of history. Those usurping leaders, who in the war between the unbelievers, such as Israel and Saddam, and the Muslims have sided with unbelief and who deal a blow to Islam and the Muslims, must leave the Islamic scene and step down from their positions as rulers of the Muslims.

Imam's message dated 1 August 1981 (10 Mordad 1360 AHS). *Sahifeh-ye Imam*, vol. 15, pp. 53-5.

The Day of Quds, the day of the deprived

The nation, government, parliament, army and other armed forces of Iran, which today stand in unified rank demonstrating Islamic unity and divine order, are determined to stand against any satanic power and violator of human rights, to defend the oppressed and support beloved Lebanon and Quds until Quds and Palestine are returned to the Muslim fold. The Muslims of the world should view Quds Day not only as a day for all the Muslims of the world, but one for all the deprived, and from that sensitive point, they should stand against the oppressors and the world-plunderers and should not rest until the oppressed have been set free from the oppression of the power-wielders.

Imam's message dated 1 August 1981 (10 Mordad 1360 AHS). *Sahifeh-ye Imam*, vol. 15, p. 56.

The nations' duty on Quds Day

It is the duty of the nations, with the arrival of Quds Day and the anniversary of the martyrdom of that great man in the history of mankind (Imam Ali [pbuh]), in their gatherings and marches to earnestly demand that their governments rise up against America and Israel using their military might and their oil weapon. And if they (the governments) pay no heed to this demand and instead support the criminal Israel which threatens the whole region, even the noble cities, and the depth of whose aspirations are now apparent, they must force them into action through pressure, strikes and threats. In a situation when Islam and its holy sites are under threat of aggression, no Muslim can remain indifferent. That which the governments of the region are doing at this time, when Israel is encroaching extensively on Muslim lands and is killing innocent, defenceless Muslims, is nothing other than uttering empty, conciliatory words. And more disastrous than this is that they turn to America, the criminal kingpin, for protection against Israel, in effect like turning to a dragon out of fear of a snake, and even though they have the means with which to fight them, they are not prepared even to utter a hostile word against them or threaten them. In such a situation, everyone should prepare himself for obliteration and throughout his life consent to any form of humiliation. ?

Imam's message dated 16 July 1982 (25 Tir 1361 AHS). *Sahifeh-ye Imam*, vol. 16, p. 330.

The Repudiation of Polytheists during *Hajj*

Oh pilgrims to the House of God, inform the people of the world about the plots of America and Israel

Oh pilgrims to the House of God, inform the people of the world about the plots of the left and right, especially those of the plunderer and aggressor America and the criminal Israel. Seek their help, count the crimes of these criminals and seek the help of God the Exalted to remedy the situation of the Muslims and sever the hands of the criminals. Then, by the will of God Almighty, I will be able to give you glad tidings of victory.

Imam's message dated 21 November 1979 (3 Aban 1358 AHS). *Sahifeh-ye Imam*, vol. 10, p. 239.

From the Saudi dynasty's point of view, presenting the Palestinian problem for consideration at hajj is tantamount to introducing a heretical doctrine into Islam

The Hijaz was at one time the centre of Islam and the centre for the mobilisation of Islamic forces. But now all we hear is 'what has it got to do with us what goes on in the world and what Israel is doing?' Mr. Musawi Khoeiniha[40] said that after a lot of pressure was brought to bear on the Friday Prayer leaders there to speak about Palestine, they contented themselves with a few words of prayer asking God to deliver the Muslims from the menace Israel. The motive behind all the beatings which our pilgrims received, the imprisonments and effrontery they were subjected to was to stop them mentioning Israel's name, for as the authorities put it, a pilgrimage of such a kind goes against the tradition of the messenger of God and is tantamount to introducing a heretical doctrine into Islam.

Imam's remarks dated 14 October 1982 (22 Mehr 1361 AHS). *Sahifeh-ye Imam*, vol. 17, pp. 36-7.

Repudiation of polytheists is one of the sacraments of hajj

These visitors (the Iranian pilgrims to the holy House of God) have come there so that along with performing the *hajj* ceremonies they can obey the call of Abraham, the friend of God, and Muhammad, the messenger of God - may the peace and blessings of God be upon him and his descendants - for obeying them is the same as obeying God the Exalted. Treat those who have migrated towards God and His great messenger from all directions with kindness, pleasantness, affection, loyalty and as brothers in Islam. Do not torment the visitors of God and the Messenger. These people have come to perform the *hajj* ceremonies and to repudiate polytheists and unbelievers whom God and His messenger have also repudiated. Respect these committed visitors, use the power of a strong Islamic regime to crush the enemy of Islam and Muslims: the usurper Israel, and sever the hand of its overlord America, the leader of the enemies of Islam and the Islamic states, and with the help of the pilgrims from all over the world, change noble Mecca into a centre for shouts against tyrants, for this is one of the sacraments of *hajj*. And God has no need for man's obedience and acts of devotion.

Imam's message dated 3 September 1983 (12 Shahrivar 1362 AHS). Sahifeh-ye Imam, vol. 18, pp. 85-6.

The call of repudiation

In the Name of God, the Compassionate, the Merciful

"When anyone leaves his home, migrating to God and His Messenger, and is then overtaken by death, it is incumbent on God to reward him."

Thanks be to God for all His blessings and may peace and blessings be upon all His prophets, especially the last and most excellent, and upon His Imams and chosen worshippers, especially the last and living one for whose advent the inhabitants of the world will devote their souls.

Pens, tongues, speeches and writings are unable to thank God for the endless blessings He has bestowed upon mankind. He is the Creator, who, with His own effulgent manifestation, has given the blessing of existence to the unseen and seen worlds, the secret and manifest worlds, and through the blessings of His chosen ones He has revealed them to us, for: "God is the light of the heavens and the earth," and by making visible these worlds He has unveiled His splendour for "He is the First and the Last, the Outward and the Inward." (Quran 57:3)

Through His sacred books, which He revealed to His prophets from Adam to Abraham and from Abraham to Muhammad - upon whom be peace - He taught us the way to attain perfection and obliterate the self in absolute perfection.

He pointed out the path we must follow to reach Him as in the Quranic verse: "When anyone leaves his home migrating to God" (Quran 4:100), and taught us how to treat our fellow believers, our friends, the unbelievers, the arrogant ones and our enemies in the verse: "Muhammad is the messenger of God and those with him are firm of heart against the unbelievers, compassionate among themselves." (Quran 48:29).

Boundless thanks that He made us of the nation (*ummah*) of His last Prophet Muhammad Mustafa - peace and blessings be upon him and his descendants - the best and most noblest of his creatures, and followers of the sacred Quran, the greatest and most illustrious of the holy books, the written expression of the visage of God, and the place where all perfections are collected together in a unified whole. God alone has guaranteed to safeguard it against meddling by devils, human beings and jinn: "We have without doubt sent down the message, and we will assuredly guard it from corruption." (Quran 15:9).

The Quran has neither a word added nor a word taken away. It is a great book which has showed us how the great divine prophets treated the oppressors of the world and the world-plunderers throughout history. It has informed us how the last Prophet - peace and blessings be upon him and his descendants - treated polytheists, tyrants, unbelievers and, at the head of them all, hypocrites. And this treatment serves as an eternal example, for all times and all lands.

In this eternal book we see that God says: "Say, if it be that your fathers, your sons, your brothers, your mates or your kindred; the wealth that ye have gained; the commerce in which ye fear a decline; or the dwellings in which ye delight are dearer to you than God, or His Apostle, or the striving in His cause, then wait until God brings about His decision and God guides not the rebellious." (Quran 9:24). He is addressing the pragmatists, the compromisers and those who express sorrow when the young are martyred, when wealth and life are lost and other losses are incurred. It is interesting to note that after love for God the Exalted and the Most Noble messenger - peace and blessings be upon him and his descendants - striving for the cause of God (*jihad*) has been mentioned as one of the divine commands, and indeed it has been pointed out that *jihad* in the way of God is at the head of all the commands for it is the guardian of all principles. In addition, God has stated that if you refrain from *jihad*, then you must be prepared for the consequences which are degradation, bondage, having Islamic and human values scattered to the winds and the other things that you fear, from the massacre of your young and old to the captivity of your spouses and kinsfolk. It is self-evident that such are the consequences of refusing to wage *jihad*, especially one waged in defence like that in which we are presently embroiled. The following verse from the Quran refers to this: "Therefore let those beware who go against His order lest a trial afflict them or there befall them a painful chastisement." (Quran 24:63). And which disaster or calamity is worse than that which the enemies of Islam, especially at this time, are doing to deracinate the foundations of Islam, establish governments like oppressive monarchies, return the predatory advisors and destroy the agriculture and progeny of the nation, and inflict upon the country and people of Iran that which they have brought upon the country of Iraq and its innocent people over these past few years.

Endless praise and thanks be to the divine being of godship who, through His spiritual teachings, has saved the Iranian nation from the tyrannical monarchy's whirlpool of corruption, and has showed them how to live independently in the shelter of the glorious banner of Islam. Today in the world there is no country apart from Iran which is free of interference from the superpowers, and which can reject foreigners and independently determine its own destiny based on the principles of Islam. God has indeed favoured us by allowing us to live in the shadow of these people.

Endless thanks be for the favours of the Glorious and Exalted God, who, as the respected Iranian pilgrims set out for the temple of love and the shrine of the beloved on their migration towards God the Exalted and His venerable messenger - peace and blessings be upon him and his descendants - made it possible for the voice of Islam to ring out in even the most remote areas of the world; for the spiritual flag of Islam to flutter throughout the regions of the world, and for the eyes of the world to be turned towards the country of the friend (Imam Mahdi) of God the Supreme, may our souls be sacrificed for his advent.

Contrary to the pipe dreams of those malicious people and those renegades - whose infamy is well known - which gave them and their overlords the promise of the downfall of the Islamic Republic within three months to a year, and much to their despair, today, many years on, our dear Islamic country of Iran is more stable than ever before. Its great nation is prouder, its armed forces more powerful, its young and old people more resolute, its sacred theological centres under the guidance of the august *maraji* and the learned *ulama* (may God increase their number) more spirited, the ties between the theological centres and the universities stronger, its three forces more active, and its political, cultural and military spheres more developed. Its enemies too, who in reality are the enemies of Islam and the independence of the country, have become weaker and have been rendered powerless. The palaces of the arrogant rulers are shaky and the ignominy of the 'Black' House has been made more public than ever before. The confusion and apprehension of those in the House have increased, and the bewilderment of the world's media - which reflects the confusion of those in the House - is more conspicuous. The Muslims, along with the oppressed and weak of the earth, should take advantage of these current circumstances in an intelligent and perspicacious manner, and all Muslim sects and oppressed peoples should join hands together and free themselves from the shackles of bondage to the superpowers.

Now I would like to make a few points: Declaring one's repudiation of polytheists, which constitutes one of the fundaments of monotheism and is one of the political duties of the *hajj* pilgrimage, must take place during *hajj* in the form of demonstrations and marches held with the utmost firmness and dignity. The respected Iranian and non-Iranian pilgrims, while co-operating fully with the pilgrimage officials and my representative Hujjat al-Islam Karrubi, must take part in all the ceremonies and let their trenchant shouts repudiating the polytheists and atheists of global arrogance, at the head of who stands the criminal America, ring out beside the house of monotheism. They must not fail to express openly their hatred for the enemies of God and humanity. Is carrying religion into effect anything other than announcing one's devotion and loyalty to truth and expressing one's anger at and repudiation of falsehood? The sincerity of the monotheists' love may not possibly be expressed in any other way save a vehement expression of hatred for the unbelievers and the hypocrites. And which house is more suitable than the Kabah, the sacred sanctuary for the people, at which to repudiate both by word and by deed all manner of aggression, tyranny, exploitation, slavery, degradation and cowardliness, and in renewing the oath "Am I not your Lord who cherishes and sustains you? They said Yea!

We do testify!" (Quran 7:172) break the idols and the different overlords and keep alive the memory of, indeed recreate the greatest and most important political movement of the Prophet: "And an announcement from God and His Apostle to the people (assembled) on the day of the great pilgrimage, that God and His Apostle dissolve (treaty) obligations with the pagans." (Quran 9:3). For the traditions of the Prophet - peace and blessings be upon him and his descendants - and the declaration of repudiation do not age. Indeed, one's repudiation of such things should not be limited to the time and ceremony of *hajj*. Rather, the Muslims should create a global atmosphere which overflows with devotion and love for God and a hatred for His enemies which is translated into action.

The Muslims must not listen to the devilish insinuations of the tempters nor the sophisms of the casuists, of the reactionaries and the apostates. They must not for one moment turn a deaf ear to this holy, monotheistic and global tune, for most certainly from here on the world plunderers and the enemies of the people will not sit by quietly but will resort to every trick in the book and all kinds of disguises to get what they want. They will turn to pseudo-clergymen and court-affiliated preachers, mercenaries hired by the court, nationalists and hypocrites, using them to deliver false and misleading philosophies, commentaries and interpretations of Islam. They will do anything to disarm the Muslims and deal a blow to the unyieldingness, pride and power of the nation of Muhammad - peace and blessings be upon him and his descendants.

And many indeed are the ignorant ones who claim piety yet say that the holiness of the venerated Kabah, the house of Truth, would be defiled by demonstrations, marches, the shouting of slogans and declaring one's repudiation (of pagans), therefore this should not happen. They assert that the *hajj* is a time for worship and contemplation not a theatre for battle or arraying troops. Equally dishonourable religious scholars may also intimate that struggle, disavowal of pagans, battle and contention are things in which the worldly people and the materialists become involved and that to concern oneself with political issues, especially at the time of *hajj*, would be beneath the dignity of clergymen and the religious scholars. Such suggestions can themselves be considered part of the secret political strategy and machinations employed by the world plunderers.

The Muslims must use everything they need to rise up in a serious defence of divine values and of their interests. They must stand firm and strong in the battle lines of such a sacred defence, not giving the unaware, spiritless followers of Satan the opportunity to attack further their ranks of belief and dignity. From every place and every country, especially from the Kabah of Truth, they must join the armies of God. The dear pilgrims must set out from the best and holiest domains of love, awareness and *jihad* to an even loftier Kabah. Like the Lord and Leader of the martyrs, Hadrat Abi Abdullah al-Husayn (Imam Husayn), upon whom be peace, they must turn away from the sacred land of pilgrimage and head towards the sacred battlefield, they must leave the circumambulation of the Kabah and the sacred precinct to circumambulate the master of the house, and they must turn away from the ablution at the Zamzam well to bathe in martyrdom and blood, transforming themselves in the process into an unyielding nation exhibiting great cohesion such that neither the superpower of the East has the strength to confront nor that of the West. For most certainly the spirit and message of *hajj* is nothing other than to provide the Muslims with instructions for struggle against the appetitive soul and a programme for struggle against unbelief and polytheism.

Be that as it may, announcing one's repudiation of polytheists during *hajj* renews the promise of struggle and provides an exercise in organising the combatants for continuing the battle with unbelief, polytheism and the idol worshippers. It will not end with slogans, for these are only the beginning and make known the decree for battle and organise the armies of God against those of Satan and his people, this being considered one of the basic principles of monotheism (*tawhid*). And if the Muslims cannot declare repudiation of God's enemies in the house of the people and the House of God, then where can they do so? If the sanctuary, the Kabah, the mosque and the mihrab[41] cannot serve as a fortress and buttress for the soldiers of God and the defenders of the sanctuary and sanctity of the prophets, then where is their place of safety and refuge?

In short, the declaration of repudiation constitutes the first stage of the struggle and is a continuation of those other stages which it is our duty to perform. In each period of history, the form this struggle takes and the strategies and programmes involved are determined by the conditions of that time. One must see what one must do in a period like today when the leaders of unbelief and polytheism have endangered the very essence of monotheism (*tawhid*) and have made all the national, cultural, religious and political aspects of the nations a plaything of their fantasies and carnal desires. Should one sit at home and through incorrect analyses, through affronting the position and rank of human beings and inspiring a spirit of helplessness and weakness in Muslims, in practice actually tolerate Satan and his offspring and prevent society from attaining purification which is the utmost degree of perfection and the ultimate aim? Should one give the impression that the struggle of the prophets against the idols and the idol-worshippers was limited to inanimate stones and wood, and that, God forbid, prophets such as Abraham, although the pioneer of idol-smashing, left the battle scene when it came to waging war against the tyrants? Whereas in fact the destruction of the idols, all the struggles and battles of Hadrat Abraham with the followers of Nimrod and the worshippers of the sun, moon and stars, were a prelude to a great migration. And all those migrations he undertook, the hardships he endured, such as settling in a barren valley, building the House (the Kabah) and the trauma of the sacrifice of Ismail, were a prologue to a mission or message in which the words of the first and last builders and founders of the Kabah are repeated by the Seal of the Messengers and whose eternal message is conveyed with the eternal words: "And truly I am innocent of (your blasphemy of) joining others with Him." (Quran 6:19). For if we offer any other analysis or explanation, then in the contemporary period idols and idol-worshipping would not be seen to exist at all, whereas in truth which right-minded person has not recognised the new and modern type of idol-worshipping in all its bewitching and beguiling forms, and who is not aware of the domination such idol-temples as the 'Black' House have acquired over the Islamic countries and over the blood and dignity of the Muslims and the people of the third world.

Today our cries repudiating the polytheists and the unbelievers are cries against the oppression of oppressors. They are the cries of a people whose homes, countries and wealth have been plundered and who have now had enough of the aggressions of the East and West, at whose head stands America and its henchmen.

Our cries of repudiation are the cries of repudiation of the people of Lebanon and Palestine and all the other nations and countries to which the superpowers of the East and West, in particular America and Israel, have turned a covetous eye, whose wealth they have plundered, on whom they have imposed their servants and agents, into whose lands they have dug their claws from distances of thousands of kilometres and whose countries' borders, both on land and at sea, they have occupied.

Our cries of repudiation are the cries of repudiation of all the people who can no longer tolerate the haughtiness of America, and in particular its hegemonic nature; who don't want their anger and hatred to remain stifled and stuck in their throats for ever; and who have resolved to live in freedom and die in freedom and be the rescuers of future generations.

Our cries of repudiation are cries defending honour, dignity and a school of thought, they are cries defending resources and wealth, they are the painful cries of nations whose hearts have been lacerated by the dagger of unbelief and hypocrisy.

Our cries of repudiation are the cries of the indigence of the hungry, deprived and destitute who after working night and day have the product of their sweat and toil stolen by the international thieves. Greedily and in the name of capitalism, socialism and communism these thieves have sucked the blood of the poor nations, of the farmers, labourers and others who toil, have grafted the world's economic jugular vein onto their own, and have prevented the people of the world from attaining the least of their legitimate rights.

Our cries of repudiation are the cries of a nation for whom all the unbelief and arrogance (in the world) are waiting in ambush ready for the kill, all their bows, arrows and bayonets aimed at the Quran and the great family. How preposterous it is to imagine that the nation of Muhammad - peace and blessings be upon him and his descendants - those satiated with the waters of the *Kawthar*[42] of Ashura and those awaiting the inheritance of the virtuous ones would yield to a humiliating death and to servitude to the West and East. And how preposterous to imagine that Khomeini would remain quiet and calm in the face of attacks by the fiends, the polytheists and the unbelievers on the inviolability of the Most Noble Quran, on the family of the Messenger of God and the nation of Muhammad - peace and blessings be upon him and his descendants - and the followers of Abraham, the true believer, or that he would be simply an onlooker to the humiliation and degradation of the Muslims.

I am prepared to spill my valueless blood and sacrifice my unimportant life in order to carry out the obligatory duty and the precept of defending the Muslims. I am waiting to achieve the greatest accomplishment: martyrdom. The powers, superpowers and their servants can rest assured that even if Khomeini were to be left to stand alone, he would continue along the same path, which is that of struggle against unbelief, tyranny, polytheism and idol-worship, and with the help of God, alongside the crusaders of the Islamic world - these bare-footed people exposed to the wrath of dictators - he would still not let the world plunderers and their agents who persist in their oppression and tyranny rest peacefully.

Yes, our slogan 'neither East nor West' is the principal slogan of Islamic revolution in the world of the hungry and the oppressed. It is the designer of the true policy of non-alliance for the Islamic countries and those which in the near future, with the help of God, will accept Islam as the only school of thought capable of saving mankind.

This policy will not be deviated from in the slightest. The Islamic countries and the Muslim people of the world must not be dependent on the West, on Europe and America, neither must they depend on the East, on Russia. God willing, they (are not and instead) place their trust in God, His Messenger and the Imam of the Age. To turn one's back on this international policy of Islam would most surely and decisively mean turning one's back on the aspirations of the school of Islam and betraying the Messenger of God - peace and blessings be upon him and his descendants - and the guiding Imams - upon whom be peace; it would end in the death of our country and nation and that of all the Islamic countries.

No one should suppose that this slogan is a temporary one. For this is the eternal precept on which the actions of our people, our Islamic Republic, indeed all Muslims throughout the world are based. For the condition for entering the path which leads to God's blessings is that one repudiates idols and distances oneself from the path followed by those who have lost the way; and this should be put into practice in all areas of the Islamic world and in every Islamic community.

After participating in the marches to declare their repudiation of idols and announce their solidarity with the brave people of Iran, the Muslims must direct their thoughts to ridding their Islamic lands of imperialism and must strive to drive the armies of Satan out of their countries and extirpate the Western and Eastern military bases there. They must not allow the world-devourers to use their facilities for their own advantage and deliver a blow to the Islamic countries. For the greatest disgrace and shame for Islamic countries and their leaders is for foreigners to find their way into the Muslims' top secret and military centres. Let the Muslims not fear the hullabaloo and the tormenting but hollow announcements they make, for, like a spider's web, the palaces and military and political powers of world arrogance are fragile and are falling apart.

The Muslims of the world must direct their thoughts to educating and controlling those heads of state who have sold their souls to the devil and to making them reform themselves. They must awaken them, through either advice or threats, from the deep slumber which is destroying both themselves and the resources of the Islamic nations. They must warn these agents and servants. Indeed they themselves must also be alert to the danger posed by the hypocrites and the middlemen of world arrogance; they must be perspicacious and must not be heedless of this danger. They must not sit idly by, spectators to scenes of Islam's destruction and the plunder of the wealth, resources and dignity of the Muslims.

The Muslim nations must direct their thoughts to freeing Palestine and show the world the extent of their repugnance for the conciliatory and compromissorial policies adopted by the shameless, venal leaders who, using the name of Palestine, have dashed the hopes of the people in the occupied lands and the Muslims of this region. They must not allow these traitors to sully the reputation; esteem and honour of the heroic people of Palestine at the negotiating tables and in the various meetings, for these venal, pseudo-revolutionaries of little dignity have, in the name of freeing Quds, turned for recourse to America and Israel.

How strange it is that with each day which passes on the bloody tragedy of Palestine's usurpation, the silence and conciliation of the heads of the Islamic countries and the accommodating plans with the usurper Israel increase and nothing more is heard of the slogans about Bayt al-Muqaddas. And if a government or a people of a country such as Iran, which has itself presently been laid to siege and is fighting a war to defend itself against aggression, should rise up and shout in support of the Palestinian people, they (the heads of Islamic states) condemn them. Not only that but the very fact that a day should be called 'Quds Day' strikes fear into their hearts. Perhaps they think that the passing of time has changed the nature and form of Israel's and Zionism's crimes and the blood-drinking wolves of Zionism have stopped thinking about making inroads into and usurping the lands from the Nile to the Euphrates. The respected authorities of Iran, our people and the Islamic nations will not give up their struggle to deracinate this evil tree.

The dispersed groups of Islam's followers, the spiritual power of the nation of Muhammad - peace and blessings be upon him and his descendants - and the means which the Islamic countries have at their disposal must, with the help of Almighty God, be put to use, and, through forming Hizbullah centres of resistance throughout the world, Israel must be forced to repent its criminal past and the Muslims' usurped lands snatched back from its clutches.

As I have warned many times before over the years both before and after the revolution, I once more point out the danger of this filthy, cancerous tumour of Zionism enveloping the whole body of the Islamic countries. I declare my unsparing support, along with that of the nation, government and officials in Iran, for all the Islamic nations, the zealous youth and the

Muslims in their struggles to free Quds. I thank the dear youths of Lebanon who have brought honour to the nation of Islam and abjectness and ignominy to the world plunderers. I pray for the success of all the beloved people in the occupied lands and those in areas neighbouring this occupied country who by relying on the weapon of faith and holy war deliver blows against Israel and its interests, and I assure them that the people of Iran will not abandon them. Rely on Almighty God, utilise the spiritual power of the Muslims and attack the enemy with the weapons of piety, holy war, steadfastness and resistance, for *"If ye will aid the cause of God, He will aid you, and plant your feet firmly."* (Quran 47:7).

The message for repudiation, dated 28 July 1987 (6 Mordad 1366 AHS). *Sahifeh-ye Imam*, vol. 20, pp. 294-303.

Without the repudiation demonstrations, our pilgrimage would not be a true pilgrimage

This year, God willing, 150,000 people will leave Iran for the pilgrimage (*hajj*). There, these pilgrims will execute their duty which is to express their repudiation of polytheists, America and Israel. It is not possible for our pilgrims to go to *hajj* and not embark on demonstrations against world arrogance. Repudiation of polytheists is one of the fundamental political duties of *hajj*, without which our pilgrimage would not be a true pilgrimage. The Saudis should know that if they act against this, they will be standing against all the Muslims of the world, but if they act correctly, it will be to their advantage.

Imam's remarks dated 11 April 1988 (22 Farvardin 1367 AHS). *Sahifeh-ye Imam*, vol. 21, p. 20.

The Islamic epic: Palestine, is the result of the repudiation of polytheists demonstration in *hajj*

The beloved, brave nation of Iran can rest assured that the incident in Mecca[43] will spark great changes in the Islamic world and will provide suitable grounds for the eradication of corrupt regimes in Islamic countries and for the removal of pseudo-clergymen. Even though not more than a year has passed since the epic repudiation of polytheists demonstration, the scent of the innocent blood of our dear martyrs has spread throughout the whole of the world and we are seeing its effects in the farthest reaches of the earth. The epic events which have occurred for the Palestinian people are not accidental. Could the world ever imagine who has composed this epic and at present what ideals the people of Palestine lean towards such that fearlessly, with bare hands, they resist the brutal attacks of the Zionists? Is the only cause that of nationalism which has made them so strong? Is it from the tree of those political players who have sold their souls that the fruits of perseverance and the olives of light and hope fall into the lap of the Palestinians? If this were the case then for years now they have been alongside the Palestinians and getting their daily bread in the name of the people! Without a doubt it is the call of *Allahu Akbar*' which has achieved this. It is the same call that rang out from our people and that brought the Shah in Iran and the usurpers in Bayt al-Muqaddas to despair. This call is the fulfilment of the slogans of repudiation shouted loudly by the Palestinian people, who shoulder to shoulder with their Iranian brothers and sisters took part in the demonstrations during *hajj*, slogans calling for the freedom of Quds and death to America, Russia and Israel. They too sacrificed their blood on the same land of martyrdom that the blood of our dear ones was spilt, and as martyrs lay down to rest.

Yes, the Palestinians found the path they had lost by going along our path of repudiation. And in this battle we witnessed how iron fortifications fell apart, how blood triumphed over swords, faith over unbelief, raised voices over bullets; how the dream of the Bani-Israel (the Jews) to occupy the lands from the Nile to the Euphrates was shattered and once again the Palestinians' star of knowledge shines brightly (this time) from our blessed tree of neither East nor West. Today, in the same way that widespread activity is taking place throughout the world in an attempt to make us compromise with unbelief and polytheism, so too in the same manner efforts are continuing to dampen down the flames of anger of the Muslim people of Palestine. This serves as just one example of how the revolution has progressed. ?

Imam's message dated 20 July 1988 (29 Tir 1367 AHS). *Sahifeh-ye Imam*, vol. 21, pp. 80-1.

SECTION FOUR
THE ENEMIES' EFFORTS TO PREVENT THE ISLAMIC REPUBLIC OF IRAN FROM LEADING THE STRUGGLE

The enemies' efforts to prevent the islamic republic of iran from leading the struggle

The Imposed War and the Plots by some Countries against Revolutionary Iran

Saddam, the enfeebler of Islamic fronts against Zionism

Saddam should be put on trial just as Carter should. Carter acted in his own interests and this cursed man (Saddam) acts in the interests of America. It is not simply for the sake of a few kilometres of arid land that he (Saddam) has sent in his troops, forcing all these Muslims on both sides to do battle and be killed, all these billions of Iraqi dinars and Iranian tumans to be spent to the detriment of both countries and these weapons which we should be using against the enemy, against Zionism and imperialism, to be turned against one another. This is the treason that Saddam has perpetrated (in the interests of America).

Imam's remarks at a gathering of ambassadors of Islamic countries, dated 21 October 1980 (28 Mehr 1359 AHS). *Sahifeh-ye Imam*, vol. 13, p. 242.

The imposed war: the result of collusion between Zionism and the Baath Party

What we find most regretful about this imposed war is that the forces which should be used to put an end to Israel and save the great Bayt al-Muqaddas have, through the collusion of the great Satan and international Zionism with the Iraqi Baath party, been used and continue to be used to attack the stubborn enemy of Israel and America. I now repeat that as long as the Islamic nations and the oppressed of the world do not rise up against the oppressors of the world and their offspring, particularly the usurper Israel, their criminal hands will not be severed from Islamic countries, this cancerous tumour will not be thrown out of Bayt al-Muqaddas and Lebanon, and the likes of Saddam and Sadat will continue with their crimes and to drag Egypt and Iraq towards destruction. The way to repel these tyrants is to turn to Islam, to follow (the teachings of) the Quran resolutely and rise up in unity and harmony beneath the banner of *tawhid* (divine unity).

Imam's remarks dated 18 September 1981 (27 Shahrivar 1360 AHS). *Sahifeh-ye Imam*, vol. 15, pp. 203-4.

Creating an opportunity for Israel

What is most regrettable is that the superpowers, America in particular, by deceiving Saddam into attacking our country, have kept the powerful government of Iran busy with defending its land in order to give the usurper and criminal Israel an opportunity to push forward its evil plan to create a greater Israel from the Nile to the Euphrates.

Yitzhat Shamir, the new American pawn, immediately upon becoming a candidate for prime minister to replace Begin, another pawn, and before doing anything else, revealed Israel's plan. He said the

Palestine Liberation Organisation must be wiped out and made it clear that he would remain an advocate of a greater Israel.

Imam's message dated 22 September 1983 (31 Shahrivar 1362 AHS). *Sahifeh-ye Imam*, vol. 18, p. 122.

We are ready to do battle on both fronts

Here today we are suffering because of that party and there we are suffering because of the corrupt regime of Israel, and we are ready to do battle on both fronts. Here we are fighting to defend what is ours, we consider there (Palestine) too to be ours and we are ready to fight to defend it. But do we have to give you something before you will open the way for us to make our move? Should we have nothing more to do with this criminal (Saddam) and sit down and make our peace with him, throw our arms around him and give him a pat on the back for perpetrating all these crimes because now you want to work with us? He says we have to give him something so that he will work with us! No, this is all very illogical and will never come to pass.

As far as the matter of opening the way is concerned, you should be pleading with us to come and help. We are volunteering to help, but you must ask us to come and help you to stop them (the Israelis), that is of course if you are speaking the truth when you say you oppose Israel. Otherwise, the circumstances would suggest that you are not opposed to Israel and you do not want us to go there. You are putting down conditions in such a way so as to stop us from going there.

Imam's remarks at a gathering of commanders and a group of army officials, Jumhuri Islami newspaper dated 13 June 1982 (22 Khordad 1361 AHS), vol. 16, pp. 78-9.

Seeking a bribe from Iran to help it fight against Israel

Our country has placed its great wealth, including its youth, who are there on the scene to deal with any situation which may arise for the Muslims, at the disposal of devotion and has embarked on a holy war (*jihad*) for Islam, for the religion of God the Blessed and Exalted. But when our government suggests that you open the way for us to go and fight with your enemies, Saddam lays this down as one of the conditions (that we first have to make peace with him) because he has no hope in you. This is simply ludicrous. They say we have to forget whatever they have done before they will open the way for us. What kind of opening the way is that? Is it not a tragedy for Islam when a group of self-sacrificing people want to go and fight the enemy of the Arabs, the enemy of Islam, the enemy of the noble sanctuaries, the enemy of the whole region - while they (the Arab governments) sit back and are indifferent, or more to the point side with this enemy - but before they will open the way for them to go and fight for them they first seek a bribe from us?! It's like someone going to save a man drowning in the sea and when he reaches him the drowning man says: 'What will you give me for allowing you to save me?'!

These people in the Iraqi government are using the issue of Israel as an excuse to escape the grip of divine revenge and justice. They are using it as an excuse saying: 'If you want us to give you permission to go and save us who are drowning, you must first overlook the crimes we have committed against you'...

The path Saddam wants to lay before us is one that (he hopes) will lead to him being saved, not one that will lead to Israel. Those involved have studied the matter, if we accept, then peace will be established and the Saddams of this world will be saved, and if we refuse, then it will be clear that we do not really want to embark on a holy war, that we do not want to fight against Israel. We are telling them that we accept. You move aside and let the experts come to assess what you have done to this country, what crimes you have perpetrated; indeed let them come and decide who has perpetrated these crimes. But for us to condone the crimes because we want to do something for you, this is one of the absurdities that will remain in the annals of history. History will record that Iran wanted to save the Arabs from Israel, Israel which bears particular animosity towards the Arabs, it wanted to save the holy sanctuaries and the Islamic countries, for they are all threatened by Israel, and go and do battle against this malignant cancer, but the (Arab) governments first wanted a bribe from it. These are all matters which will be recorded in history and they are shameful deeds which will be recorded on the foreheads of these people.

Imam's remarks dated 13 June 1982 (23 Khordad 1361 AHS). *Sahifeh-ye Imam*, vol. 16, pp. 283-5.

With the final defeat of Iraq, the way will be open to advance on Quds

Today, the dear nation of Iran, relying on divine power, advances despite the ignorant ones who thought that because of their inhuman crimes and the martyring of the nation's esteemed personalities the people would leave the scene, and who could not and cannot understand the secret of their presence (on the scene). We hope that by defeating America's recent plot for preserving Saddam and the Aflaqite party, our brave forces will, with the final defeat of the Iraqi government, pave the way for an advance towards Bayt al-Muqaddas, just as it is hoped that we will not witness indifference from the countries of the region whose every possession is now in danger of destruction after the recent attack by Israel on the Islamic country of Lebanon and the murder and plundering perpetrated there.

The Muslim nations should realise that with this lethal silence of some of the regional governments and this unquestioning submission of theirs to America and Israel, today beloved Lebanon is being put into the gullet of these world-devourers and their vassals, and the same will happen to the other dear countries in the near future. If today the regional governments stood against these criminals using the oil weapon and guns, the problem of Israel, and subsequently of America and any other rapacious power, would be solved. We express our severe disapproval of some of the Muslim governments who have stretched out their hands to America, which is the original criminal and the main plotter, in an attempt to seek their deliverance from something which is nothing other than a man-eating wolf, and we condemn them absolutely. Indeed, if it were not for this problem of the war with Iraq, this plot to distract us from the existing problems that face us, and the plan to defeat us on two fronts, the brave nation and revolutionary government of Iran would adopt another course of action.

For the umpteenth time we turn to the Muslim governments, particularly the regional governments, and ask them, indeed advise them most categorically to rise up to preserve the dignity, lives, honour and wealth of the Islamic nations; to unite with us, the Syrian government and the Palestinians and present a single front to defend the glory and honour of Islam and the Arabs; and to sever for evermore the hands of these criminals from their rich countries. Do not miss the opportunity, for tomorrow will be too late.

Imam's speech dated 27 June 1982 (6 Tir 1361 AHS). *Sahifeh-ye Imam*, vol. 16, pp. 313-4.

Egypt and Israel unite against Iran

The Egyptian government openly says that this Islamic Republic must not be and joins forces with the Israeli government to suppress Islam. They both agree to help Iraq against Iran. Why should the Islamic countries find themselves in a situation such that when Israel attacks Lebanon they are indifferent and some of them even forge friendships with Israel? We must continue to follow our own path and struggle on.

Imam's remarks dated 6 June 1982 (16 Khordad 1361 AHS). *Sahifeh-ye Imam*, vol. 16, pp. 263-4.

The order for holy war (*jihad*) with a country which opposes Israel!

In the Name of God, the Compassionate, the Merciful

Surely we belong to God and to Him shall we return (Quran 2:156)

I use the sacred phrase "Surely we belong to God and to Him shall we return," not with reference to Israel's crimes and the martyrdom and injury of many innocent Muslims in the dear land of southern Lebanon, even though it would be appropriate to use it here too; nor do I use it with regard to the occupation and destruction by the criminal Zionists and heathen regime of Israel of the cities and villages of that Islamic land, even though here too it would be appropriate; nor with reference to the displacement of thousands of the brothers and sisters of that oppressed, Islamic region, even though here too it would be appropriate; nor with regard to the oppressed Palestinians suffering under Israeli tyranny, even though here too it would be appropriate; nor regarding the martyrdom by the criminal supporters of Saddam of more than forty men, women and suckling infants of Ilam[44] as they shouted out slogans against America and Israel, the blood-sucker, who were the targets of a bomb which also injured more than two hundred innocent Muslim tribes people and destroyed a mosque, a religious centre, a hospital and the homes of the oppressed, even though here too it would be appropriate; rather I use it with reference to the indifference of the Muslim governments, and wish it were only indifference they displayed!

I use the phrase in reference to the support extended to Israel and Saddam, these two illegitimate children of America, by many of the (Muslim) governments. I and Muslims everywhere must utter "Surely we belong to God and to Him shall we return" in reference to the spiritual and material help the governments of Islamic countries give America - the head of the criminals - Israel and the Aflaqite Baath Party of Iraq which is the executer of America's and international Zionism's evil plans.

Every self-respecting Muslim must utter this phrase in reference to the suggestion - put forward on the false accusation that Iran is receiving arms from Israel - that the command for *jihad* be issued against a country (Iran) which is opposing Israel, and also with regard to the efforts to get officially recognised Israel that attacked the Islamic country of Lebanon martyring thousands of innocent Muslims in the south of that land. Israel, the aggressor and criminal, must be endorsed, America, the head of the aggressors, must get material help from the resources of the oppressed and needy Islamic countries and, through the efforts of the mass media in the Islamic regions, obtain spiritual and political help, while Palestine and Syria must stand alone!...

I beseech God the Most High to awaken these governments that are neglectful of the interests of Islamic countries and heedless of the commands of the Noble Quran, from the sleep of indifference, and crush the enemies of Islam and the Muslims.

Peace be with you and God's mercy and blessings.

Imam's message on the occasion of the attack on southern Lebanon by the regime occupying Quds, 7

June 1982 (17 Khordad 1361 AHS). *Sahifeh-ye Imam*, vol. 16, pp. 268-9.

Instead of cleansing the region of the stain of Israel's existence...

Although the Iranian nation and government have seen much improper opposition from many governments of the region, they do not wish to disregard Islamic brotherhood and turn to force. The regional governments devote all their efforts to opposing the government and people of Iran instead of joining hands together with them to free the region from the clutches of the big powers, who look on them as being dependent on them; instead of standing against these people who take their copious wealth, in particular their oil, free of charge; and instead of cleansing the region of the stain of Israel's existence. ?

Part of Imam's message on the occasion of the *hajj* pilgrimage and the auspicious Feast of Sacrifice (Id al-Qurban), dated 29 August 1984 (7 Shahrivar 1363 AHS). *Sahifeh-ye Imam*, vol. 19, p. 26.

Groundless Accusations

(The rumour that the Islamic Republic of Iran has relations with Israel)

Ties between Iran and Israel: an absurd and childish accusation

We do not expect anything else from the likes of Sadat and Saddam who are the agents of powerful countries, of America, and who are building, or rather allowing to be built, bases for the infidels, the oppressors and America or allowing them to be built in Islamic lands. We do not expect anything else from them since they do not believe in Islam. They are servants, servants of America, who will do whatever it bids. They launched this attack on an Islamic country, without any reason, on the orders of the big powers, America in particular. We do not expect anything else of them. Of course they are obliged to oppose us through different means, and we are sitting here, listening, and will neutralise their opposition.

They accuse us of getting arms from Israel; they accuse a country that has been opposed to this accursed band of Zionists from the beginning; they accuse us who even before this revolution at the time of the now defunct, vile Pahlavi regime continually voiced our opposition to that corrupt regime. We do not even consider Israel as being part of mankind, let alone have relations with it. For more than twenty years now one of the issues which has been at the top of my agenda in my speeches and written declarations, wherever I may have been, has been Israel and its tyranny, while many of the heads of Islamic countries have not been prepared to take even one step in opposition to Israel. Take Saddam for example, who has brought all this trouble about. It is said that in order to try to save face after the shame he brought on himself by attacking Islamic Iran and encountering defeat, and in order to cover up his crime, he made Israel bomb the (nuclear) centre so that it would appear that Israel opposed Saddam, opposed the Baathist government of Iraq. After this they had their excuse, an absurd excuse, and they began to publicise that Israel opposes Saddam but has ties with Iran. This is an absurd, childish statement by dint of which they hope to make the Islamic states consider us a supporter of Israel, whereas the truth of the matter is that from the time we first embarked on this movement one of our most pressing concerns was the elimination of Israel. They cannot prove such a false claim. Therefore, these brothers who have come here from abroad should investigate this matter and discover whether we are fighting with Israeli-made weapons or with the weapon of faith.

Imam's remarks dated 24 August 1981 (2 Shahrivar 1360 AHS). *Sahifeh-ye Imam*, vol. 15, pp. 109-10.

The accusation that Iran and Israel have ties is a means to an end: to cause division

The plan for creating dissension among the Islamic sects is one of the crimes planned by the power-wielders and their ungodly agents, among them the court-affiliated preachers who are more contemptible than the oppressive kings, who benefit from dissension among the Muslims. Every day they fan the flames of dissension and arouse emotions. In the hope of destroying the very foundations of unity among Muslims, they use every opportunity they get to promote their plan for creating differences. Just recently, calumnious accusations were made over the propaganda loudspeakers that Iran has relations with Israel and buys weapons from it. This was done in the hope of driving a wedge between the Arabs and Iranians, of creating animosity among the Muslims, and of opening the way for the superpowers and increasing their influence to the full. For which informed individual is there who does not know that Iran has been in the past and still is the staunch enemy of Israel, and that one of the reasons for our dispute with the deposed Shah was his friendly relations with Israel? Who does not know that for more than twenty years now in my speeches and declarations I have placed Israel in the same category as America for its oppression, and after America, have condemned it for its aggression and plundering? Who does not know that throughout the Islamic revolution and in the fervent million-strong demonstrations, the Muslim people of Iran proclaimed Israel their enemy, one in the same category as America, and that they turned the oil off to them both and reviled both.

It is not surprising that this ominous tune is emanating from the throats of America, the mother of the illegitimate child Israel, and Saddam, the younger brother of Begin, and that their propaganda loudspeakers, America's in particular, are trying to disseminate it extensively. For the blows these two have received from the real Islam, others have not received, and the anxiety the prospect of unity between the Arab and Iranian Muslim brothers causes them, others do not experience. America is worried about its interests in the region and Saddam is worried about his downfall and eternal disgrace.

The Muslims, and in particular our Arab brothers, should realise that the issue is not simply Israel and Iran, the main issue for the world plunderers of the East and West is Islam. For it is Islam that can bring together the Muslims of the world under the honourable banner of *tawhid* (divine unity), that can sever the hands of the criminals from the Islamic countries and curtail their domination of the deprived and weak of the world, and that can present the world with a valuable, progressive and divine school of thought. The Arabs of the world should realise that the blow dealt them today by Saddam and Sadat is so severe that only through their unity will they be able to recover from it.

Today Sadat, with the widespread arrest of our Muslim brothers in Egypt, has completed his service to Israel. His union with America and Israel has caused loss of face for the Arab nation. His union with an Israel which in addition to the crimes it perpetrates in the region has recently turned its hand to another great crime: excavating at the al-Aqsa mosque, the first *qiblah* of the Muslims. And by weakening the foundations of this mosque, God forbid that the first *qiblah* of the Muslims should be destroyed and Israel should achieve its vile desire.

Imam's message dated 6 September 1981 (15 Shahrivar 1360 AHS). *Sahifeh-ye Imam*, vol. 15, pp. 145-6.

Saddam's scheme to lay the blame on Iran

Every day it is different, every day another novel scheme is carried into effect. One day he (Saddam) comes to an agreement with Israel which then bombs a place, an institution, in Iraq. He then puts the blame on Iran and accuses Iran of being Israel's accomplice. He accuses us who before the revolution opposed Israel and who from the beginning of the revolution to the present have always opposed Israel, have declared our opposition and have boycotted it and its allies in every respect. This Iran, he says, is not opposed to Israel, rather it is Israel's accomplice.

Imam's remarks dated 9 October 1981 (17 Mehr 1360 AHS). *Sahifeh-ye Imam*, vol. 15, p. 245.

Buying arms from Israel: a song sung by America

They make whatever accusations they like against an Islamic country, against Iran, whose people from the time this movement first emerged, and even before that, opposed Israel. Indeed one of the differences the Iranian people had with the now defunct Muhammad-Rida was over him helping Israel. Now Iran is accused of buying arms from Israel by the self-serving propaganda trumpeted over the loudspeakers of America and its dependants.

Imam's remarks dated 16 December 1981 (25 Azar 1360 AHS). *Sahifeh-ye Imam*, vol. 15, p. 372.

Propaganda by Muslim leaders against Muslims

What has happened to the Muslims, what has happened to the Muslim leaders that have made them sacrifice all their dignity and self-esteem for the sake of America? What has happened to them that has made them offer up to America the great wealth of Islam, which belongs to the bare-footed and weak nations, while in response to this offering, America supports Israel and declares that it will not sell it out for them? What has happened to the Muslims? Why should the Muslims be this way? Why should the Muslims' propaganda machines work against a group of Muslims who only want to free themselves from the grip of foreigners and international thieves? Why do they take sides against Iran? What has Iran done to deserve this? What has happened to make some of the court-affiliated clergymen accuse Iran of heresy? The Quran clearly stipulates that if someone claims to be a Muslim, he must be recognised as such and not be rejected. What do these people know about Islam? We shout out that we are Muslims, that we want to implement the laws of the venerable Quran and the commands of the Most Noble Prophet in this country, and for over twenty years now we have been announcing our opposition to Israel and America, yet still these writers in their magazines and newspapers and these broadcasters on the radio accuse us of having friendly relations with Israel. Are we the friends of Israel or are those who sit by and watch while Israel does what it does to the Muslims? What has Israel done to Lebanon and what is it doing to Syria? It has annexed the Golan Heights and it aspires to do much more than this, yet still you say you want to recognise it. Do we have friendly relations with Israel when for more than twenty years we have been calling on you to come together and throw this cancerous tumour out from amongst the Muslims' midst, to take Bayt al-Muqaddas from it and deliver the Islamic countries from this cancerous tumour? Or do you? You who are using all kinds of tricks and deceit to officially recognise Israel and who are supporting a country which is against Islam and whose tyranny is clear to the whole world?

You have the audacity to stand against God, you seek to give His enemy and the staunch enemy of the Muslims the upper hand, you want to officially recognise it and give it peace. But even if you do officially recognise Israel, it will not recognise you. You are just sitting back waiting until Israel, God forbid, rules over you all.

Imam's remarks dated 10 February 1982 (21 Bahman 1360 AHS). *Sahifeh-ye Imam*, vol. 16, pp. 31-2.

The rumour about Iran's co-operation with Israel is merely to dance attendance upon America

An aeroplane passes over one place and comes down some place else and they circulate a rumour that Israel was helping out and the documents exist (proving this). Which documents?! This of a country which has opposed Israel for twenty odd years, which has stopped Israel from touching its oil, has cut relations with it completely, which proclaims it a usurper and calls on the Muslims to unite together to drive it out of Muslim lands?! Israel and the immoral America both are laughing at the Muslims' folly. Once again these Muslims have let Israel alone and some of them are seeking to strike up friendly relations with it in accordance with America's command. They have concentrated all their efforts on propagandising against Iran. They don't stop for a moment to ask themselves what is really going on. All of this kow-towing to America, all of this kow-towing and fear, you give your resources to America; you have relations with it, apologise to it and dance attendance on it.

Imam's remarks dated 15 March 1982 (24 Esfand 1360 AHS). *Sahifeh-ye Imam*, vol. 16, p. 97.

Anti-revolutionary runaways are behind the rumours about arms purchases from Israel

Pursuant to their evil and futile ambitions, these miserable people who have run away from Iran or were already abroad (at the time of the revolution) are sitting there, conversing and fabricating and spreading lies. One of their big lies, which is aired perhaps every night on the radio - just last night it was mentioned two or three times - is that Iran is buying instruments of war from Israel. They are accusing people who for twenty years have been at war with Israel, who have lambasted Israel. They are accusing an Iran which, according to its religious laws, cannot have any kind of relationship with Israel and will not have. A few times last night it was repeated that these people are buying arms from Israel. These people are no different from Saddam.

Imam's remarks dated 9 March 1982 (18 Esfand 1360 AHS). *Sahifeh-ye Imam*, vol. 16, p. 82.

Opposition to Israel and America has been the essence of our revolution

We have opposed Israel from the very first day, and these people who have paid attention to worldly affairs - to what goes on in the world - know this. For more than twenty years now in my speeches I have always spoken about Israel and said it should not become an independent state, that this oppressor should be removed from the face of the earth. I warned of the danger it poses but hitherto these very countries that say 'we are Muslims, we are Islamic,' have regarded us as Israel's accomplice! Hitherto it has been said of us that we are America's accomplice! This is said of us who from the beginning have recognised America as a tyrant and an oppressor, who, when we saw that due to the treason of the former government our country was in America's grip, voiced opposition to this, the people rose up shouting 'death to America,' they took matters into their own hands, seized that nest of spies[45], dismissed the people there and sent them packing. It is like saying we are working with America to carry on a dispute with America! Is this anything other than a sign of the moral decadence of the heads of these countries? Many of these countries are slipping morally, that is why they pushed Saddam into attacking this Islamic country.

Imam's remarks dated 3 April 1982 (14 Farvardin 1361 AHS). *Sahifeh-ye Imam*, vol. 16, pp. 147-8.

If Israel touches the ocean, the ocean will become unclean

I hereby notify you of a danger which faces you too, and it is that I would not put it past Saddam, this Saddam whose rule is fast expiring, to at some time kill a number of you and lay the blame on Iran in order to force you into opposition.[46] There is much fear that this will happen. Do not underestimate this criminal and presume that he will not do anything. This criminal can perpetrate many crimes. In my opinion, this crime is imminent. Just as he bombs a place then says Iran has done it, just as he accuses us of obtaining weapons from Israel while it is he himself who is the ally, friend and brother of Israel, so too will he perpetrate this crime. Now also the superpowers and their broadcasters have taken up this ridiculous scheme (accusing Iran of buying arms from Israel). One says it was done with America's knowledge, America claims it said not to go so far while the Congress asks why it was done at all. For sure, they will all take up this issue, in order to make the people think that Israel has sent arms to Iran. All of them have upheld this claim, including Israel itself, who knows that in the eyes of the Muslims if it touches the ocean with its finger, the ocean will become unclean, consequently by claiming to have helped Iran it can give Iran a bad name. It knows that claiming to have an agreement with Iran will give Iran a bad name. Israel itself has perceived this.

Imam's remarks dated 1 June 1982 (11 Khordad 1361 AHS). *Sahifeh-ye Imam*, vol. 16, p. 245.

Why do they accuse the Islamic Republic?

Do you think Israel will be content with this? Israel's intentions are to eliminate all these Muslims and America's intentions are to make sure Islam is not implemented. They all oppose the Islamic Republic because it bears the name 'Islamic' and because it wants to act upon Islam. They oppose it through their propaganda saying that we are pro-American or pro-Israeli! They say this of us who for twenty years now - in fact it must be more than that now - have been shouting out that the people's problems are caused by America and Israel. Yet we are pro-Israeli, while those who are sitting there watching as Israel destroys their countries are not, no, they are all opposed to Israel! If you are truly opposed to Israel then what have you done to show it? What actions have you taken?

Imam's remarks dated 22 August 1982 (31 Mordad 1361 AHS). *Sahifeh-ye Imam*, vol. 16, p. 375.

The true colours of those who claim Iran supports Israel have been revealed

In the past year the plotters, the newspapers and players of the media connected to America and Zionism have, with the utmost impudence, accused Iran of bringing in weapons from Israel and of supporting this criminal regime. Now, however, at the Fez conference it has been revealed and is now clear who supports Israel: Saddam the criminal and most of the governments in the region. They support a criminal regime which after all the crimes it has committed and the services (it has received) from the small governments in the region has brazenly made a laughing stock of them, humiliating them enough to make any human being other than themselves ashamed, ashamed not because they are the heads of these governments but because of their connection to Islam and the fact that the affairs of the Muslims are, unfortunately, in their hands.

The result of these services to this criminal was the massacre of innocents in Beirut, a crime the depth of which we do not know. The magnitude of this crime was such that according to news reports it provoked global outrage. Even the world's master criminals such as Reagan and Hosni Mubarak were forced to appear to condemn it. Its magnitude was such that even those news agencies and newspapers which usually side with Israel condemned it describing it as the biggest criminal act since World War Two. It was such that even the world's criminal archetypes such as Israel, the Phalangists and their collaborators blamed each other for it.

The greatest misfortune for the Muslims is that the heads of the regional governments do not breathe a word (in protest), and more tragic and disgraceful than this is the unlimited and unconditional support given by some of the rulers in the region and the fact that once again in the Hijaz the crimes of Israel and its grandfather America cannot be mentioned.

With praise and thanks to the nourisher of mankind we again receive divine help from Islam and the Islamic republic. God made this trick of theirs - presenting the Iranian government as a supporter of Israel - backfire on them and revealed their true colours before the nations. He also revealed the true face of Saddam the Aflaqite who found an excuse not to confront Israel and then wanted to use this to free himself from the warrior defenders of Iran and who, at the Fez conference, tried to provoke emotions in a bid to gain support and official recognition for Israel and ensure its security. *"And the unbelievers plotted and planned, and God too planned; and the best of planners is God."* (Quran 3:54)

Imam's message dated 12 September 1982 (21 Shahrivar 1361 AHS). *Sahifeh-ye Imam*, vol. 16, pp. 442-3.

Imperialist propaganda loudspeakers spread the rumour of arms purchases from Israel

And more lamentable still is the Israeli affair that the imperialist propaganda loudspeakers have hitherto been spreading, accusing Iran of buying arms from Israel, of being an Israeli ally and even sometimes of being an ally of America. They accuse Iran of bringing these things in from Israel, Iran whose notable speakers have for about the past twenty years now in all their discourses given top priority to Israel and opposition to Israel, while Iraq, which supports Israel and is in turn supported by Israel, they claim is not an ally, no, indeed Iraq opposes Israel!

The tragedy of it all is that the Muslims sit back with eyes, ears and hearts open yet blind to the realities. What must be done? Oh Friday Prayer leaders of Islamic lands, what must be done? Why have we reached this sorry state where America comes from the other side of the world, determines our countries' destinies and the destinies of the Islamic *ulama* - albeit through other people - states quite clearly that it has interests in the region and interferes openly in the region's affairs while the Muslims simply sit back and look on? Oh Friday Prayer leaders of all Islamic countries! Make the people aware, make them ask why, this 'why' is applicable both to the West and the East.

Imam's remarks dated 2 January 1983 (12 Dey 1361 AHS). *Sahifeh-ye Imam*, vol. 17, pp. 195-6.

Israel will not turn over a new leaf

We will be steadfast to the end and will not establish relations with America other than if it turns over a new leaf and desists in its oppression, leaves Lebanon alone and goes back to the other side of the world whence it came, and does not stretch out its hands against the Persian Gulf. So long as America acts this way, South Africa employs such practices and Israel exists, we cannot accept them. Israel will not turn over a new leaf.

Unfortunately you see how the devils persist in claiming that Iran has relations with Israel and America, even though since twenty years ago, at the time of the Shah, we have been shouting out and calling on the Muslims to comprehend the danger posed by Israel. We must remember that we are a country that wants to be independent, we do not want others to interfere in our affairs and so long as our relations with God the Blessed and Exalted are strong, no one can harm us. ?

Imam's remarks dated 28 October 1984 (6 Aban 1363 AHS). *Sahifeh-ye Imam*, vol. 19, p. 85.

A Short History of Palestine

A look at the ancient history of the land of Palestine up to the advent of Islam

The land of Palestine, which in ancient times was known as Canaan, covers an area of 25,000 square kilometres, lies on the eastern coast of the Mediterranean Sea and borders Egypt, Syria, Jordan and Lebanon. Palestine is a fertile land enjoying a temperate climate. It witnessed the advent of such great prophets as Jesus (pbuh) and Moses (pbuh) and was the land through which Hadrat Abraham (pbuh) traversed and where he lived. From a geo-political point of view too, it is a very sensitive and strategic country.

The city of Jerusalem (Yerushalayim (Hebrew), known by Muslims as the city of Bayt al-Muqaddas or al-

Quds or simply 'Quds' meaning 'the holy') was built in the Judean hills and is situated, along with a temple to Jehovah, atop Mount Moriah. It is one of the important sites of Palestine, to its east lies Mount Zion[47] and on its west the Mount of Olives.

The eventful history of Palestine begins with the names of the prophets of our forefathers. The prophet Jacob was also known by the name Israel and the Bani-Israel are the descendants of Jacob who enjoyed power about thirteen centuries before the birth of Christ. At the time of the Pharoah's rule and before the advent of Moses (pbuh), the Israelis formed a huge community in Egypt. Four hundred and thirty years after Jacob's arrival in Egypt, Hadrat Moses led the Bani-Israel tribe away from bondage in Egypt across the desert towards the Promised Land.

The journey was to take forty years and was not without incident. One of the most notable was while Moses (pbuh) spent forty days away from his people on Mount Sinai where he was inspired by God to write down the Ten Commandments on tablets of stone. In his absence, his tribe once again turned to idol worship and it was because of their disobedience that they had to spend forty years in the desert. Throughout this long period, Moses did not desist from guiding his people, but time and again the Bani-Israel rebelled and transgressed.

After his death in Moab, within sight of the Promised Land he had never reached, Joshua, his successor, led the Bani-Israil through Jordan towards the Promised Land. Their arrival there signalled the start of a campaign for conquest which included the plunder and killing of the local people. The ruler of Jerusalem united with the rulers of five other cities against Joshua and his men, but all were defeated and hanged. The people of Palestine, however, continued to resist the invasion and eventually prevailed over the Bani-Israel. Bloody battles persisted between the two sides in which the inhabitants of Palestine continued to impose defeat. Eventually, however, the Bani-Israel amassed power and gained control over the main cities and in c. 1010 BC Hadrat David was able to snatch Jerusalem from the Palestinians and found the Bayt al-Muqaddas or the House of God there. This building was completed by Hadrat Solomon.

Bayt al-Muqaddas was built about 1100 years after the building of the Kabah in Mecca by Hadrat Abraham (pbuh) and 970 years before the birth of Christ. Hadrat David is a fourteenth generation descendant of Hadrat Abraham, the founder of the Kabah, and according to the Gospel of Matthew, Hadrat Jesus' lineage reaches back twenty-eight generations to David. Consequently, Mecca (the Kabah) is the first sacred place of the monotheists and the al-Aqsa mosque in Quds the second.

The Ark of the Covenant: The Ark of the Covenant in Muslim tradition is the box in which Moses was laid by his mother and cast into the waters of the river Nile. Moses placed his stone tables, his chain mail and the tokens of his prophethood in this box so that no one could touch them. At the time of Hadrat David, this box was lined both within and without with gold and transferred from Hebron to Mount Zion where an altar was built to keep it. For a while it lay in the hands of the victorious Palestinians but was eventually handed back to the Bani-Israel. It was kept on Zion until the time of Hadrat Solomon when upon completion of the Bayt al-Muqaddas building; the ark was transferred to Quds. Solomon ruled for forty years and returned peace to Quds, but following him the oppression and plundering of the Bani-Israel began again.

About 730 BC, King Shalmaneser invaded Israel, imprisoned the Bani-Israel and settled Babylonians in the area. In 586 BC, the land of the Jews was attacked once again, this time being overrun by the Babylonian ruler Nebuchadnezzar. During this assault, most of the population was expelled or imprisoned, the Jewish monarchy was overthrown and the First Temple built by Solomon razed.

Since the arrival of the Bani-Israel or the Israelites in Palestine 480 years before the founding of Quds (about 1300 years before Christ) under the leadership of Joshua, this land has been afflicted with strife. Today, 3300 years later, Palestine has still not found peace.

Subsequent Jewish prophets such as Jeremiah, Isaiah and Daniel, whose words and prophecies are recorded in the Old Testament, comforted the Jews during years of suffering and imprisonment and the destruction of Jerusalem, continuously promising deliverance and offering glad tidings of the coming of a great messiah. The conquests of Cyrus, the Achaemenian king who rose in the East and created his empire taking one land after another, pleased the Jews and their rulers. Cyrus went on to take Babylonia, where he freed the Jews from their captivity, and Palestine and Jerusalem, to where he allowed them to return. Cyrus ruled his empire with moderation and treated all tribes and religions well. It was on his orders that the House of God was once again constructed.

Peace reigned in Jerusalem until towards the end of the reign of Darius III, when in 333 BC the Persians in Palestine were overpowered by Alexander, king of Macedon. Upon his succession, Alexander had immediately set about the invasion of the Persian empire, wresting Egypt, Syria and Phoenicia from the hands of the Persians, leaving a trail of death and destruction in his wake. Much of Iran's treasures were plundered during this period and in revenge for the destruction of Athens by Xerxes, Takht-e Jamshid, the seat of Persian government, was sacked and burned and

Alexander's commanders made rulers over conquered Persian cities.

After Alexander, Palestine fell into the hands of his successors. In 63 BC, Roman domination began with the capture of Jerusalem by the Roman general Pompey. Twelve thousand Jews were killed in the siege and the walls of the city were destroyed. Under such conditions, the advent of Jesus was eagerly awaited by the people of that region who saw in him the fulfilment of their hopes.

The promised messiah was born in Nazareth, a town of lower Galilee, to a mission which came to be marked, as the Bible relates, by many miracles. In Jerusalem, Jesus spent all his days teaching and learning at the temple, thus provoking the jealously of the Rabbis who set about trying to get rid of him. Eventually, on the instigation of the Jewish Council, which issued a ruling against him, Jesus was crucified by the Roman procurator, Pontius Pilate, who, it is said, actually liked Christians.

The Most Noble Quran actually rejects the story of Christ's crucifixion as believed by the Christians and states instead: *"But they killed him not, nor crucified him, but so it was made to appear to them... Nay, God raised him up unto Himself."* (Quran 4:157). Be that as it may, Christianity, the religion of which Jesus is the central figure, lived on and went on to attract many followers.

Repressive Roman administration sparked numerous revolts by the Jews which the Romans dealt with harshly, resulting in the deaths of many Jews. In 70 AD, Titus, the elder son of the Roman Emperor Vespasian, put down a Jewish revolt in Judaea with an army of 80,000, and after a siege lasting a few months, destroyed Jerusalem causing the Jews to disperse once again.

About three hundred years after the death of Christ, when Constantine I (the Great 306-337 AD), emperor of Rome, converted to Christianity making it the official religion, Jerusalem underwent a revival. The Church of the Holy Sepulchre, begun in 325 AD on the site believed to be that of Jesus Christ's crucifixion at Calvary, was completed ten years later and Jerusalem became a holy Christian city. For more than five centuries, from 135 AD when the Roman Emperor Hadrian seized and destroyed the city reconstructing it as a Roman colony and banning all Jews, only a small number of Jews ever lived there.

At the time of Chosroes II Aparvez, the Sassanian king, war between the two empires of Iran and Byzantium broke out. It lasted from 604 to 630 AD and saw the defeat of the Byzantines by the Iranian armies. With the help and guidance of Jews who lent their assistance to Iran during the war, the Persians captured Palestine in 614 AD. However, after the death of Chosroes, this land once again fell into the hands of the

Christians with its capture by the Byzantine Emperor Heraclius in 628 AD.

Jerusalem after Islam

In the first thirteen years of his mission, when Hadrat Muhammad (upon whom be peace) lived in Mecca, the al-Aqsa mosque (the Remote Mosque) in Jerusalem was the Muslim's *qiblah* (prayer direction), the first. Two years after his migration to Medina, at the Bani Sulameh mosque in Medina, the *qiblah* of the Muslims was changed on God's command from the al-Aqsa mosque to the al-Haram mosque (the Sacred Mosque containing the Kabah) in Mecca. Perhaps the most important reason for the change was to rob the Jews of the excuse to pour scorn on the Muslims for praying in this direction.

After the death of the Prophet, at the time of the first caliph, the Muslim army was sent to face the Byzantines in Syria and Palestine. It was during the rule of the second caliph, however, that the Byzantine armies were defeated and Syria and Jerusalem fell into Muslim hands. The inhabitants of the city initially put up strong resistance and a siege lasted for many months leading to food shortages and the spread of disease which, among other things, finally forced their surrender.

The second caliph entered the conquered city to conclude a peace treaty wearing simple even shabby raiment and riding an unembellished mount, much to the surprise of the inhabitants. The caliph treated his subjects with tolerance and moderation. Under his rule, Jews were allowed to return and Christians given freedom of worship.

From 637 AD (15 AH) until the twentieth century, Palestine was to remain in Muslim hands. The population of Jerusalem comprised mostly Muslim Arabs and because it had been the first *qiblah* for Muslims, it was held in great esteem and was recognised as a holy place.

The Crusades

With the attack by western European Christians led by Godfrey of Bouillon on the Muslims in 1096 (488 AH), resulting in the capture of Jerusalem, the wars known as the Crusades began and lasted for nearly two centuries. Several motives for the start of these wars have been cited, not least among them the Christians' desire to exact an earthly revenge for advances made by the Muslims on the western front; the lure of eastern wealth and land; and in some cases, though by no means all, the genuine religious belief that heaven awaited those who ascended there from the site of Christ's tomb. However, as historians have concluded, what lay at the heart of the matter was the issue of Palestine and the city of Jerusalem, the tributary status of the Christians of this city and the unpropitious treatment they came to be exposed to.

In the Middle Ages - the period of European history from the fall of the Roman Empire in the West (476 AD) to the fall of Constantinople (1453 AD) at the hands of the Ottoman Sultan Muhammad II the Conqueror - Europe was ruled despotically by the Church. The pope of the time, Pope Urban II, in order to start the first crusade, resorted to deceit. Priests spread the rumour that signs of Christ's coming had appeared in Palestine. Consequently, large numbers of Christians set off for Jerusalem in the hope of witnessing the second coming of Christ. It didn't happen, but every year the priests preached that it had been postponed until the following year, in this way increasing the number of pilgrims to Palestine.

In the early days of this affair, the Pope set off on a pilgrimage to Jerusalem, accompanied by seven hundred pilgrims. He turned back for Europe upon reaching Cyprus and spread the rumour that the Muslims had stopped him entering the holy city. With such tricks the flames of war were fanned and for nearly two centuries claimed their victims.

In the first crusade, seven hundred thousand men, mostly from the masses of poor to whom, with their depressed economic and social conditions, taking the cross was a relief rather than a sacrifice, set off towards Jerusalem with a number of knights. Along the way, as the story goes, others joined them increasing their number to millions. However after three years of fighting, plundering and a slow advancement, only forty thousand men reached Jerusalem, the others either having been killed in battles with the Muslims or having succumbed to illness. After a month's siege and a difficult battle, the besiegers finally stormed the city and perpetrated an indiscriminate massacre involving all ages and both sexes, and plundered everything in the name of booty. Godfrey their leader, who shortly after the victory was crowned king of the Crusader state in Palestine, in a report to the Pope wrote: "As to those who fell into our hands in Jerusalem, know this, our men rode in a sea of Muslim blood as deep as the horses' knees."

So it was that for the next ninety years, Palestine lay under the sway of the Christians. Although the first crusade resulted in the capture of Jerusalem and the establishment of Crusader states in the Holy Land, the second (1147-9 AD / 542-544 AH) failed to stop a Muslim resurgence and Jerusalem fell to Salah ad-Din (Saladin) Ayyubi in 1187. Following this victory, most of the remaining Christian strongholds in the region were seized in a series of brilliantly executed campaigns. The Christians were swept out of the conquered lands and only Antioch, Tripoli and Tyre, besides certain smaller towns and castles, remained in their possession.

The fall of the holy city aroused Europe. The Pope, who saw the fall as a humiliation for the Christians, issued a religious edict for holy war. In response, hostilities among Europe's rulers were buried and Frederick Barbarossa, emperor of Germany, Richard I Coeur de Lion, king of England, and Philip Augustus, king of France, took the cross. These three were the most powerful sovereigns of Western Europe, and with them the third crusade (1189-92 AD / 585-588 AH) began.

Frederick, who was the first to set off, was drowned while crossing the River Calycadnus in SE Asia Minor. Most of his followers subsequently returned home. But the kings of England and France entered the fray, capturing some lost ground (although Jerusalem eluded them) and leaving a trail of slaughter in their wake, harrowing accounts of which European chroniclers have recorded. Peace between the two belligerents was finally achieved and following the death of Salah ad-Din Ayyubi, which came only a few months after the peace, the sultanate he had built was divided amongst his various heirs of the Ayyubid family.

In Europe, after much conflict between the popes and the kings, Pope Innocent III (1198-1216 AD) won maximum authority, excommunicated the kings and issued a religious edict for holy war with the Muslims. After only a few short years of peace, the flames of war were rekindled. The crusaders set upon their fourth crusade (1202-1204 AD) capturing Constantinople.

The fifth crusade (1217-21 AD / 614-618 AH) was started once again at the instigation of Pope Innocent and his successor. The Church wanted the European kings to return Jerusalem to the Christian fold. They, however, were not inclined to embark on such a campaign and thus a religious decree for holy war with the Muslims was once again issued. This crusade resulted in a Christian defeat.

Papal incitement was once again behind the start of the sixth crusade (1228-9 AD). In 1229, due to serious disputes which had arisen among the Ayyubids, Jerusalem was yielded to Frederick II of Germany, leader of the Crusaders, as the result of an infamous treaty which guaranteed one Ayyubid leader Frederick's aid against the others. The al-Aqsa mosque, however, remained in Muslim hands. Jerusalem remained under Christian control until 1244 when a contingent of Khwarizm Turks, previously dislodged from their Central Asian abode by Chengiz Khan, restored the city to Islam.

The seventh crusade (1248-54 AD / 646-652 AH) ended in disaster for the Christians in Egypt. Their leader Saint Louis (Louis IX) of France had embarked on the campaign in revenge for the defeat of the Christians in Gaza. His army, however, was entirely destroyed and he, along with most of his nobles, was taken prisoner. After a month of captivity, he and his men were released on the payment of a ransom and the restoration of Dimyat (an Egyptian city that had earlier surrendered to his forces). In 1270, he led another futile crusade, the eighth and last (1270-1 AD), now to Tunisia, where he died.

Following the seventh crusade and the death of the last Ayyubid king, the Mamluks (a dynasty of slaves) took over the reins of power, dominating for about two and three-quarter centuries (1250-1517 AD) one of the most turbulent areas of the world. These slave sultans cleared their Syrian-Egyptian domain of the remnants of the Crusaders and checked for ever the advance of the redoubtable Mongol hordes of Hulagu and Timur.

Meanwhile, in Anatolia the Ottoman dynasty, founded by Uthman I (Osman) 1259-1326 AD, was busy securing its power. At the end of the thirteenth century, Uthman established the Turkish state which was expanded by his successors, by dint of many battles and victories, to include all of Asia Minor and much of SE Europe. Jerusalem came under Ottoman rule in 1517 where it remained until it was captured by British forces in December 1917. But it was the capture of Constantinople - an important Christian trade centre and the capital of the Easter Roman empire - earlier in 1453 (857 AH) by Uthman's descendant Muhammad II the Conqueror (1451-81 AD) which formally ushered in a new era, that of the Ottoman Empire.

The capture of Constantinople was a watershed in European history. It marked the end of the Middle Ages and, just as the Crusaders had transferred the knowledge and civilisation of the Muslims to Europe, so too this city, which remained the capital of the Ottoman empire for five hundred years, would inspire changes during the Renaissance and subsequent periods. Following its capture, important strides were made in the fields of industry, literature and architecture, and the lands under Ottoman sway flourished as Europe looked on with a wary eye.

The rise in Iran of the Safavid dynasty, which made the Shiite branch of Islam the official state religion, and the overt and covert machinations devised by the European governments, in particular the British government, led to bloody battles between Iran and the Ottomans which lasted for more than two centuries. Consequently, at a time when Europe had embarked on its movement to revive art and learning (the Renaissance) after making peace with the Ottomans, the world of Islam was cleft by a great schism, the power of the Muslims was exhausted in these lengthy wars and instead of turning their thoughts to the defence of the Islamic civilisation, they were distracted by civil war and religious rancour.

Jerusalem and Palestine in the Twentieth Century

After the Industrial Revolution, the face of Europe changed rapidly and the Europeans began to surpass the Muslims in the different fields of science and art. During this period, the East had fallen into a stupor while Europe created modern industrial methods and mass produced manufactured goods. Domestic markets came to be saturated so foreign markets were sought to which surplus goods could be exported and raw materials obtained. Thus the era of colonisation and appropriation of other countries was begun.

Preparations for the establishment of an Israeli state and Palestinian and Arab reaction

At the end of the 19th century, revolts took place in Palestine, and the British, who up until that time had supported the Ottomans, suddenly shifted their allegiance and stood against them in support of the agitators. The reason behind this switch in allegiance lay in Britain's need to protect India, its most important colony at the time and the source of its wealth and power, against possible incursion by Russia and France, two of her most powerful adversaries. In her attempts to do this, Britain saw no choice but to wrest sovereignty over certain Asian countries from the Ottomans, and in particular to gain control of the Suez Canal. The British government thus embarked on a policy of inciting the Arabs to rebel against the Ottoman Turks. Amongst its targets was the opportunist Ottoman representative in the Hijaz, Husayn, the Sharif of Mecca, who, with the promise of Britain's help, was encouraged to break away from Ottoman rule. In 1916, at the instigation of the British, he declared himself the 'king of the Arabs' and began the Arab revolt.

In May 1916 (1334 AH), a secret agreement between London and Paris, the Sykes-Picot agreement, was signed to carve up the Ottoman Empire among Britain, France and Russia after their victory in the First World War. Later, however, on seeing that the agreement ran counter to its control over the Suez Canal and taking advantage of Russia's weakened position and the revolution which was taking place in that country, Britain reneged on its agreement in 1917 (1335 AH) and made Palestine a British mandate.

These measures were taking place at a time when nationalist ideas and their circulation were being strongly encouraged by the imperialist British government as a way to dismember the Ottoman Empire and weaken the Ottoman government. Such ideas, which gradually displaced the Islamic identity in many Muslim countries, became the main weapon used by imperialism, of which the British government at that time was the standard-bearer, to secure and further imperialist policy interests. The result was the development of ethnic tendencies and the rise of divisive and separatist movements in Islamic lands, particularly in the domains of the Ottoman government.

As nationalist movements emerged in the Middle East, fanciful claims about the unity of the world's Jews, which had no basis in historical realities, began to be propounded and promoted. The Zionist movement espousing the idea of transforming the Jewish religious community into a nation with an independent state was sparked by the publication of Theodore Herzl's The Jewish State in 1896. When a number of Jews began to take steps towards the establishment of such a state and the settlement of Jews there, they were encouraged and supported by Britain, which in the early 1900s gradually became the principal centre of Zionist activity. They began to acquire financial support from wealthy Jews and in order to further their political aspirations they formed an organisation taking its name from the hill in Palestine where the prophets David and Solomon, along with a number of others, are buried: Zion. The British were not adverse to the Zionist's plan, as they needed bases from which to perpetuate their control over the region. The imperialists in the Foreign Office saw an important advantage in having a friendly community in the region since the First World War had exposed the vulnerability of the Suez Canal, Britain's lifeline to its empire in India.

Initially, the aims of the nationalist Jews of the Zionist movement did not attract much sympathy from other members of the Jewish community, and at the end of the 19th century attempts to start the flow of Jews into Palestine were foiled when a number of Jewish rabbis, aware of the political motives behind the moves and the link to imperialist policies, vehemently opposed them. However, as opposition to and persecution of the Jews increased, the solution to the Jewish problem was more and more sought in the creation of a Jewish state in the ancient homeland of the ancestors of the Jews. Although the Zionist Organisation still faced opposition from other Jewish bodies over this plan, it was opposition it could check through its branches in European countries. During the First World War political Zionism became dominant and the Zionists asked Britain and America to give them guarantees that after the war, if the Ottoman government, which was aligned with Germany against Britain and in whose hands Jerusalem lay, was defeated, this ancient land would be changed into a Jewish state.

The Zionists' endeavours proved fruitful. They were able to secure the support of Lloyd George's government in Britain, whose motives for doing so were mainly self-interest, and influential figures in America. When Turkish and German forces were defeated by the British at Megiddo in 1917, the land passed into Britain's hands and the name 'Palestine' was revived as an official, political title for the land west of the Jordan. In November 1917, the Balfour Declaration, named after Lord Balfour, the then British Foreign Secretary, was issued, pledging official backing for the creation of a

Jewish national home in Palestine. In April 1920, at a meeting of the Supreme Council of the League of Nations in San Remo, Italy, Britain insisted on and acquired a mandate over Palestine. It was approved by the League in July 1922 and went into effect in September 1923. Incorporated into it was the Balfour Declaration. In issuing this Declaration, the British neglected their conflicting commitments to the Arabs. Sharif Husayn of Mecca, now king Husayn, who was aligned with Britain, requested an explanation from the British government. In reply Britain assured him that the decision to help the Jews return to Palestine was not inconsistent with the rights and freedoms of the inhabitants of Palestine. No mention was made of the plan to create an independent Jewish state.

The British were, at the outset, committed to the Jews, believing as they did that a Jewish national home would best serve their interests in the region. They allowed immigration and purchase of land, defended the Jewish community from riots, and permitted the organisation of Jewish political institutions and the formation of a Jewish army. They also suppressed the Arab-Palestinian population. Under British rule, the Jewish community in Palestine grew rapidly from 50,000 in the early days to almost half a million in some 250 settlements by 1939, after the immigration floodgates had been opened. Arab opposition and uprisings were the response to occupation by the British and the Jews.

Winston Churchill, then Britain's secretary of state for the colonies, was given the task of reassuring leaders of the Arab community that Britain had no intention of turning its Palestine mandate into a Jewish state and that immigration would continue only to the point where a Jewish national home was formed and only as far as Palestine's economy allowed. Independent Jewish trade, economic and cultural agencies and even terrorist organisations were quickly set up in Palestine with the help of financial aid from wealthy Jews around the world. The Jews were highly organised through the Zionist Organisation, the Jewish Agency, the Vad Leumi or representative body of the Yishuv (the Jewish community in Palestine), Jewish political parties and a Jewish labour movement.

In 1920, however, the Palestinian Arabs were not organised. The Arab community was deeply divided by numerous clans and groups of affiliated clans, by strong class distinction between landlords, tenants and sharecroppers, and by religious divisions among Muslims and Christians. The Arabs as a whole were beset by division and discord and other than talking about helping their brothers in Palestine they did nothing. In the course of the struggle against the British and the Zionists however, parochial ties among the Palestinian Arabs began to give way to a sense of regional identity and the Greek Orthodox Christians came to see themselves as part of the Palestinian Arab people.

In the summer of 1929, the first bloody confrontation between the Palestinian Arabs and the Zionist immigrants took place. The Zionists and British troops opened fire on the Palestinians martyring about 351 people. Many more were injured or arrested and faced life sentences or execution. From the late 1920s till 1935, the armed rebellion of Shaykh `Izz al-Din al-Qassam, the first Arab leader in Palestine to advocate an armed struggle against foreign colonisers and rulers, took place. In 1935, al-Qassam gathered some 800 armed men in Haifa and began marching towards the hills of the West Bank in an effort to overthrow the British forces and make Palestine independent. They were confronted by the British army and the Zionists in an uneven battle in which al-Qassam, along with some of his followers, was martyred and many more were arrested.

In 1937, Abd al-Qadir Husayni took over the leadership of the struggle and he too, after many battles, was martyred along with his followers. In 1944, Hasan Salameh assumed responsibility of commanding the guerrilla warfare against the combined British and Zionist forces, and he too was eventually martyred.

In the late 1930s and during the '40s, the Palestinian problem became an Arab problem and was at the top of the list of headaches for the international community. In the face of the Palestinian struggles and Arab political reaction, the British government began to change its policy in Palestine and in the White Paper of 1939, it decided to restrict Jewish immigration and land purchases. This policy was to find even wider implementation after World War II. Zionist reaction to this change was bitter and a campaign of terrorist activities was launched against the British in Palestine.

Throughout the Second World War however, Palestine was relatively quiet. The Arab rebellion died down and, in the early stages of the war at least, the Zionists co-operated with the British, despite the latter's enforcement of the provisions of the White Paper, in the hope of being able to form a Jewish army to fight Nazism. Their hopes proved to be in vain, and as the war progressed, the Zionists increasingly turned against Britain, resorting once again to terrorist tactics in an attempt to achieve their aims.

In December 1946, the Zionist Organisation demanded an independent state in Palestine. The issue was placed before the United Nations General Assembly which recommended in August 1947 that Palestine be partitioned - with 45.4% of the area going to the Arabs, who made up 70% of the population and 53.5% to the Jews, who constituted just 30% of the population and owned 6% of the land. The remaining area, covering

Jerusalem and its suburb, was to be placed under international control.

On 29 November, the UN General Assembly adopted Resolution 181 specifying partition. The Jews accepted the partition plan warmly while the Arabs, with good reason, rejected it angrily. Interethnic violence erupted immediately and intensified as 15 May 1948, the date Britain was to resign its mandate, approached. On 14 May 1948, as the last British troops left, a Jewish National Council was established in Tel Aviv and the State of Israel proclaimed.

During the war, international Zionism had shifted its main effort from Britain to the United States, where it gained the support of both major political parties. Subsequently, in accordance with a prior undertaking, a few hours after the proclamation of a Jewish state, Harry Truman, the US president of the time, officially recognised the new Israeli government.

As the British withdrew, they left valuable arms and equipment to the Jews. From then on UN intervention proved fruitless and attempts to stop Zionist attacks on Palestinians were in vain. The usurping Zionists began to seize towns and villages driving the Palestinian inhabitants out of their homes. Faced with the resistance of the poor, innocent people, they perpetrated massacres like those carried out in the villages of Deir Yasin and Kafar Qasim in April 1948.

Arab villagers, terrified by reports of such events, left their homes en masse to Transjordan. Early on 15 May, units of the regular armies of Syria, Transjordan, Iraq and Egypt entered Palestine in support of the Palestinian Arabs. They scored some initial successes, but the Israelis launched a violent counter-offensive with the support of Europe and America and the flood of arms and planes with which they supplied them. The battle ended with an Arab collapse and the exodus of over a million Palestinian Arabs.

On the one side the Israeli government ignored the United Nations' partition plan while on the other different guerrilla groups and organisations were set up by the Palestinians to defend their natural and indisputable rights. In early 1964 the Palestine Liberation Organisation was formed following a proposal made at a summit of the Arab League. The PLO held its first congress on 28 May 1964 in Jerusalem at which the Palestine Liberation Army was created, giving the struggle a new form and impetus. From that time on thousands of people were to sacrifice their lives for the freedom of Palestine. Despite continuous Jewish immigration, the Arabs and Muslims continued to be overwhelmingly superior in population.

The Six-Day War

On 5 June 1967 (1387 AH), with a surprise attack on airfields in Egypt, Jordan and Syria, Israel sparked the third Arab-Israeli war, which became known as the Six-Day War, and occupied the West Bank of the Jordan River and the Gaza Strip in Jordan, the Golan Heights on the Syrian border and the Sinai Peninsula in Egypt. In a resolution, the United Nations called on Israel to withdraw from the territories they had occupied, Israel refused and went on to annex East Jerusalem and Bethlehem, formerly under Jordanian control, and another twenty-seven villages.

The direct lesson of the Arab defeat was that the Arab regimes could not destroy Israel in a classic war situation, especially since it employed the most up-to-date weapons supplied by America and Europe, and therefore the Palestinian guerrilla organisations had to be strengthened in order to confront it. After the 1967 defeat, the Palestinians reached a collective conclusion that the restoration of their country depended on their own efforts.

On 11 August 1969, the al-Aqsa mosque was extensively damaged by a fire said to have been started by a short circuit in the wiring, but which in fact was arson. The construction of Jewish settlements in the occupied territories was swift, and the Israeli government strived to transform the appearance of such cities as Jerusalem from Islamic to Jewish. Efforts were made to change the 3,000 minority population of Jews in Jerusalem to the majority, consequently the Jewish population of this town rose to 190,000.

Extensive excavations at the Dome of the Rock shrine and the al-Aqsa mosque were begun by the usurping government using the excuse that they had found archaeological relics and inscriptions there dating back to the time of the prophets and the old tribes. It was through this means that in addition to making more Arabs homeless, the Zionists could destroy the grounds of this site and rebuild it. Eventually with the powerful backing of America, Britain and Europe and after months of extensive efforts on their part, and despite much opposition from the Arabs and even the United Nations, the Israeli government succeeded in transferring the Israeli capital from Tel Aviv to Jerusalem.

The Battle of Karameh (1968)

Following the Six-Day War of June 1967, which ended in humiliation for the Arabs, the Palestinian resistance organisations based and trained in bases in Syria and Lebanon intensified their offensives. The town of Karameh, situated 25 km to the west of Amman (the Jordanian capital) in the Jordan valley, was home to a number of Palestinian refugees before the June 67 Arab-Israeli war. As a consequence of this war, its refugee population of 25,000 doubled and the town found itself only 4 km from the new Zionist truce line, well within the range of the Israeli army, a proximity which led the Fath organisation to establish its base there and the Zionist defence minister at the time to announce that it had become the main base of Palestinian resistance. One of their reasons for standing against the Israelis from Karameh was that they would communicate to the Jordanian regime that the shedding of Palestinian blood in Karameh would give them the right to remain in this land and broaden their armed offences from the Jordan valley.

In March 1968, in an attack by a fully armed Israeli raiding force on the town of Karameh and the hand to hand battle which ensued with three hundred Palestinian guerrillas, aided for the first time by the Jordanian army, the Zionists suffered severe losses and were forced to retreat. The success at Karameh greatly boosted Palestinian morale, opened up new ways for the victory of the Palestinian nation and gave the Fath guerrilla organisation new prestige and increased membership. In reality, however, 1968 was a false dawn for the Palestinian guerrillas. Although during the battle of Karameh, the guerrillas enjoyed extensive support from the Arab governments and for the first time joined forces with the Jordanian army, this co-operation was to prove transient.

The growth of guerrilla organisations based in Arab states came to pose a severe internal threat to regimes such as those in Jordan and Lebanon, where they formed a type of 'state within a state.' In Jordan, agreements between the Palestine Liberation forces and the Jordanian government broke down almost as soon as they were made. In September 1970 a bloody civil war broke out between the two sides. Fighting ended with a truce agreement sponsored by Arab heads of state which apparently left neither side the victor. But over the following months the Jordanian government gradually asserted its authority over the country and restricted the commandos' base areas. By July 1971 the Palestinian resistance had been virtually liquidated as a guerrilla force in Jordan.

The Ramadan War (October 1973)

In October 1973, the Egyptian army with shouts of *Allahu Akbar* (God is the Greater), launched a surprise attack against the Israelis, crossing the Suez Canal in three sectors and capturing the entire Bar-Lev line, which at that time was deemed to be impenetrable, and with aerial support attacked Israeli positions in the occupied Sinai desert. At the same time from the east a force of 500 Syrian tanks and two infantry divisions advanced deep into Israeli-held Syrian territory to advance almost to Israel proper, and the Syrian air force launched raids on Israel. In the first days of this attack dozens of Israeli aircraft were destroyed and thousands of Israelis killed or taken prisoner and the myth of the Israelis' impregnability was exploded.

The West's reaction was quick and in response to desperate appeals from Tel Aviv, the US quickly began a large airlift of sophisticated equipment to Israel.

Twenty thousand tons of weapons were sent to Israel (this amount had increased to 33,500 tons by the end of the airlift on 15 November) plus 40 Phantom bombers, 48 A4 Skyhawk ground attack jets and 12 C-130 transporters, while by comparison Soviet arms shipments to Egypt and Syria amounted to 15,000 tons. Consequently, the Israelis soon succeeded in turning their setbacks of the first week of the war into a military victory. By 12 October they had forced the Syrians back to their main defence lines, which at their nearest point were some 24 miles from Damascus, and on the night of 15 October, they succeeded in making a thrust across the Suez Canal and consolidating a bridgehead on the West Bank. Eventually on 25 October, with only 601 km between them and Cairo, a cease-fire framed in UN Security Council Resolution 340 went into effect marking a formal end to the hostilities.

Following the 17-day Ramadan war, Anwar Sadat, who had taken over as president in Egypt after the death of the national leader Gamal Abdul Nasir, set a course for compromise with America and the West.

Recognition of the PLO in 1974

In 1974, the United Nations officially recognised the Palestine Liberation Organisation as the sole representative of the Palestinian people. In September, the UN General Assembly agreed without a vote to include 'the Palestinian question,' for the first time since the creation of Israel, as a separate item on its agenda and then invited the PLO to take part in the debate. On 13 November Yassir Arafat, accorded the honours of a head of state, addressed the UN General Assembly with a pistol in one hand and an olive branch in the other saying: "I have come bearing an olive branch and a freedom fighter's gun. Do not let the olive branch fall from my hand." His presence there was warmly welcomed by the representatives, especially those of the developing world.

The Palestinians' Conflict in Lebanon

Following the Jordanian regime's suppression of the Palestinian resistance in Jordan in 1970-71, Lebanon became the last remaining centre of Palestinian guerrilla activity. With the arrival of the Palestinian guerrillas and the PLO in the early 70s and an influx of Palestinian refugees, traditional rivalry between left-leaning Muslims and rightists, mainly Maronite Christians, was accentuated. The stance of the Israeli-backed Christian militia on the presence of the Palestinians in Lebanon differed sharply with that of the Muslims who felt it was Lebanon's duty to lend them all possible assistance.

Civil war was sparked in May 1975 by an attack on a bus carrying Palestinians in a Christian quarter of Beirut by the Christian Phalange (officially: the Lebanese Kataeb Social Democratic Party) militia, who worked in close co-operation with the US and Israeli intelligence agencies. Violence spread throughout the country reaching a culmination in atrocities with the attack in August 1976 on the besieged Tel el-Zaatar Palestinian refugee camp in East Beirut by right-wing forces as a result of which thousands of civilians were killed or injured. The civil war lasted until 13 October 1990 and influenced the political structure of Lebanese society and government.

The Camp David Accord

One of the most important events to occur in the history of the Palestinian revolution and one which constituted a turning point in Israeli-Arab relations was the signing of the Camp David Accords in September 1978. Following the demise of Gamal Abdul Nasir in September 1970 and in particular after the Ramadan War of October 1973, Egypt was led down a path of reconciliation.

In 1974 and '75, Sadat, who had taken over the reins of power after Nasir's death, signed two agreements with Israel over the Sinai; in 1977 he unilaterally abrogated the Egyptian-Soviet Friendship Treaty, increasingly turning to the US for aid; and in November of the same year in a dramatic move he addressed the Israeli Knesset in Jerusalem. Eventually in 1978, at the US presidential retreat of Camp David in Maryland, he concluded a peace treaty with Israeli Premier Menachem Begin under the auspices of US

President James Carter, making Egypt the first Arab country to officially recognise the usurper regime and causing a rift in the Arab world. This event took place on the threshold of the victory of the revolution in Iran.

Although past events and the treason of Camp David had created a widespread feeling of despair and shame amongst the Arabs and Muslims, the victory of the Iranian revolution in 1979 and the overthrow of the most powerful western policeman in the region and Israel's staunchest ally: the regime of the Shah, breathed new life into the struggle against the Zionists and created a rare joy in Lebanon and Palestine, moreover since calls of 'Today Iran, Tomorrow Palestine' were one of the revolution's main slogans.

Attacks by forces of the Zionist regime on Palestinians in Lebanon

On 6 June 1982, the Zionist regime launched a widescale land, sea and air attack against Lebanon with the ostensible aim of clearing southern Lebanon of Palestinian guerrillas (who in any case had for nine months maintained a US-mediated cease-fire). Initially the Zionists announced that strikes would be carried out only against the Palestinian guerrillas that they would last for only 48-72 hours that they had no intention of attacking Syrian positions in Lebanon or of occupying any part of Lebanese soil, and that they would retreat as soon as their operations had ended. It was soon apparent, however, that the Zionist objective was in reality the annihilation of the entire Palestinian quasi-state that had been created in Lebanon and the establishment of a docile and friendly neighbour under right-wing Maronite domination.

The assault lasted not 48-72 hours but 80 days. Heavy civilian casualties occurred among both Lebanese and Palestinians; property was destroyed; Syrian positions were attacked in the Beqaa valley and their missile positions destroyed; and Beirut was subjected to a callous saturation bombardment which coupled with the severing of water and electricity supplies as well as fuel and food helped the Zionists secure a stranglehold on the PLO headquarters in Beirut.

Arab and Soviet assistance for the Palestinians was, during these events, minimal. The Zionists had chosen the best time for their attack, a time when Iran and Iraq were wrapped up in a full-scale war. Consequently, the Palestinian issue, which until then had been the focus of the region's attention, was now relegated to a position of secondary importance and the reactionary Arab regimes, with the excuse of supporting Iraq in a war deemed to have first priority, procrastinated in their support for the PLO and Syria.

Following the Israeli invasion of Lebanon, the PLO was forced out of Beirut and the Palestinian fighters were dispersed to eight Arab countries. The

PLO headquarters was moved to Tunis. This invasion and the ensuing war not only weakened the PLO's military might it also destroyed the organisation's political clout driving some of the Palestinian leaders to seek solutions in conciliation and the development of closer relations with Egypt and Jordan.

Another important effect of this war was that it intensified differences within the PLO - in particular in the ranks of Fath which constituted one of the biggest and most influential constituents of this organisation, even being considered its backbone - which inflicted a serious blow to its international standing. Internal differences in the organisation began on 9 May 1983 with a rebellion within Fath in the Beqaa valley. Fath opponents of Arafat under the command of Colonel Abu Musa and Abu Salih, members of the PLO Central Council and the Fath Revolutionary Council, with the support and encouragement of Syria, rebelled against Arafat and demanded a reconsideration of Fath's political policy and an improvement in relations with Libya, Syria and Algeria.

This rebellion resulted in a bloody confrontation between supporters and opponents of Arafat, a confrontation which ended with the expulsion of Arafat and his followers from Lebanon. They left Tripoli for Yemen, Tunisia and Algeria aboard five Greek ships flying the UN flag and protected by the French navy. From the very beginning the Fath rebels were supported by left-wing factions who were themselves supported by Libya and Syria. The backing of these two countries for Arafat's opponents led to the PLO chairman developing closer ties than ever with Jordan and Egypt (whose own relations with Syria and Libya were strained). From then on new branches were created in the organisation amongst them the Intifada Fath Organisation, under the leadership of Abu Musa, which was a wing of the Fath organisation.

The explosion at the US marine and French contingent headquarters in Beirut (23 October 1983)

The invasion of Lebanon on 6 June 1982, during which Israeli forces pushed through the country to the outskirts of Beirut, opened the way for the deployment of multi-national forces (American, French and Italian). As the invasion commenced, the Zionists announced that their objective was to establish a security zone 40-45 kilometres inside Lebanese territory. However it soon became clear that what they were really after was to drive all Palestinian forces from the country and install a regime in Beirut that would conclude a peace treaty with it. To this end the Israeli forces advanced on West Beirut where the PLO was based. The city was subjected to heavy bombardment and water and electricity supplies were severed as were supplies of food and fuel. During the 63-day siege of West Beirut thousands of Palestinians and Lebanese were brutally massacred provoking condemnation from the international community but no practical attempts to stop the slaughter.

Eventually the PLO was forced to agree to a withdrawal of its forces from Lebanon. Evacuation began on 22 August under the supervision of a multi-national force comprising 800 French and US troops and 400 Italian soldiers. The last of the 8144 PLO commandos, 3500 Syrian-controlled Palestine Liberation Army troops and 2700 Syrian soldiers left West Beirut on 1 September 1982 having secured a solemn promise from the US that Palestinian civilians would be protected after the fighters had withdrawn. However, after completing its task, the American contingent of the multi-national force which, in accordance with the explicit American commitment, was obliged to safeguard the civilian population as well, withdrew, two weeks before its original mandate ran out, forcing the French and Italians to also pull out and effectively terminating the multi-national commitment to protect the civilians.

Following the assassination on 14 September of Bashir Gemayel, the Lebanese President-elect, Israeli troops moved into West Beirut ostensibly to 'maintain order.' Two days later atrocious massacres of Palestinian civilians by Lebanese right-wing militiamen took place in the Sabra and Shatila refugee camps in areas now under Israeli military control and without any Israeli attempt to prevent them.

US marines returned to Lebanon on 20 September 1982 as part of an international peacekeeping force with similar Italian, French and much smaller British contingents. On 29 September 1982 the Israelis left Beirut.

After the Israelis' withdrawal from the Shouf region of Lebanon the following year on 3 September 1983, their positions were taken up by the Phalange militia and the Lebanese army. This led to fighting between them and the Druze-PLO alliance. The United States and France intervened with warplanes and warships on the side of the Lebanese army. A cease-fire was mediated by Saudi Arabia on 25 September, but the US continued its reconnaissance missions over west-central Lebanon from its aircraft carriers. On 23 October 1983 the multi-national forces in Lebanon became the target of a suicide attack by revolutionaries from the Islamic Jihad Organisation. The headquarters of the US Marines in Beirut was blown up followed six minutes later by the French military headquarters. In all 241 US marines and 59 French paratroopers were killed.

This attack constituted one of the heaviest military and political blows the American forces had sustained since the Vietnamese war and the French since their war with Algeria. In addition to destroying the power and might of the multi-national forces in Lebanon and lifting the fear they had created for the Muslim and progressive forces by their presence, the attack strengthened the spirit of resistance and struggle in the Muslims, the Lebanese revolutionaries and the Palestinians.

On 7 February 1984 the US withdrew its troops from Beirut. The other members of the Western MNF followed suit.

The Camp Wars

From 19 May 1985 until early 1987 a one and a half year war broke out between the Amal movement, a Lebanese Shiite organisation, and Palestinian guerrillas in Palestinian refugee camps in Beirut, resulting in the siege of the two sides' camps. The repercussions of this war were intense, the unity of the Palestinians was affected and differences among the Palestinian organisations aggravated.

The Amal organisation strongly opposed the Palestinian presence in Lebanon and viewed it as an incitement to Israeli attacks against the country especially since this presence, and the fact that many Palestinian operations against the Zionists were launched from Lebanese soil, had provided the excuse for the 1982 Israeli invasion of Lebanon. Although the Palestinians sympathised with Amal's position, they argued that they needed help to return to their homeland.

The dispute resulted in bloody clashes between the Palestinians and an important section of the Shiite forces in Lebanon, a dispute which served only the interests of the Quds-occupying regime. The different Palestinian factions adopted a common stand against Amal, but the Fath *intifadah* organisation, which harboured the most hostility towards Arafat, the Fath leader, blamed him for the continuation of the camp wars saying he was encouraging them in order to bring himself out of political isolation. Within the Amal organisation too, criticism and uncertainty over the leadership centring around its performance and the stances adopted by it resulted in the formation of new, more militant groups.[48]

And so the events which took place in Lebanon from the early 1980s onwards led to a general purging of the battle front against Israel of impurities. This process, which was greatly affected by the experience of the Islamic revolution in Iran, ended with the most genuine and unyielding of the forces - who viewed the struggle with Israel to be an Islamic duty - finding a new relentlessness and power and becoming the staunchest opponents of conciliatory moves. And up until the present, it is these forces which have created serious setbacks for the realisation of US and Israeli hopes and plans.

The birth and development of groups such as the Hizbullah in Lebanon is the most obvious manifestation of this process. The large volume of propaganda produced by the enemy against these groups and the machinations devised against them are proof of the fear and alarm which have come to prevail over the enemy camp.

It is clear that regardless of the slight possibility of transient success for the conciliatory plans one can be certain that the sowing of the seeds of Islamic resistance in Lebanon has borne fruit and as long as the domestic fronts of resistance in the occupied territories have the endurance and strength needed, then the enemy's failure will be serious.

The advent of the intifadah or the uprising of the Palestinian people

Introduction: What is certain is that the Islamic resurgence movement, which had entered a new phase with the struggles of Sayyid Jamal al-Din Asadabadi in the Islamic countries and also with the Tobacco Movement in Iran, was continued by Muhammad Abduh and Sayyid Qutb in Egypt, resulted in the uprising of the Muslims against the British in India, was continued in Pakistan by Iqbal Lahori, and brought about the revolution in Algeria in 1962. The revolution in Iran in the late 70s was also a continuation of this movement.

The two decades before the Iranian revolution were a period of stagnation for the Islamic resurgence movement in the Islamic countries. The reason for this was two-fold. On the one side this ideological movement was subdued by oppressive governments which held sway over the Islamic countries, forcing priority to be accorded to political action and political struggle against oppression and dictatorship and less attention being paid to theoretics and the propagation of the resurgence as a result. And on the other, this movement was overshadowed by the phenomenon of Arab nationalism during the years preceding the revolution in Iran, a phenomenon which itself gave rise to other factors - among them the creation of the Baath party in Iraq and Syria by the Christian, Michel Aflaq, which became the most powerful political party in the Middle East region - which, with the creation of the government of Israel and the ensuing Arab-Israeli wars, were instrumental in turning the solution to the Palestinian problem into a purely Arab issue.

The 1979 Islamic revolution in Iran was a watershed in the Islamic resurgence movement. On the one hand it breathed new life into the movement while on the other it gave it a political content which it had hitherto lacked. For until the Iranian revolution, the Islamic resurgence movement had been an ideological-cultural movement, one of religious scholasticism whose call was for a return to the self, the Islamic identity and the values which all the Islamic nations shared. It was only natural then that the message of the Islamic revolution in Iran would move the Muslims and excite their sentiments, that the positions adopted by the Leader of the Revolution, Imam Khomeini, would be the focus of attention of the Muslim combatants around the world, including the Palestinian fighters, and that Islamic fundamentalism would be revived.

Before the revolution in Iran the Muslim Palestinians were bound together by the ties of their Arab nationality, Islam being relegated to second place. This is why Palestinians of different beliefs: Islamic, Christian or Marxist came together in one group or organisation. With the victory of the Islamic revolution in Iran, belief that the power of Islam could unite and bring victory gained strength, and Islam once again excited the attention of the Muslim combatants. Links between the Islamic revolution movement in Iran and Palestine were forged long before the victory on the common battle fronts against Israel, and Iranian guerrillas often went to Palestinian bases where they underwent training to help them in their struggle against the Shah. Indeed, many years previously Imam Khomeini had given permission for a third of sahm-i imam[49], *zakat*[50] and khums[51] monies to be used to support the Palestinian movement.

The slogan 'Today Iran, Tomorrow Palestine" which was shouted in the thick of the revolution, struck fear into the hearts of the Zionists and offered hope to the Palestinians. The best evidence of this is to be found in the statements made by Palestinian leaders and members of the PLO's Central Council concerning the Islamic revolution and Imam Khomeini during the early years of the revolution, statements which were carried in the domestic and foreign press. For further reference refer to volume five of the anthology *Sahifeh-ye Imam* which covers the talks held between Palestinian leaders and Imam Khomeini.

The struggle with Israel was not limited to the Iranian revolution movement. Before the victory of the revolution in Iran, the Eastern bloc powers under the leadership of Russia and also some progressive countries put on a show of supporting the Palestinians. However, this support stemmed from the conflict of interests and the rivalry which existed between the world powers and at its best advocated the right for the Palestinian nation to exist. None of these powers opposed the existence of Israel; on the contrary they formally recognised it but considered it an aggressor country. The Islamic revolution of Iran and Imam Khomeini were, on the other hand, opposed to the very basis of the existence of the Zionist regime as a country. The saw it as a usurper and considered the perpetuation of the Zionist government in any shape or form to mean the perpetuation of conflict in Islamic lands. And it was this thinking which carried the sense of national and religious pride amongst the Palestinians to new heights and caused a surge in Islamic awakening, while at the same time striking fear into the hearts of Israel and its supporters.

Intifadah: another link in the chain of Islamic resurgence

In November 1987, a summit of the Arab League was held in Amman, and unlike on other occasions, no stance was adopted on the struggle against the Zionist regime. In this conference, all attention was directed at the war between Iran and Iraq, and on the whole it progressed along lines favourable with the Camp David agreement.

For years the Palestinian refugees had waited for the Arab nation (ummah) to deliver them from their homelessness while those in the occupied lands had sat back expecting the Arab governments to act. However, the preoccupation of the Palestinian groups and parties with their continuous differences and splits, along with the obvious indifference on the part of the Arab regimes to the Palestinian plight, dashed all hope of effective action ever being taken on their behalf or of the efficaciousness of Arab nationalism. Consequently, attention was turned to Islam and action from within, which the victory of the Islamic revolution in Iran had shown to be successful.

It was under such circumstances that agents of the Saudi government killed pilgrims visiting the House of God. In this bloody tragedy, more than 400 pilgrims, ten of whom were from the occupied territories in Palestine, were slaughtered for the crime of expressing their disavowal of pagans and shouting death to America and Israel. Ceremonies for those martyred were held in Ramallah and al-Khalil (Hebron) and in other occupied areas of Palestine.

These events formed the basis of a new kind of uprising and struggle against Israel that was started in autumn 1987 by the residents of the occupied lands: the *intifadah*. Intifada in a word means uprising; it stems from the Arabic word meaning to shudder, to shake off, like a wet bird shaking off the drops of water that lie heavy on its feathers in order to lighten its wings for flight, or an uprising which shakes off the impurities in order to ascend to new heights. Hitherto each uprising (*intifadah*) had been connected to a certain group, such as the uprising in Fath during which, in May 1983, a group calling itself the Fath Intifada - to distinguish itself from the main Fath group under the leadership of Arafat - broke off from the main Fath organisation. This time, however, in 1987, *intifadah* had no prefixes or suffixes; it was simply the *intifadah*, the uprising of the people in protest at the continued occupation of Palestinian lands. This movement had the following aims and results:

1 - It brought the Palestinian issue back from the brink of oblivion.

2 - It attracted the attention of world public opinion.

3 - It occurred simultaneously with the wave of Islamic resurgence in the region, which lent it a special attractive quality.

4 - It emphasised the need to find a solution to the Palestinian problem.

5 - It made Western Europe attempt to get closer to the Palestinian issue.

6 - It cast doubt on the soundness of Israel's policy, even amongst the American Jews, in such a way as to cause a number to come to believe that in order to prevent Israel's image from becoming even more tarnished (after the Zionist forces' reprisals for the uprising of the people) concessions must be given to the Palestinians.

7 - It created a threat to the internal security of the Zionist entity.

8 - The differences of the Palestinian groups were overshadowed and they began co-operating, and the governments and organisations, which had hitherto determined the fate of Palestine along lines conducive to their own interests, were forced this time to follow the lead of the people.

For the first time, after more than 40 years of occupation and Zionist rule, the Palestinians were on the offensive and the Israelis on the defensive.

A comparison of the characteristics of the intifadah with those of the Islamic revolution in Iran

In some aspects, the *intifadah* movement is very similar to the Islamic revolution movement in Iran, notably in the fact that it did not stem from one particular group or organisation. One of the characteristics of the Islamic revolution movement in Iran was that before its culmination, different Islamic, non-Islamic and nationalist organisations and individuals of various ideological leanings struggled against the Shah's regime and each one believed the future of the revolutionary movement to lie in their hands. When on 17 January 1978, in demonstrations protesting against the publication of a calumnious article about Imam Khomeini in the Ittila`at newspaper, a number of people in Qum were martyred, a chain reaction was started. Ceremonies marking the seventh and fortieth days after their martyrdom were held in Tehran, Tabriz and other cities, each one of which turned into a demonstration which resulted in clashes and the martyrdom of a number of other people. This in turn set the stage for further seventh and fortieth day ceremonies and consequently further demonstrations. By the latter half of the year, the demonstrations had become a national uprising which all the political groups: the Marxists, nationalists and religious groups of different leanings, joined in. No one had expected such a large scale uprising of the people to have taken place without the intervention of some political group or another.

All groups joined the ranks of the people, and pictures and drawings of different personalities were held up. However, that which was important for the people in general and was a unifying factor in the uprising was the common aim: the overthrow of the Shah, and, as the slogans and demands of the people showed, the prevailing tendency of the movement was towards Islam, since Islam was and is the religion of the majority of people in Iran. The *intifadah* movement had precisely the same characteristics.

Many opinions have been expressed about the *intifadah*, opinions which only future events can verify. What can be claimed with some certainty is that the spontaneous and popular nature of the *intifadah* was its most salient feature and its most dominant was its Islamic aspect. It is this which struck fear into the hearts of the Israelis.

The arrest and imprisonment of Shaykh Ahmad Yasin in the first few months of the *intifadah*, stemmed from this fear, and the expulsion and sending into exile of 415 Palestinians from the occupied territories in December 1992 was done with the aim of stamping out the *intifadah*. Those expelled were mainly committed Muslims who supported Hamas and were considered by the Zionists to be the leaders of the uprising. On the one hand, this move is demonstrative of the Islamic aspect of the *intifadah*, while on the other it shows that it was an uprising of the people which lacked complete dependence on any group or party, even Hamas, for after the expulsions not only did the movement continue, but a short time later more than 300 Palestinians from the occupied territories were either killed or injured in a confrontation with Israeli forces. This shows that the uprising was a spontaneous, popular one, not one organised by a group or party, and leadership of it found its way into every home.

The prolonged continuation (1987-93) of the uprising shows that even if certain people had played a role in setting it off, they were not necessarily needed for it to keep its momentum. The *intifadah* did not have a centralised political command and no one particular organisation formed its central nervous system; all the organisations were its followers and supporters and each one strove to direct its modus operandi. Each one of the Palestinian organisations spoke as if command of the *intifadah* lay in their hands, however one should remember that most of them were based outside Palestine in Tunisia, Syria or Jordan. The people in Palestine heeded their words and acted towards achieving the common aim they shared with them i.e. freeing the occupied territories from Israeli occupation, however it did not mean that had all these organisations withdrawn their support the *intifadah* would have ceased to be.

Another similarity between the *intifadah* movement and that of the Islamic revolution in Iran,[52] which was seen for the first time in the history of the Palestinian struggle, was the use of the mosques and Friday Prayer ceremonies as bases for demonstrations. The struggle of the Palestinians has always depended on guerrilla operations, weapons and organisation, during the *intifadah*, however, Palestinian women and children were active in a striking way, and fists, sticks and stones were used against bullets. This time the struggle was dubbed 'the revolution of stones' or the 'uprising of the stone-wielding youth.' The desire for martyrdom and the willingness to forgo one's life, weapons which have no likeness, no substitute and no equal, were other important characteristics of the *intifadah* movement.

Another point to note is that the *intifadah* was a reaction of the people to the failure of the different methods of struggle adopted by many and thought to hold the key to the Arabs' problems. These included Arab nationalism - which reached its peak at the time of Nasser but which in recent years has lost its appeal - and communism and leftist tendencies which received a fatal blow with the break up of the Soviet Union. Eventually, after all the roads the Palestinian movement had travelled down came to a dead end, the conclusion was reached that Islam was the only solution. The path that political philosophies could not find, arriving mostly at defeat, surrender and compromise instead, is being sought through Islam today, and it is a path which will return the follower 'to the self', and one that is now pursued not in Palestine alone but through the surge of Islamic awakening witnessed in all the Islamic and Arab countries.

In the past, Islamic resurgence had only ideological and cultural aspects, but with the victory of the Islamic revolution in Iran in 1979 under the leadership of Imam Khomeini - as a religious scholar and *marja-i taqlid* (sole source of religious guidance) - a political and practical dimension was added. The Palestinian struggle, which was for years characterised by its political and military aspects combined with nationalist ideas, had by the mid-nineties acquired an ideological aspect and an Islamic dimension. As Dr. Fathi Shaqaqi, the secretary general of Islamic Jihad in Palestine said: 'The victory of the Islamic revolution brought back confidence in ideology and religion for all Muslims of the world and proved that Islam is an unbeatable force. Islam brought alive the power of uprising in the Palestinian people.'[53] With the people's movement (*intifadah*) in Palestine, even those who are still influenced by the ideas of Arab nationalism are looking to Islam as an energy source and a means to bring the Arabs together for saving Palestine, and some have even started to genuinely re-evaluate their ideas.'[54]

Some of the Palestinian forces felt that the Palestinian issue was not simply one of settling Jews on occupied land. Rather, in addition to helping the political and economic aims of the imperialists in the Middle East region, they saw the whole affair as part of a new western crusade against the Islamic ummah and as a way to take revenge for the defeat of the Christian and western forces in the Crusades of 1096-1254 and for the conquest, humiliating as it was for the West, of Constantinople in 1453 by the Ottoman Turks.[55]

It was a new idea formed after the Palestinian movement reached the many dead ends in its struggle, or rather to be more accurate it was an idea which found renewed strength. So in this way one can say that the *intifadah* had a lot of similarities with the Islamic revolution in Iran, in particular in its Islamic aspect, and Imam Khomeini was one of the respected role models for the Palestinian people and they paid great attention to his opinions. For this reason, the collection of his views and thoughts should be afforded considerable attention and scrutiny for he is an effective personality and role model in the Palestinian struggle and someone whom the Palestinian Muslims regard as having revived the Islamic movement.

The compromise of Gaza and Jericho

The *intifadah* brought hope for the Palestinian refugees and created a serious danger for Israel which it felt acutely. The fear that the movement would continue agitated the occupying government and made it ready to compromise. The Israelis never recognised the

Palestinian nation as one with an historical identity. Consequently, before the *intifadah* they had always obstinately refused to accept any resolution or peace plan that tried to find a political solution, however limited the rights and concessions for the Palestinians it may have given. Security Council resolutions 242 and 338 and Reagan's peace plan offer clear proof of this obstinate stance. Eventually though, America's and Israel's fear of the *intifadah* forced them to give in to negotiations with the PLO.

The break-up of the Soviet Union and the shift from a polarised international system to one fully dominated by the US compelled the Americans to adopt new policies. In order to block the way for the infiltration of European and Japanese influence, and even that of Islamic fundamentalism, and open the way for installing the new world order and establishing American world dominance, they were forced to direct their attention to controlling and extinguishing tension in the world's flash points, especially in the Middle East region - whose volatile situation was seen to have international repercussions - to grabbing the Middle East peace initiative and damping down tensions in areas prone to crises.

The more conciliatory groups in the Palestinian struggle saw the *intifadah* as their trump card, one that would secure hitherto unachieved concessions in negotiations. They felt that because of the *intifadah*, they could now enter negotiations in a much stronger position. Consequently, they began to use it to their advantage. On 9 September 1993, Yassir Arafat, chairman of the PLO, in a letter to Israeli premier Yitzhak Rabin, formally recognised Israel's right to exist in peace and security. He also renounced violence and announced the PLO's agreement to the Declaration of Principles (accord) and Security Council resolutions 242 and 338 (which formally recognised the existence of the occupying regime and called on it to withdraw to borders in place before 1968). He also stated that those articles in the Palestine National Charter that denied Israel's right to exist and contradicted the PLO's commitment to renounce terrorism and other acts of violence would henceforth be 'inoperative and no longer valid.' The day after Yitzhak Rabin, also in a letter, officially recognised the PLO as the representative of the Palestinian people and in the Israeli parliament announced that he had agreed to start negotiations with them. The 17-point draft of the accord - which provided for Palestinian self-rule for the Gaza Strip and the West Bank town of Jericho - was signed by Arafat and Rabin during negotiations. One of the aims of America and Israel in giving in to this agreement was to create a split among the Palestinians and damp down the flames of *intifadah* using Palestinian hands.

Another of the results of this agreement was to smooth the way for the official recognition of Israel by the Arab governments and transform Israel into a legitimate base in the region. This agreement, brought about because of the acute worry the *intifadah* caused Israel, may have constituted a limited retreat on the part of Israel from its previous stance of nonacceptance, but it was still a long way from securing the elevated goals the Muslim nation of Palestine aspired to in their struggle.

Recognising Israel's right to exist will turn out to be the source of many tragedies for the Middle East and the Muslims in the future, and the fault does not lie only with the PLO and Arafat. If we look at this agreement issue from a wider perspective and judge it from the viewpoint of Imam Khomeini, then the fault for these tragedies lies also on the shoulders of all the Muslim governments, all of them have helped bring about this humiliating situation. Even though the results and future of these new moves for compromise cannot be given final judgement without more time and it is up to posterity to make known the realities, it is obvious now that the seeds of resistance in Palestine have found fertile soil in ideological and Islamic ground, and the faith and motivation of the Muslim people of Palestine form a gushing spring which is responsible for irrigating this ground. So the most natural assumption is that the tree of steadfastness and struggle will grow ever taller and prolific. Indeed, the signs are already there. This is the future that Imam Khomeini anticipated and throughout his life and struggles he took determined steps and bore much hardship along the road to realising this future. ?

"If ye will aid (the cause of) God, He will aid you and plant your feet firmly." (Quran 47:7).

*

Notes

[1] An interview with Imam Khomeini, 7 December 1979 (16 Azar 1358 AHS). *Sahifeh-ye Imam*, vol. 4.

[2] Quds is the Arabic word for Jerusalem and means 'the holy.' Jerusalem is revered as the third holiest city in Islam, after Mecca and Medina.

[3] 22 September 1982 (31 Shahrivar 1362 AHS). *Sahifeh-ye Imam*, vol. 18.

[4] The al-Aqsa mosque: the site in Jerusalem where the Prophet ascended to heaven in the eleventh year of his mission (Quran 17:1); also the complex of mosques and buildings erected on the site. The chief of these was extensively damaged by arson in 1969, two years after the Zionist usurpation of Jerusalem.

[5] Taken from *Islamic Government* translated by Hamid Algar, p. 116.

[6] *Ummah*: the entire Islamic community, without territorial or ethnic distinction.

[7] *Sahifeh-ye Imam*, vol. 12, p. 282. Speech dated 9 August 1981 (18 Mordad 1359 AHS).

[8] *Marja-i taqlid*: a scholar of proven learning and piety whose authoritative rulings one follows in matters of religious practice.

[9] *Sahifeh-ye Imam*, vol. 10, p. 93. Speech dated 1 November 1979 (10 Aban 1358 AHS).

[10] *Sahifeh-ye Imam*, vol. 8, p. 235. Speech dated 16 August 1979 (25 Mordad 1358 AHS).

[11] The direction of prayer which is towards the Kabah in Mecca.

[12] It is to be noted that here by *Sahifeh-ye Imam* we mean its English version (not the Persian one).

1 The feast of sacrifice, one of the greatest feasts in the Muslim calendar.

1 The scholars of Islam.

[15] Referring to Ali ibn Abi Talib, cousin and son-in-law of the Prophet, and the first of the Twelve Imams of Shiite belief. The word *Hadrat* is used as a respectful form of address.

[16] One of the *ahl-adh-dhimma*, a non-Muslim citizen of the Muslim state whose rights and obligations are contractually determined.

[17] *Taghut*: one who surpasses all bounds in his despotism and tyranny and claims the prerogatives of divinity for himself, whether explicitly or implicitly.

[18] Meaning the Zionists who are different from the true followers of *Hadrat* Moses: the Jews.

1 *Shariah*: the all-embracing laws of Islam derived from the Quran and normative practice and authoritative pronouncements of the Prophet, and a number of secondary sources.

1 At the Arab League Summit held in September 1964 in Egypt, in addition to discussing the differences that Egypt had with Yemen and Saudi Arabia, and the aims which each of the Arab governments had in their relationship with the newly established Palestine Liberation Organisation (which formally announced its existence in 1964), the most important matter discussed was how to divert the sources of the river Jordan in order to forestall the Israelis' irrigation scheme. The Israelis had at that time completed the work needed to enable them to divert some of the waters of the river Jordan, which runs through Syria, Occupied Palestine and Jordan, to irrigate the Negev Desert. The disagreement between the Arab countries was so intense that at the beginning of the conference the open session was closed and the heated discussions carried on behind closed doors. The conference eventually ended with no results.

[21] *Zakat*: the tax levied on various categories of wealth and spent on the purposes specified in Quran 9:60.

[22] Share of the Imam: *sahm-i imam*, monies paid to the Imam, or, in the period of his occultation, to the *ulama*, for charitable disbursement.

1 The feast of breaking the Ramadan fast, one of the greatest feasts in the Muslim calendar.

[24] Referring to the signing of the Camp David accords.

[25] See footnote 5.

[26] Referring to the Camp David accords.

[27] Referring to the peace plan of Crown Prince Fahd of Saudi Arabia.

[28] A city in Chaldea, site of a decisive battle between the Arabs and Persians.

[29] The Camp David agreement is the name given to accords signed in September 1978 (1358 AHS) by the president of Egypt at the time, Anwar Sadat, and the prime minister of the usurper Israeli regime, Menachem Begin, with the mediation of James Carter, the then US president, at Camp David, a US presidential retreat in the Appalchian Mountains in Maryland. These accords constituted the greatest act of betrayal to be carried out in the wake of the bloody and heavy battles between the Arabs and Israel and the first step towards compromise. So greatly offended were the sensibilities of the Arab nations by the move that Egypt was expelled from Arab circles. In the early days of the victory of the Islamic revolution, a revolution which had given self-confidence, a fighting spirit and a new aggressiveness to the Islamic nations, while at the same time weakening the position of Israel and its supporters, this great act of betrayal led to Sadat's assassination (October 1981) at the hands of a number of soldiers who were supporters of the Islamic revolution. A few years later, however, the compromising Arab governments, on conciliatory grounds, once more welcomed Egypt back to the fold.

[30] On January 28, 1981, at the invitation of Khalid, the king of Saudi Arabia, the third conference of Islamic heads of states was

held in Taif near Mecca, with the participation of thirty-eight countries. It became known as the Taif conference. Because of Egypt's signing of the Camp David accords and because the communist regime in Afghanistan was brought to power by Russia, these two countries were not allowed to participate in the conference. Iran and Libya declined to take part. Along with other matters, agreements on Afghanistan and the continuation of the struggle against Israel were approved.

[31] The Camp David plan.

[32] Referring to the peace plan proposed by the then Crown Prince Fahd of Saudi Arabia.

[33] Husni Mubarak, the president of Egypt; King Hassan of Morocco; King Husayn of Jordan and Sultan Qabus of Oman.

[34] On August 3, 1981 (1359 AHS), Egypt, America and Israel reached an agreement on accords dealing with the stationing of troops in the Sinai peninsula (which was occupied by Israel) after the withdrawal of Israel in 1982. About this time, that is on August 7, 1981, Fahd, the present king of Saudi Arabia, who at that time was the Crown Prince, proposed a plan which contained the following points:

1- Israeli withdrawal from all occupied territories including the Arab section of Bayt al-Muqaddas.

2- The rights of the Palestinians who do not wish to return to their homeland are to be guaranteed by recompensing their losses.

3- Guaranteeing the right of all countries in the region to live in peace with one another.

These were just some of the points contained in the plan. The third point was seen by many politicians as being a cunning, implicit recognition of Israel's existence and provoked opposition from the radical Arab flank.

[35] Two summit meetings of Arab leaders were held in Fez, one of the cities of Morocco, during this period. At the first, held on November 25, 1981, the eight-point plan of Fahd, the then Crown Prince of Saudi Arabia, was put forward for consideration. Only a few hours after the start of proceedings, the meeting was ended by King Hasan of Morocco because of deep differences of opinion over the proposed Fahd Plan. The heads of eight countries (Algeria, Syria, Iraq, Oman, Sudan, Mauritania and Tunisia) failed to attend. The summit meeting resumed in Fez on September 9, 1982 with the presence of Yassir Arafat, the Palestinian leader, and this time the Arab states, including Syria, agreed on their own set of proposals which, apart from asking that the UN Security Council should guarantee peace and secure borders among all nations of the region, were the same as the 1981 Fahd Plan.

[36] *Sahm-i Imam*: Share of the Imam, or monies paid to the Imam, or, in the period of his occultation, to the *ulama* for charitable disbursement.

1 Another name by which Arafat is known.

[38] Referring to Saddam's false claims that he seeks peace.

[39] The night in which, according to *Surah* 97, the Quran was revealed.

[40] Imam's representative for *hajj* affairs.

[41] A recess in a mosque indicating the direction of prayer (*qiblah*).

[42] *Kawthar*: the heavenly fountain of unbounded grace and knowledge, mercy and goodness, truth and wisdom, spiritual power and insight, which was granted to the Holy Prophet, the man of God, and in some degree or other, to all men and women who are sincere devotees of God. That fountain quenches the highest spiritual thirst of man; it confers overflowing benefits of all kinds.

[43] Referring to the vicious attack by the Saudi regime's security forces and police on Iranian and non-Iranian pilgrims to Mecca performing the repudiation of polytheists ceremony in 1987. In this attack, hundreds of pilgrims were martyred for the crime of shouting their repudiation of America and Israel.

[44] A city in Iran.

[45] Referring to the seizure of the American embassy in Iran on 4 November 1979 by Iranian students.

[46] In 1982 a conference of the organisation of heads of Islamic states was due to be convened in Iraq. In a move aimed at domestic consumption as much as at attracting foreign support and uniting the Arab governments against Iran, the Iraqi regime

began to exhaustively use this issue to its advantage. Imam Khomeini's speeches caused doubt for some of the countries about attending the conference, and eventually, when the conference was convened it was done so without the participation of some of the Muslim and Arab governments such as Syria and Libya.

[47] Zion means the sunny hill or the dry hill. The name came to signify Jerusalem itself and is mentioned in the Old and New Testaments.

[48] Saidi, Zamel, Palestine Liberation Front, p. 114.

[49] Refer to footnote 24.

[50] *Zakat:* Obligatory alms tax which constitutes one of the five pillars of Islam.

[51] *Khums:* A tax consisting of one-fifth of agricultural and commercial profits.

[52] The exaggerated propaganda being disseminated by the Western countries, in particular America, on the *intifadah* having as its role model the Islamic revolution in Iran, and on their similarities, was not without malice. In addition to trying to detract from the genuineness of the uprising, they wanted to create an excuse to carry on an angry struggle against the Islamists. Bearing in mind that international public opinion could not accept all the repression brought about by the Zionists, this kind of propaganda gave the Israelis some justification for suppressing the *intifadah*. Now they could say to

the westerners: 'If we don't quash this uprising, Palestine, the gate to Europe, will become a base for the development of Islamic fundamentalism and the tragedy of Spain will be repeated.' In this way America and Israel could alarm Europeans with the prospect of a dangerous neighbour with fundamentalist bases, and thus facilitate their attempts to quash the Palestinian uprising.

[53] *Hamshahri* newspaper Monday 8 February 1992 No. 45. Dr. Shaqaqi was born in 1951 in Gaza city. He published the book *Imam Khomeini wa Tarh-e Islam-i Novin'* in 1979 and in 1988 he was sent into exile from occupied Palestine and is now leading the movement from abroad.

[54] Ahmad Jibril, one of the famous Palestinian personalities, said in a conference in Tehran in 1992: "Why do we say we need all Muslims? Because we know that the Palestinians cannot free Palestine on their own, and we also know that Arabism and Arab nationalism alone cannot free Palestine either." He said that while in the past his ideas had their roots in patriotism, racism and nationalism, following the victory of the revolution in Iran his attention had been drawn to revolutionary Islam. Imam Khomeini, the aged leader of the Islamic revolution in Iran, describing America and the West as the Great Satan, had, he said, influenced him greatly, and had made him change many of his previously-held views. *Amal al-mutamir al-Islami al-awwal hawl-i Filistin*, p. 45.

[55] Ahmad Jibril says: Sisters and brothers, we now see that the issue is nothing other than a crusade in different clothes and forms. The European and western governments want to take their revenge on Islam for their past defeat. Same source p. 47. Also Munir Shafiq says: The Palestinian issue is an Islamic issue and this is not contradictory to patriotism and Arabism, and because the Palestinian issue is fundamentally an Islamic issue, a remedy should be sought accordingly. The Palestinian issue has become the focus of the battle and disagreements between the Islamic *umma* and its enemies, as it is at the centre of the plans of our enemies, namely the Zionists and western imperialists. For this reason, it is impossible for the uprising of the nation to occur, its independence, its unity and the raising of the flag of *La ilaha illa llah* (there is no god but God) to be materialised as long as the Palestinian issue is not a central part in the Islamic strategy of all the Islamic countries. Same source, p. 109.

Source: The Institute for Compilation and Publication of Imam Khomeini's Works

International Affairs Department

2

www.ingramcontent.com/pod-product-compliance
Lightning Source LLC
Jackson TN
JSHW070021160726
105219JS00005B/226
* 9 7 9 8 2 4 0 9 5 4 9 3 1 *